ART AND MOURNING

Art and Mourning explores the relationship between creativity and the work of self-mourning in the lives of twentieth-century artists and thinkers. The role of artistic and creative endeavors is well known within psychoanalytic circles in helping to heal in the face of personal loss, trauma, and mourning.

In this book, Esther Dreifuss-Kattan, a psychoanalyst, art therapist, and artist, analyses the work of major modernist and contemporary artists and thinkers through a psychoanalytic lens. In coming to terms with their own mortality, figures such as Albert Einstein, Lucian Freud, Louise Bourgeois, Paul Klee, Eva Hesse, and others were able to access previously unknown reserves of creative energy in their late works, as well as a new healing experience of time outside of the continuous temporality of everyday life.

Dreifuss-Kattan explores what we can learn about using the creative process to face and work through traumatic and painful experiences of loss. *Art and Mourning* will inspire its readers to understand the power of artistic expression in transforming loss and traumas into perseverance, survival, and gain.

Art and Mourning offers a new perspective on trauma and will appeal to psychoanalysts and psychotherapists, psychologists, clinical social workers and mental health workers, as well as artists and art historians.

Esther Dreifuss-Kattan, Ph.D., is a senior faculty member at the New Center for Psychoanalysis in Los Angeles, a psychoanalyst in private practice in Beverly Hills, a clinical specialist at the Simm/Mann UCLA Center for Integrative Oncology, and a practicing artist and curator of art.

"In *Art and Mourning*, Dreifuss-Kattan asks—how can the conflict between the wish to survive and the realization of death be overcome? In answer to this question she demonstrates that a creative approach to loss has inspired some of the most important art work of our time. By critically examining the works of Louise Bourgeois, Alberto Giacometti, Paul Klee, Eva Hesse, and others, the author shares a fresh art historical perspective with great empathy towards the artists and her readers."—Suzanne Isken, Executive Director of the Craft and Folk Art Museum, Los Angeles, USA.

"Dreifuss-Kattan does a brilliant job of placing Freud and Modernism in the cultural and biographic context of twentieth-century art, abstraction, and Expressionism. The book demonstrates how art can transcend the past in an attempt to secure a balanced future. Dreifuss-Kattan draws on her clinical experience and a familiarity with a wide range of artistic, cultural, and scientific figures, including Paul Klee, Lucian Freud, René Magritte, and Albert Einstein. *Art and Mourning* is an aesthetic experience. She writes with compassion, clarity, and immediacy. The illustrations are sumptuous, powerful, and telling. The book is a 'must read' for art lovers, cultural historians, mental health professionals, and readers interested in loss, mourning, and the dynamics of creativity."—Peter Loewenberg, Professor Emeritus, UCLA, European Intellectual and Cultural History and Former Dean, New Center for Psychoanalysis.

"*Art and Mourning* presents an entirely unique view of the intricate relationship between art, time, death, trauma, and mourning. Grounded in individual psychobiographies of a diverse range of artists including Paul Klee, Eva Hesse, Lucian Freud, René Magritte, Ferdinand Hodler, and Dina Gottliebova Babbitt, the chapters trace specific forms through which individual artists process and transform trauma and mourning in their work. Theoretically informed by a sophisticated use of psychoanalytic theory as well as larger philosophical and artistic considerations, *Art and Mourning* is one of the most interesting books about art I have read in the past years and opens up an entirely new perspective on the rich body of work on trauma and mourning."—Gabriele Schwab, Chancellor's Professor of Comparative Literature, Faculty Associate of Anthropology and Theory and Culture, University of California Irvine, author of *Haunting Legacies: Violent Histories and Transgenerational Trauma.*

"*Art and Mourning* is a remarkable achievement. The author uses her own psychoanalytic training, her work with terminally ill patients, and her artist's eye, to create new links between these artists' own personal stories and their creative output, and in the process creates a wonderful and illuminating book. Dreifuss-Kattan uses Sigmund Freud's own writings of psychobiographies as a starting point. Through a thoughtful focus on the lives, and particular traumatic experiences, of a series of artists, from Paul Klee to the Holocaust survivor Dina Gottliebova Babbitt to Freud's own grandson Lucian Freud, she creates something entirely new and deeply satisfying. Using her extensive, insightful knowledge and experience, Dreifuss-Kattan has written an important book that sheds light on the harrowing effects of trauma and loss, and the role that art can play in the healing process."—Carol Seigel, Director, Freud Museum, London.

ART AND MOURNING

The role of creativity in healing trauma and loss

Esther Dreifuss-Kattan

Routledge
Taylor & Francis Group
LONDON AND NEW YORK

First published 2016
by Routledge
2 Park Square, Milton Park, Abingdon, Oxon OX14 4RN

and by Routledge
711 Third Avenue, New York, NY 10017

Routledge is an imprint of the Taylor & Francis Group, an informa business

British Library Cataloguing in Publication Data
A catalogue record for this book is available from the British Library

Library of Congress Cataloging in Publication Data
Names: Dreifuss-Kattan, Esther, author.
Title: Art and mourning : the role of creativity in healing trauma and loss / Esther Dreifuss-Kattan.
Description: 1 Edition. | New York : Routledge, 2016.
Identifiers: LCCN 2015035519 | ISBN 9781138886933 (hardback : alk. paper) | ISBN 9781138886940 (pbk. : alk. paper) | ISBN 9781315714470 (ebk)
Subjects: LCSH: Bereavement—Psychological aspects. | Death in art.
Classification: LCC BF575.G7 D735 2016 | DDC 155.9/3—dc23
LC record available at http://lccn.loc.gov/2015035519

ISBN: 978-1-138-88693-3 (hbk)
ISBN: 978-1-138-88694-0 (pbk)
ISBN: 978-1-315-71447-9 (ebk)

Typeset in Bembo
by Swales & Willis Ltd, Exeter, Devon, UK

Printed and bound in the United States of America by
Edwards Brothers Malloy on sustainably sourced paper

To Sarit and Jonathan, their children Daniela, Sophie and Max, and to Gabriela and Pavel

CONTENTS

PREFACE

I would like to dedicate this book to the memory of my mother, who passed away in 2008 at the age of 92. Only after so much time has passed do I feel ready to write about "time and mourning," struggling as I was with the unthinkable, fearing the impending loss of her and then the strong force of mourning. My work in these pages is intimately connected with my mother's life and death.

Despite a distance that spanned an ocean my brothers and I felt very close to her in the last few years of her life, as my once strong and competent mother became more physically and psychologically dependent upon us. In her final years, she resided at the very Jewish Home for the Elderly in Zürich, Switzerland, that she and my father had directed together 25 years earlier. I spent much of my childhood living in that very same home, from the time I was 10 years old until my nineteenth birthday. It was an uncanny experience to grow up in a house with so many old people, most of whom never left the premises except to go to the hospital or to be buried in the cemetery. After a resident died they would be actively mourned, especially by my mother and the deceased's family, and my parents would perform all of the proper Jewish rites. In my frequent visits in the last few years to the nursing home where my mother grew older and weaker, my childhood came rushing back to me.

During one of my final visits with my mother, we attended a piano concert with many of the other elderly residents in the large living room of the facility. As I sat next to my 92-year-old mother, my eyes flicked across the room and my memory did somersaults. I used to sit in this very same room as a young child some 50 years earlier, when my parents directed the nursing home and my family resided on the fifth floor.

While I attempted to make my mother comfortable on the wooden chair, my eyes wandered from the young Russian man preparing his music to Mrs. Fisher. A retired pianist in her late nineties, now slumped in her wheelchair beside my mother, she had performed here in the same residence 40 years prior. Under a halo of white hair, her pale face twitched. Each discordant note seemed to line up and march against her memory. Her fingers tapped the rhythm on her armrest and her eyebrows moved up slightly with each mistake the young pianist made. Back and forth, watching Mrs. Fisher and my mother, I studied each of their pale, tired faces and their pairs of trembling hands.

Suddenly it felt as though time itself divided, and I saw myself sitting in the same hall at the age of 10: the familiar sight of the crumpled faces and purple sweaters throughout the room, and the strong odor of the nursing home in the air brought me back to an earlier time. When the piano played back in those days 50 years earlier, "my" forty grandparents in the room saw their bygone childhoods in me and hoped to partake in my childhood and in my life that was still to come. In me—the child whose life had just begun—they must have also recognized their own lives coming to an end.

Suddenly the music pulled me back to the present and the room full of very old friends and strangers. Mrs. Fisher, the erstwhile musician, now seemed out of sorts, staring across the room. My eyes followed hers to a door where a nurse entered with Mrs. Ginger, the oldest resident in the home. I realized that my mother's anxiety was rising now as well, as she looked nervously at the two women entering. As though frozen in time, Mrs. Ginger sat up straight in her wheelchair, one of her hands clutching a yellow tennis ball. She stared into what seemed to be another universe, her eyes locked in mid-air. The piano music did not appear to affect her dark mood—the nurse must have forgotten to bring her hearing aid. I could not take my eyes off the yellow ball. Something about that yellow ball triggered my memory.

The yellow ball in Mrs. Ginger's wrinkled hand now seemed to roll down the long incline of my memory, bouncing down the steep steps all the way to the first floor and into the backyard. I ran after it, a little girl in a white dress and red boots. I wanted to catch the ball so badly. When it came to an abrupt stop, I bent down to pick it up. What was this thing I saw lying next to my ball, I wondered, hiding in the wet, uncombed lawn? I picked up a twig and tried to move the unfamiliar object, but I suddenly started to tremble. I ran up the stairs to the administrative office, sinking into my mother's arms. She looked up at me for a brief minute, and then immediately returned to the phone. I tugged on her skirt; she gestured and, slightly annoyed, hung up the phone and followed me to the backyard. My mother finally spotted my yellow ball, and then her eyes followed to the strange object in the grass. "Dentures!" she cried, laughing uproariously. I did not understand. My mother slowly explained to me that old people often lose their teeth, and sometimes even lose their dentures. Bewildered, I stared at the artificial teeth, feeling confused about old age and the place I now was to call my home.

As I looked at the ball stuck in Mrs. Ginger's hand, I was pulled back and forth between the past and the present. My childhood memories stood like uninvited guests, lingering shadows behind each of the old residents. The image of Mrs. Ginger as a motionless statue pulled me further back in time, to the age of 12, the age when a Jewish girl is considered an adult. I was home alone one night when the night nurse Nina, who always wore a big silver cross on her chest, woke me up to tell me that one of the old women, Sarah Feldman, had just died. Unable to reach either my parents or the doctor, she asked that I sit with the body for a short time while she attended to all of the other needy patients. I was dumbfounded, but agreed, remembering the many times my mother had explained to me what a privilege it was to sit with the dead. It was a special, peaceful experience based on *kavod hamet*, the Jewish commandment to watch over the departed, as they must not be left alone from the moment of passing until their burial. Still, I shuddered as I stared at the motionless Mrs. Ginger.

The piano still played, vibrant with life, as my weak mother slowly seemed to crumble in the chair next to me. Not even the beautiful music could arrest her overwhelming feeling of exhaustion. She could barely keep herself upright and was no longer quite sure who I was, her daughter from America. The once strong, energetic, and competent director of this very nursing home was now my weak, incapable, and frail child-mother. With two hands outstretched, I guided her slowly away from the music to her room on the same floor, to the edge of her own bed. I lifted her blouse over her head and slipped her pink nightgown on her. Where had her steadfast determination gone, or her devotion to religious principles, I wondered. Had her kindness and compassion for her fellow human beings and her intellectual rigor disappeared? As I lifted her legs and helped her into bed, she extended her hand to me and commented on her failing strength. She, too, wondered what had become of her and how she would ever make it over time.

How would I fare without her? Her body slowly moved farther and farther away, setting loose love, longing and mourning. I sat next to her bed and read aloud one of her favorite poems. As her breath became calmer and her eyes closed, I tried to seal my sadness away.

Two nights before my mother's death, while she was suffering from overwhelming pain, my mother recalled by heart the poem "Mondnacht [Moonlight]" by the Romantic poet Joseph von Eichendorff. Not only was she able to access her wish and need to "fly home," but she could identify with the comforting, embracing feeling of the limitless universe so beautifully expressed by the poet:

Mondnacht	**Moonlight**
Es war als hätt der Himmel	It was as though heaven's glimmer
Die Erde still geküsst,	Silently kissed the earth
Dass sie im Blütenschimmer	That in its blossoms' shimmer
Von ihm nun träumen müsst.	She dreamed of his worth.
Die Luft ging durch die Felder,	The breeze moved through the wheatfields
Die Ähren wogen sacht,	And swayed the heads of grain
Es rauschten leis die Wälder,	The forest softly rustled
So sternen klar war die Nacht.	So starry the night was again.

Und meine Seele spannte Weit ihre Flügel aus, Flog durch die stillen Lande, Als flöge sie nach Haus.	And, oh, my soul expanded Far, wide, its wings to roam, Sailing through hushed lands As if my soul was flying home.[1]

My mother's recollection of this particular poem that was stored in her memory helped both of us, in the final days of her life, to connect to her creative inner core and to her mourning for her own life. A creative, transformational object, this poetic imagery fostered a reverie that helped her rise for a short while beyond her pained body, accessing for an extended moment the standstill of time. It helped me to connect to her in a very safe and intimate way, bringing me back in time to my vibrant mother who was forever reciting poems. The poem's formal structure provided both of us with a creative defense against the fear of death and against the potentially destructive force of timelessness.

The innumerable poems my mother knew by heart were like colorful beads that strung together the experiences of her life, her personal and her historical time, in concentric layers of memory. For my mother, reading, studying, and reciting poetry were a means of self-expression: the poems connected her to her own internal life and creativity. From the time I was a girl and throughout my life, these poems have helped me understand my mother's emotions, and they have been my guide on the path to her unconscious.

Note

1 Translated by the author.

ACKNOWLEDGMENTS

I am so very pleased to be able to express my appreciation to the many people who have helped and supported me in writing this book.

The first to believe in me when I arrived in Los Angeles was Ruth E. Iskin, now Associate Professor of Art History at Ben Gurion University of the Negev. She invited me to teach at the University of California Extension Division in the Visual Arts Department. Her support, encouragement, and later friendship allowed me to put my thinking about art into writing. Her own stellar career showed me that it is never too late to start something new and succeed in it. Her last book *The Poster: Art, Advertising, Design, and Collecting, 1860–1900* is proof of her great talent and focus that is so inspiring to me.

Many thanks go to my good friend Diana Kormos-Buchwald, Director of the Einstein Papers Project at the California Institute of Technology, who enthusiastically invited me to come to the Einstein Papers Project to read and research personal letters sent between Albert Einstein and his two sons, Hans Albert and Eduard. My weekly visits to Pasadena over the course of a year were exciting and stimulating, and Diana's thoughtful guidance and discussions allowed me to get to know Einstein from an entirely new, more personal perspective.

Gabriele Schwab, Chancellor's Professor of the University of California in Irvine and a Research Psychoanalyst at the New Center for Psychoanalysis involved me in thoughtful conversations about artistic expression and trauma. Her careful reading of my entire manuscript improved it greatly. Her own amazing creative productivity helps me to see that one can successfully accomplish different projects at the same time and still have a life. Her powerful book *Haunted Legacies: Violent Histories and Transgenerational Trauma* taught me much about literature and trauma. I value our friendship and sharing of our European background.

Many thanks go to friend and colleague Laurie Wilson, Ph.D. Art Historian, Research Psychoanalyst and Professor Emerita of Art Therapy at New York

University for inviting me for several years to present my work in progress to *The Psychoanalysis and Visual Art Group* at the annual American Psychoanalytic Association Meeting in NYC. The feedback and lively group discussions with my colleagues were stimulating, and thought-provoking questions made my thesis better. Laurie's excellent book: *Alberto Giacometti: Myth, Magic, and the Man* have inspired part of my first chapter and stands as a prototype of what scholarship in art and psychoanalysis can be like.

Much gratitude goes to Suzanne Isken, former Director of Education at the Museum of Contemporary Art (MOCA) in Los Angeles and now Director of the Craft & Folk Art Museum (CAFAM), as well as to Thomas Brod MD, Psychoanalyst at the New Center for Psychoanalysis, for organizing and sponsoring panel discussions with psychoanalysts at MOCA for the following exhibitions: *Lucian Freud*, *Wack! The Feminist Revolution*, and *Louise Bourgeois—Sculpture*. Participating in these panel presentations at MOCA and the dialogue with the audience, some of them practicing artists, deepened my thinking about the process of art-making, and inspired three chapters of this book. Suzanne's support and curatative guidance in our collaborations have also been enriching and meaningful to me.

Thanks to Michael Gales, MD, the Program Committee Chair of the New Center for Psychoanalysis, who invited me to present over the last years my papers on Dina Gottliebova Babbitt, René Magritte, Albert Einstein, and time and timelessness, as part of the monthly scientific lectures at the New Center for Psychoanalysis. His friendship and trust in me makes the Institute a warmer place. My friend and fellow research psychoanalyst, Jeffrey Prager, Sociology Professor at UCLA and Debora Silverman, Professor of History and Art History at UCLA, are my good friends, supporters and cheerleaders, and Jeff's comments after he read my manuscript in progress were helpful. I would like to thank the leadership, staff and membership of the New Center for Psychoanalysis as a whole for their encouragement and support during my work on this book.

Appreciation goes to my friend Barry Fisher, Human Rights Lawyer in Los Angeles, who introduced me to the artist and Holocaust survivor Dina Gottliebova Babbitt. The visit to her home in a beautiful forest in Northern California was very moving, and allowed me to interview her about her experience as a prisoner and artist in Auschwitz. Barry's expertise on the history and culture of the Roma people was very helpful and educational and contributed greatly to my understanding of Gottliebova Babbitt's circumstances both in her hometown Brunn in Czechoslovakia and later in the concentration camps. This encounter with Gottliebova Babbitt inspired me to write Chapter 3.

My friend and mentor, Peter Loewenberg, Professor Emeritus of History at UCLA, convinced me when I arrived in Los Angeles from Israel and Switzerland to become a research psychoanalyst; the chapter on Paul Klee was generated as part of these studies. Peter's many years of scholarship in German, Austrian, and Swiss modern and cultural history serve as a model to me, and he and his wife Josephine's warm, supportive manner made me feel welcomed in LA.

While at the Southern California Psychoanalytic Institute, my paper on Paul Klee received the Best Thesis Award. I give grateful thanks for the support of my late professor Victor Wolfenstein, UCLA, who was one of my most inspiring teachers at the Southern California Psychoanalytic Institute, and I miss him.

It was so important for me to meet the very accomplished English sculptor Jane McAdam Freud, daughter of the English artist Lucian Freud. Her early childhood memories of her grandparents Lucie and Ernst Freud, youngest son of Sigmund Freud and parents of Lucian Freud, offered me new insights into the Freud family and connected me more personally to her father, Lucian. Due to this encounter with Jane, my thinking about Lucian came to life in a more personal, compelling way.

Dominique Bondy, the program chair at the Freud Institute in Zürich, invited me a few years ago to present a chapter in progress of this book. Having my former colleagues and friends sitting in the audience, as well as my two brothers and sisters-in-law from Israel and Switzerland was a wonderful experience, both moving and meaningful, as the past and the present seemed to merge.

Anne Coscarelli, Ph.D., director and founder of the Simms/Mann UCLA Center for Integrative Oncology as well as Suzanne Levanas LCSW and Randi Grossman MPH, Director of Chai Lifeline West Coast, offer me the opportunity to use art as a tool for healing trauma for adults and children with cancer. Their loving devotion to their patients and their families is humbling and never ceases to impress me, and they both serve as role models to me.

Cheers go to the Paul Klee Archives in Bern, Switzerland, whose friendly staff allowed me to see the original drawings by Paul Klee hidden in many locked drawers. The archivists not only made sure I did not walk away with one of these small treasures, but also guided me along in a most professional way to find what I was looking for.

I would like to thank the following people and organizations for the copyrights and rights of reproduction for the images used in this book:

Cécile Brunner, Kunsthaus, Zürich; Sylvia Bandi from Hauser & Wirth Galleries, Zürich; Ariana Dannacher from the Museum zu Allerheiligen Schaffhausen/Sturzenegger-Stiftung; Heidi Frautschi from the Zentrum Paul Klee, Bern; Jacqui M. Chambers from the Norton Simon Museum, Pasadena; Alice Jaeckel from the Swiss Institute for Art Research SIK-ISEA; Maria E. Murgula from Artist Rights Society (ARS), New York; Véronique Mamelli from the Réunion des Musées Nationaux Agence GNGP, Paris/Estate Brassai-RMN; Julie Schilder from Visual Artists and Gallery Association (VAGA), New York; Robbi Siegel from Art Resource: Images/Easton Foundation; Agnieszka Sieradzka from the Auschwitz-Birkenau State Museum; Christian Schnellman from the Kunstmuseum Bern; and Leslie Wong from Bridgeman Images.

Many thanks go to my first editor Alyssa Wiesel, who carefully read through the first draft of my manuscript and helped me to shape up my English. Corinne Lightweaver edited the following draft, and aided in focusing my analysis with her intelligent questions and targeting of details, leading to progress and to the next stage of my manuscript. My editor Ben Garceau read through the entire finished manuscript with a sharp eye. His help with the reorganization improved my project greatly. His professional editing skills and most friendly, professional manner made the work so much easier. I am very grateful to him. I would also like to thank the staff at Routledge, particularly Kirsten Buchanan for supervising the publishing process, and Kate Hawes, whose encouragement made the process that much more pleasant. I would also like to thank Ruth Bennett for her careful copy-editing and good cheer, and great appreciation to Adam Bell at Swales and Willis for his outstanding help in the completion of my book.

My appreciation goes to my brother and sister-in-law Walter and Claudette Dreifuss and to my friend Karin Dreiding for their amazing generosity, which allowed me to focus on this project with some measure of peace of mind, as well as to my brother and sister in-law Alex and Marlise Dreifuss, and to Shlomo Kattan, who continuously extend their loving support. My gratitude goes to my late friend and partner Heinz Harvey Rich-Richeimer, whose loving kindness, humor and artistry carried me along for the last twelve months.

My gratitude goes to my beloved daughters, Sarit and Gabi, and their wonderful spouses, Jonathan and Pavel, who read through some individual chapters and gave me helpful feedback, many editorial suggestions, and much love and encouragement. Their amazing scholarship and focus never ceases to impress me, filling me with pride and motivating me to push to the finish line. My grandchildren, Sophie and Daniela, doubles of sorts, and little brother Max make me smile each day and thus contribute greatly to my happiness and well-being, and foster my creativity.

My late parents Max and Suzanne Dreifuss-Levy are every day still an inspiration to me. Their daily love and holistic care for older adults, their tolerance toward all people, unrelated to religion, race, social status or political affiliations, was amazing. Growing up as a little girl living in a home for the aged from 1959 to 1971 in Zürich, Switzerland, death and trauma were never far away and left a strong, unconscious imprint that informs my work and research interest to this day.

My deep appreciation goes to my patients, who use the visual arts as a tool for the self-expression of healing and transformation in their attempts to confront and accept cancer in their life and their death.

INTRODUCTION

Art and mourning

This book grew out of my 30-year involvement in art, psychotherapy and psychoanalysis with cancer patients and survivors in university hospitals in Zürich, Tel Aviv and Los Angeles. With paint and brushes, paper and scissors, fabric and ribbons, I have guided people—people who were hospitalized, in outpatient clinics for intense chemotherapy and radiation treatments, or who came to support groups before or after surgeries and other intense medical experiences—to project their fears, hopes and other complex emotional states onto paper and canvas, and then followed up with individual or group discussion and discovery. Together we have tried to understand and interpret their personal imagery and creative experiences, and sometimes discussed how unresolved conflicts from their past have stood in the way of a full psychological recovery with cancer, after cancer, or after other medical and psychological trauma.

Realizing the amazing power of creative expression when faced with trauma, loss and mourning, I guided them to become better artists. Art-making is not only a lifeline, it is also a way to reconsider life anew and even to hold off death. My psychoanalytic training taught me to see beyond the obvious, to consider the therapeutic relationship in all of its facets and to help the cancer patient or survivor face the often tragic consequences of their journeys with cancer and illness, however long or short they may be. When confronted with any loss and mourning, art can be one of the most powerful tools, as words alone often seem inadequate to the exploration of such emotionally charged and unknown territory. Art-making and creative expression of any kind serve as powerful weapons in the fight against a potentially life-threatening illness, as the pleasure experienced through creating in spite of trauma and pain—both physical and psychological—far outlasts the fear of facing the content of one's own unconscious expression.

In *Art and Mourning: The Role of Creativity in Healing Trauma and Loss*, I will demonstrate how art, literature and other creative work can "embody" a traumatic loss and its mourning. This creative, formal embodiment of a piece of art can also be a powerful tool to reawaken one's psychic life and change one's experience and perception of time (Schwab, 2007). I will discuss specific sculptures by Alberto Giacometti, Louise Bourgeois and Eva Hesse; look at poems by Rainer Maria Rilke; explore portraits by Ferdinand Hodler, Dina Gottliebova Babbitt and Lucian Freud; analyze anew paintings by René Magritte; and gain some insights on creative reverie and time as discussed by Albert Einstein in some of his letters to family and friends.

Object loss and mourning are painful and life-altering events of our normal lives. In "Mourning and Melancholia" (published in 1917 but written in 1915), Sigmund Freud explores the individual's reaction to the loss of an ideal or to the actual loss or disappointment of a loved one. Freud wrote this essay during an emotional time. Europe was in the throes of World War I, and, in 1915, two of his sons volunteered for military service and fought on the front line despite Freud's protestations (Ogden, 2007). Just as my mother used the imagery of poems to express mourning for her own impending death, Freud's essay served as a transformational object for him: he transformed his fear for the lives of his sons and his mourning for the victims of WWI into a theoretical paper.

In trying to understand the creation of a piece of art, we can take the formation of our dreams as a partial template. Fragments of a dream can turn into sensory perceptions that can then be transformed into more cohesive symbols, shaping both content and form, reconnecting bonds that were severed through loss. Indeed, it is the artistic form that integrates experiences of loss and trauma and allows for developmental growth. In its reparative function, imagination and its visual expression attempt a rapprochement with the external world, elaborating both memories and new perceptions. In transcending the distinction between time and space, they can create a picture or sculpture that can become a permanent memorial.

Each artist discussed in this book reacts differently in the absorption or metabolization of his or her trauma or loss. Major losses or trauma are often experienced as a temporal delay outside of the boundaries of a single time and space. To work through mourning and creative reparation in order to reestablish a psychological equilibrium, the artist often not only mourns the present loss, but must also revisit earlier losses as well. When dealing with major loss and mourning, if there is no integration through artistic expression, no idealization of the self can take place, and instead one suffers the "depletion of the self by the shadow of the loss of the Other" (Kristeva, 1989, p. 5). Giving a form through visualization or verbalization, however, can stabilize the self and thus reestablish the narcissistic balance that had been overwhelmed by the archaic affects of trauma, illness or loss, thus initiating both an internal and external dialogue. Aesthetic expressive abilities allow the artist not only to connect to the Other, the viewer, but to reconstruct and recollect in a visual form his or her inner experiences as well.

Art-making—with its symbolization and exteriorization at a time of personal loss and trauma—allows for a gradual modulation of affects. It fosters personal reinvention through the reconstruction of the artist's past, allowing her to become her own witness. By expressing one's own story in words or images, as Dori Laub (1995) pointed out, the artist demonstrates a wish to survive these losses and distance herself from the trauma. Looking at one's own creation and sharing it with others, one's internal witness becomes even stronger. Eventually, the newly expressed narrative can be substituted for the actual trauma, helping to regain the coherence and integration of the self. Art-making can thus transcend the past and become linked to the present in an attempt to secure a more balanced future.

The ideas Freud discussed in "Mourning and Melancholia" inspired Melanie Klein to construct her own theories of mourning and how it can inform the creative process. Setting out from the suppositions Freud put forward about the role in mourning of affects, including the aggression and guilt founded in destructive fantasies, Klein (1975) argued that in this context reparation after loss, namely a wish to restore and repair the damaged internalized object, is particularly significant. She pointed out that the creative reparation arising from loss and mourning opens up the capacity for symbol formation and generates new imagery, further promoting a more mature developmental stage.

Pathological reparation resulting in depression, however, can either take the form of a manic reparation based on the denial of aggressive feelings, or can result in an obsessional reparation based on the need to magically eliminate depressive anxiety and ignore the ambivalent aspect of mourning with its triumph, remorse and guilt. Freud suggested in "Mourning and Melancholia" (1917 [1915]) that the trauma of object loss resulting in depression can lead to a need to incorporate (or devour) the object within the ego, thus unconsciously preserving it. Nicolas Abraham and Maria Torok (1994) expanded on Freud's idea, calling this internalized object an "exquisite corpse" because it seems to lie deeply inside the psyche, waiting for the ego to revive it in the future. The "secret" of such a trauma can become entombed within the psyche, forming a "psychic enclave" or "crypt" that houses the departed love object with often devastating emotional consequences. This intrapsychic tomb allows the depressed artist to deny his or her loss, blocking the expression of strong emotions like grief, guilt, or aggression, and results in an inability to create genuine artistic expressions (Abraham and Torok, 1994).

In regular mourning, on the other hand, fantasies begin to reappear and fill the void left by trauma and loss, replacing absence and emptiness with new memories and imagery, which in turn engender creativity. Loss, bereavement and absence often trigger the imagination because they allow the affects to be expressed and thus re-solidify the cohesion of the self. Where did this creative force originate? From a developmental perspective, Christopher Bollas (1987) has pointed out that initially the mother or the primary caretaker becomes a transformational object for the infant, as both negotiate their inter-subjective experiences around the rituals of feeding, soothing, diapering and sleeping. Donald Winnicott (1965) referred to her as the "environment mother," since she provides a total environment for the infant, fostering the process of symbolization. Thus, we can see the creation of the baby's transitional object as the first creative act, negotiating the mother's absence, as self and other is recognized (Winnicott, 1971). As adults, we seek to reconnect to this early transformational process, to remember the intense affective experience of togetherness and separation, enjoying the familiar while experimenting with the new and the imaginative. This unthought and unrepresented experience can then become symbolized as an aesthetic moment (Sirois, 2008): the recollection of the maternal object, a search for an affective state, a mood, like the experience of being held.

An awareness of the finitude of our bodies—or our ideas and representations—can give rise to sublimation and idealization, paving the way for new imagery and a wish to maintain the desire for the unknown future. The work of mourning through creative means leads to a new reality, a wish to continue living in order to create something in the present out of the past with all of its memories. As Jacques Derrida remarked, "memory projects itself towards the future, and it constitutes the presence of the present" (1986, p. 57). Through reattachment with the internalized object, a future can be re-imagined in spite of a threat to life, and can thus engender hope (Dreifuss-Kattan, 1990).

Such issues of temporality are inherent to mourning and loss, as the meaning of death gives meaning to time. As the French philosopher Emmanuel Levinas (2000) noted, "Time is not the limitation of being but its relationship with infinity" (p. 19). In the artistic experience, as in the aesthetic moment, artists and audience can briefly fuse with the sensation of the early object of desire and can access a moment, a sense of infinity. The artist searches for the symbolic representation of this early transformational object, for an aesthetic environment that can hold the self in the same experience of reverie.

In his book *The Work of Mourning*, Derrida (2001) eulogized his close friends and colleagues, writing that "Death not only takes away the person we loved, but deprives us of the influence this person had on us and through which our world was changed forever by them," illustrating his concern with the singularity of death and also with its repetitions and the way we reckon with death and mourning for the many deceased people who are no longer "with us" but reduced to an image "in us" and "beyond us" (Brault and Naas, 2001, p. 2). Like Freud, and Abraham and Torok, Derrida too discussed the relationship between memory and mourning, addressing the shift of the discourse to a particular incorporation of the Other, as the dead (or loss) becomes interiorized as a fixed idealized image. Derrida (2001) suggested that if we are able to interiorize these important losses with their strong memories attached to them as a fixed, idealized image, then we might sometimes experience a sense of "infinite transcendence." It is the memory of the Other who had touched our world so significantly that allows us to reflect this loss and open up to creative expressions (Derrida, 2001).

Art and Mourning: The Role of Creativity in Healing Trauma and Loss will illustrate these theories with the work and thoughts of artists, writers and one scientist who confronted death, trauma, loss and mourning at certain times in their life. With their individual, creative expressions, they were able to change their experience of temporalization. This new experience of time can lead to feelings of transcendence and infinity. As I mentioned previously, however, when mourning cannot fully take place—due to the flooding of affects, or because of strong defenses such as splitting or disassociation—depression can settle in and the artist can experience time as something frozen or standing still.

Most of the artists chosen for this book are modernists; all were born in Europe, two were Holocaust survivors and three moved to America later in life. Modernism helped to define the social and cultural realities of the late nineteenth and early twentieth century, fostering provocative new ideas and artistic innovations. These artists explored a new visual language and nonlinear formalism, focused more on popular content and the subversion of conventions. Artists, writers and musicians were influenced by the works of Friedrich Nietzsche, Henri Bergson, Albert Einstein and most of all by Sigmund Freud (Gay, 2008). Nurtured by such new cross-cultural and multilingual ideas, an intellectual revolution occurred that exhorted people to challenge social conformity and move towards secularization.

This paradigm shift and its accompanying innovative art movements—such as the Blue Riders, the Fauvists or the Bauhaus, among many others—initiated and encouraged an anti-capitalist perspective that considered artwork on its own terms and not just as a mirror of objective reality. In this age of pluralism and dissent, Artists reevaluated the use of imagination and illusion. As the artist Paul Klee wrote, "Today we reveal the reality that is beyond the visible things, thus expressing the belief that the visible world is merely an isolated case in relation to the universe, and that there are more latent realities" (Chipp, 1968, p. 182). In their search for a new sense of self and a new reality, they experimented with innovative materials, a totally new sense of color, and the use of abstract forms.

It was during this time period that Sigmund Freud theorized a mind with a dynamic unconscious, as well as a discourse between libido and aggression. His technique of free associations and his book *The Interpretation of Dreams*, published in 1900, freed artists up to embrace an imaginative, intuitive individuality. Many modernist artists were fascinated by the "Dream Book" with its sexual symbolizations and condensations of meaning. In 1921, a book entitled *The Mental Patient as Artist* appeared, the first psychobiography of its kind complete with colored illustrations. Published by the Swiss psychiatrist Walter Morgenthaler, who trained with C.G. Jung at the Burgholzli psychiatric hospital in Zürich, Switzerland, this small book about the artist and mental patient Adolph Wölfli greatly excited the modernist artist community and influenced their practice. Morgenthaler's monograph was followed in the next year by the publication of a catalogue of the Prinzhorn collection, called *Artistry of the Mentally Ill*: its illustrations of spontaneous art such as drawings, paintings, and sculpture created by artistically untrained psychiatric patients and prisoners was immediately adopted by the Surrealists and Dadaists as their creative bible.

These creative expressions by the mentally ill showed modernist artists that access to one's unconscious through the use of uncommon expressive techniques—such as automatic writing, drawing and other stream-of-consciousness practices—could be a valuable inspiration for their own artistic work. These spontaneous techniques, later elaborated on by Anton Ehrenzweig (1967) in his psychoanalytic theory of the creative process, were not only innovative and exciting in their own right but could facilitate the expression of mood states and allow the imagery and concepts of the unconscious to surface (Iversen, 2007).

The designation of found objects as art—urinals, shovels, and so on—was most famously championed by Marcel Duchamp, but had also been a practice of the Dadaists who inaugurated their art movement in Zürich in 1916. These spontaneous, often unconscious choices of a random object influenced the more elaborate sculptural images of Abstract Expressionism and Minimalism when a new cultural revolution started during the 1960s, such as in the works of sculptors like Louise Bourgeois and later Eva Hesse. As the sculptor and curator Robert Morris wrote in "Notes on Sculpture" in 1971 when he talked about how to make and exhibit sculpture, "drop, hang, lean—in short act . . ." emphasizing the spontaneous way to create and exhibit art driven by the unconscious (Iversen, 2007).

Modernist artists like the Surrealists and Cubists embraced another creative way to foster free association in the making of collages from random book and magazine images. First introduced by Braque and Picasso, collage-making was later interpreted by the physician and artist Max Ernst (1948) in his essay "Beyond Painting, and Other Writings by the Artist and His Friends": ". . . not unlike the celluloid surface Freud (1925) elaborates on in his 'A Note upon the "Mystic Writing Pad,"' . . . the flickering up and passing by of consciousness in the process of perception" (p. 34) accommodates the accidental and random aspects of art-making and so subverts pictorial convention.

Art from different cultures—like masks from Africa and wood-block prints from Japan, to mention only two—surfaced in works of the modernist artists as visionary abstractions and symbolic expressions, just as the sculptures by Alberto Giacometti were heavily influenced by ancient Egyptian art. This renewed attention in art and sculpture was also extended to mythological figures, such as in the paintings by the Swiss symbolist Ferdinand Hodler. Other Surrealist painters, such as René Magritte, made use of puzzling metaphorical imagery, indicating both a wish and a fear that viewers would look behind it for hidden meanings.

Like all applied psychoanalytic techniques in art-making, these new ideas and tools paved the way for more introspection, spontaneous expressions and exploration of the self. They also freed up repressed feelings such as ambivalence and aggression. Artists became risk-takers, enjoyed the experimental over the routine, and started to analyze their own dreams and use dream imagery as major templates for their literary, pictorial or sculptural expressions. Access to their own intuition and their unconscious life freed them up for experimentations with new gender roles and for pursuing emancipation within a new world of sexual and political liberation as part of their yearning for artistic autonomy.

These psychoanalytic inflections were also picked up in art criticism. Freud's essay "The Uncanny" (1919), based on his interpretation of the story "The Sandman" by the Romantic German writer E.T.A. Hoffmann, inaugurated an entire tradition of psychoanalytic writing about art. In it Freud explores the permeability of boundaries between the animate and inanimate and the idea of the double in art and literature. "The Uncanny" was a major influence on the Surrealists, opening unexplored avenues of aesthetic interpretation, and elaborating a new sense of loss and mourning. Later, in *Totem and Taboo* (1913 [1912–1913]) Freud described the symbolic meaning of the fetish that disavows the traumatic knowledge of loss and castration, insofar as the fetish serves as a memorial to that loss.

Before talking a little about the artists I will discuss in the following chapters, I would like to say a few words about the writing of psychobiographies, a practice inaugurated by Freud in his essay on "Leonardo Da Vinci and A Memory of His Childhood" in 1910. In each chapter I will focus my attention on only one specific period in the artist's life and work as it relates to a particular loss or trauma and its mourning and to the artist's individual experience at that time. I will look at the aesthetic work within a historical and political context, along with its social, economic and gender ramifications and the personal history of the artist; I will also analyze such aspects of the art as the process of its creation, and its form, line, space, light and color. I believe that the work of art, the personality of the artist, and the zeitgeist mutually inform each other, indeed that they cannot truly be separated from each other. Art can be understood at times as the artist's attempts to rework a particularly challenging time period in his or her life on an aesthetic level (Izenberg, 2003). However, we should not underestimate that any work of art is also a meaningful and independent object that can be enjoyed as well when it is fully divorced from the life and emotional experience of the artist (Alfonso and Horney Eckardt, 2005).

In Chapter 1, I will address two concepts of time, *chronos* and *kairos*, both relevant to the creative encounter, focusing on the selected works of three artists—the Swiss sculptor and painter Alberto Giacometti, the German poet Rainer Maria Rilke and the French-American artist Louise Bourgeois—who actively dealt with death and issues of mourning in their artistic work. I hope to demonstrate how each of these artists employs different creative methods, imagery and techniques during times of loss to achieve a sense of *kairos* time, an experience of time that is related to the "oceanic feeling" first described by Romain Rolland and later by Freud in *Civilization and Its Discontents* (1930).

Chapter 2 will look at drawings and one painting by the Swiss painter Paul Klee, each from his final working period and thus influenced by the artist's knowledge of his terminal illness and his exile from Germany. Klee's ability to suspend reality through the process of consistently drawing allowed him to enter into dialogue with his own creations as well as with his past and present. This creative dialogue allowed Klee to secure for himself a non-threatening future in spite of his terminal illness and slow physical deterioration. The artist was able to restore a balance with the universe and counteract his fear of abandonment through death.

Considering the subject of trauma and loss in Chapter 3, I will introduce the artist Dina Gottliebova Babbitt, a very young adult Holocaust survivor. Gottliebova Babbitt was forced by the infamous Dr. Mengele to paint portraits of Gypsies in Auschwitz during World War II. A few weeks later all imprisoned Gypsies, or Roma as we call them today, were sent to the gas chamber and perished in one night. This trauma was so overwhelming for the young artist that she internalized these losses and entombed them within her psyche, thus preventing her real work of mourning, and destroying her capacity throughout the rest of her life to symbolize and recover her true creativity. In spite of her long and otherwise satisfying life, the artist could not access her full artistic potential, nor could she access a different experience of time. In an attempt to recover and mourn her dead friends, she made it her mission—though ultimately unsuccessful—to recover her original remaining "Gypsy Portraits" from the Polish government and the Auschwitz Museum.

Chapter 4 will review a cycle of small paintings and drawings that the Swiss artist Ferdinand Hodler made of his model and lover Valentine Godé-Darel between 1908 and 1915, while she was suffering from and eventually died of breast cancer. I will analyze these paintings in light of both Hodler and Godé-Darel's mourning processes. Documenting the slow decline of Godé-Darel not only revived Hodler's own early childhood losses, but also allowed the artist to finally mourn them. While painting and drawing Godé-Darel's illness, he contemplated both her death and his own, allowing him to access a different sense of time and creative space. In the process, he (and we, the viewers) are able to mourn our own past, present and future losses.

In Chapter 5, I will focus on Eva Hesse's sculpture *Hang Up* of 1966, which forms a transition in Hesse's work from the wall to the floor space, as well as a transition to a different kind of mourning for several of her traumatic losses. Hesse was separated from her parents as a toddler due to the Holocaust, after that ordeal lost her mother to suicide, and as a young woman struggled with cancer. In her early work, the feminist Hesse dealt with mourning imagery in a more playful, defensive way; the sculpture *Hang Up* and her use of new innovative materials in later sculptures, however, paved the way to a more abstract and mature acceptance of loss and of her ability to contain her feelings of mourning and emptiness in her later sculptures of various vessels.

In Chapter 6, I will explore the mourning of beauty's transience by highlighting some of the paintings of the late English artist Lucian Freud, whose incredible painterly skills allowed him to project inner affective emotions onto the external surface of the canvas in the painted flesh and skin of his models. Freud's particular use of texture, pigment and color, as well as his consistent presence over days, weeks and months with his sitters, provided a sort of second skin, a container and a form of a transitional object. The artist's ability to visually penetrate the intimate, internal space of his models allowed him, as well as the viewer, to mourn the transience of beauty, the passage of time, and ultimately the loss of life itself.

The trauma of René Magritte's mother's suicide when he was a young teenager became a major preoccupation in some of his surrealistic paintings. In Chapter 7, I will analyze how this trauma influenced the content, style and technique of a number of his paintings, and I will argue that creating these pictures reinforced his strong defense, an unconscious attempt to avoid mourning. Magritte seems to have incorporated or entombed this loss within his psyche, halting or freezing time altogether, thereby protecting himself from being re-traumatized. While his pictures are fascinating and beautifully executed from a technical perspective, they often keep the viewer at an emotional distance through their obsessive repetition of the same surreal images, thus mirroring the artist's repressed affects and the halting of time.

In Chapter 8, I will explore some of Albert Einstein's psychobiography as it relates to his interest in intuition and states of reverie, returning to the concept of *kairos* time discussed in Chapter 1. Looking at his correspondence, I will interpret these states of reverie as they relate to Einstein's relationships with the people closest to him, particularly his two sons, his wives and the close professional colleagues who became his lifelong friends. This analysis will demonstrate his great ability for emotional involvement with the individuals closest to him, and at the same time illustrate that Einstein was most comfortable with intimate, personal relationships that granted him ample space and time, mirroring his scientific theories.

In the pages that follow I will try to understand the change that occurs in the perception and experience of time when creating art in a period of loss and mourning. I will focus on the concept of the "oceanic experience" that emerged in the correspondence between Sigmund Freud and the Nobel winning novelist and social critic Romain Rolland between 1923 and 1936. Reacting to Freud's writing on religion in *The Future of an Illusion* in 1927, Rolland sent a letter to Freud discussing his personal experience of the "eternal, a feeling without perceptible limits, like oceanic . . ." (Parsons, 1999, p. 173). Freud wrote about these feelings being "limitless," forming "an indissoluble bond of being one with the universe . . . and the external world as a whole" (Freud, 1930, p. 65). Rolland put it in relation to the oceanic, defining it as limitless, timeless and boundless. While Freud stressed the more cognitive perceptual aspect of the oceanic experience, Rolland's understanding of it was more metaphysical, influenced by his studies of the Indian mystics and his own spiritual quest (Saarinen, 2012). He called this spiritual, infinite sense of self a "formless Being, nameless, homeless and timeless, the very substance and breath of all life" (Rolland, 1947, p. 10).

Anton Ehrenzweig (1967), the psychologist and art educator, expanded on these two readings of the oceanic state and recognized its significance for the artist. He suggested that this fluid, diffuse, holistic perception called the oceanic experience plays an important role in symbol formation. He felt this "low level vision" and "unconscious scanning" was necessary to involvement in artistic expression (pp. 32–46). He saw unlimited interpretation between image and content in this state, a merging of inner and outer worlds, and the ability to dissolve boundaries of space and time, while making creative use of unconscious forms and perceptions. He fostered in his students the artistic value of accessing these "manic oceanic states" encompassing a sensation of "envelopment fusion" (p. 244). Marion Milner (1987) believed that an artist can make intentional use of these oceanic states to foster deeper creative expression (p. 197).

The ability to access the oceanic state can be different for each artist and artistic period, and can serve different functions when dealing with loss and mourning, not unlike the different ways Freud, Rolland and Ehrenzweig experienced and describe this feeling. It may result in a sense of artistic reverie, alleviating a sense of terror or fear of death and moderating acute mourning into novel artistic expression: new content and form, even a different experience of time and being in the world. There are particular situations in an artist's life, however, when this all-encompassing artistic reverie and imaginative thinking, so close as it is to Freud's day-dreaming, cannot be fully accessed due to an overwhelming trauma that is too painful to experience and process artistically. Artistic expression might still take place, but the artist cannot reach this oceanic state, this state of reverie, and can never fully reach and work through her loss and mourning. Manic defenses might then prevent genuine unconscious expression, resulting in a different, less satisfying creative expression, and preventing the satisfying working through of trauma and mourning. On the difference between these two kinds of creative response to loss, Julia Kristeva has remarked that "If loss, bereavement and absence trigger the work of the imagination and nourish it permanently as much as they threaten and spoil it, it is also noteworthy that the work of art as fetish emerges when the activity of sorrow has been repudiated" (1989, p. 19).

In the next chapter, I will explore the relationship between time and timelessness as it relates to loss, bereavement and absence in the lives and works of sculptors Alberto Giacometti and Louise Bourgeois, as well as of the poet Rainer Maria Rilke. But I will begin by reaching back to the cultural archive of late antiquity in introducing the philosophical inquiries of St. Augustine, whose reflections on poly-temporality were linked to a potentially life-threatening illness. By looking at personal narratives and the artistic forms created during these specific stages of life, we will see the ghosts of the past unmasked and brought forth in art as both fetish—a more defensive engagement—and as transformation, facilitating the imaginary and thus securing a renewed and creative future.

References

Abraham, N. and Torok, M. (1994) *The shell and the kernel*. Chicago: University of Chicago Press.

Alfonso, C. and Horney Eckardt, M. (2005) Epilogue: Creativity and polysemy—on the limits of pathography, psychobiography and art criticism. *The Journal of the American Academy of Psychoanalysis and Dynamic Psychiatry*, 33: 235–237.

Bollas, C. (1987) *The shadow of the object*. New York: Columbia University Press, p. 35.

Brault, P. and Naas, M. (2001) Introduction. In *The work of mourning*. Derrida, J. Chicago: University of Chicago Press, pp. 1–19.

Chipp, H.B. (1968) *Theories of modern art*. Berkeley: University of California Press.

Derrida, J. (1986) *Memoires for Paul de Man* (C. Lindsay, et al. Trans.). New York: Columbia University Press, p. 57.

Derrida, J. (2001) *The work of mourning*. Chicago: University of Chicago Press.

Dreifuss-Kattan, E. (1990) *Cancer stories: Creativity and self-repair*. Hillsdale, NJ: The Analytic Press.

Ehrenzweig, A. (1967) *The hidden order of art: A study in psychology of artistic perception*. London: Phoenix Press, 1988.

Eichendorff, J. von (1995). Moonlit Night. *Der ewige Brunnen. Ein Hausbuch deutscher Dichtung*. L. Reiners (Ed.). Munich, Germany: C.H. Beck, p. 552.

Ernst, M. (1948) *Beyond painting: And other writings by the artist and his friends*. New York: Wittenborn, Schultz.

Freud, S. (1900) The interpretation of dreams. *The standard edition of the complete psychological works of Sigmund Freud* (Vols. 4, 5). London: The Hogarth Press, 1953.

Freud, S. (1910) Leonardo Da Vinci and a memory of his childhood. *The standard edition of the complete psychological works of Sigmund Freud* (Vol. 11: 59–138). London: The Hogarth Press, 1957.

Freud, S. (1913 [1912–1913]) Totem and taboo and other works. *The standard edition of the complete psychological works of Sigmund Freud* (Vol. 2: 1–162). London: The Hogarth Press, 1981.

Freud, S. (1917 [1915]) Mourning and melancholia. *The standard edition of the complete psychological works of Sigmund Freud* (Vol. 14: 237–258). London: The Hogarth Press, 1957.

Freud, S. (1919) The uncanny. *The standard edition of the complete psychological works of Sigmund Freud* (Vol. 17: 217–253). London: The Hogarth Press, 1955.

Freud, S. (1924) A note upon the "mystic writing-pad". *The standard edition of the complete psychological works of Sigmund Freud* (Vol. 19: 227–234). London: The Hogarth Press, 1981.

Freud, S. (1927) The future of an illusion. *The standard edition of the complete psychological works of Sigmund Freud* (Vol. 21: 1–56). London: The Hogarth Press, 1961.

Freud, S. (1930) Civilization and its discontents. *The standard edition of the complete psychological works of Sigmund Freud* (Vol. 21: 59–145). London: The Hogarth Press, 1961.

Gay, P. (2008) *Modernism: The lure of heresy from Baudelaire to Beckett and beyond*. London: W.W. Norton & Company.

Iversen, M. (2007) *Beyond pleasure: Freud, Lacan, Barthes*. University Park, PA: Pennsylvania State University Press, p. 78.

Izenberg, G. (2003) Intellectual-cultural history and psychobiography: The case of Kandinsky. *The Annal of Psychoanalysis*, 31: 21–33.

Klein, M. (1975) *Love, guilt and reparation: And other works, 1921–1945*. New York: Delacorte Press.

Kristeva, J. (1989) *Black sun*. New York: Columbia University Press, p. 5.

Laub, D. (1995) Truth and testimony: The process and the struggle. In *Trauma, exploration in memory*. C. Caruth (Ed.). Baltimore, MD: Johns Hopkins University Press, pp. 61–75.

Levinas, E. (2000) *God, death and time*. Stanford, CA: Stanford University Press.

Milner, M. (1987) *The suppressed madness of sane men: Forty-three years of exploring psychoanalysis*. London: Tavistock.

Morgenthaler, W. (1921) *Ein Geisteskranker als Künstler*. Leipzig, Germany Ernst Bircher.

Ogden, T. (2007) A new reading of the origin of object relations theory. In *On Freud's "Mourning and melancholia."* L. Fiorini, et al. (Eds.). London: International Psychoanalytic Association.

Parsons, W.B. (1999) *The enigma of the oceanic feeling: Revisioning the psychoanalytic theory of mysticism*. New York: Oxford University Press.

Prinzhorn, H. (1995) *Artistry of the mentally ill: A contribution to the psychology and psychopathology of configuration* (E. von Brockdorff, Trans.). Vienna and New York: Springer.

Rolland, R. (1947) *Journey within (Le voyage interieur)* (I. Pelt, Trans.). New York: Philosophical Library.

Saarinen, J.A. (2012) The oceanic state: A conceptual elucidation in terms of model contact. *International Journal of Psychoanalysis*, 93: 939–961.

Schwab, G. (2007) Derrida, Deleuze, and the psychoanalysis to come. In *Derrida, Deleuze, Psychoanalysis*. G. Schwab (Ed.). New York: Columbia University Press, pp. 1–54.

Sirois, F. J. (2008) Aesthetic experience. *International Journal of Psychoanalysis*, 89: 127–142.

Winnicott, D.W. (1965) *The maturational processes and the facilitating environment*. London: Hogarth Press.

Winnicott, D.W. (1971) *Playing and reality*. New York: Basic Books.

1

ALBERTO GIACOMETTI, RAINER MARIA RILKE, LOUISE BOURGEOIS

Time and timelessness in art and mourning

In this first chapter, I will discuss the concept of time as it relates to art and mourning and place particular emphasis on the change in one's perception of time brought about by the end stage of life or in trauma. I will argue that the act of creating, in particular through writing and sculpting, can serve as a powerful tool that allows the person facing death and trauma to work through the painful mourning that comes with loss or with the end stage of life. This occurs in large part because one's perceptions of time can change while being actively involved in artistic expression. Temporalization is no longer measured in a linear way, but becomes transformed by the mystery of death, bringing the movement of time towards transcendence and infinity. This change allows for time to stand still and resemble the eternal, establishing a unique relationship between the subject and his or her future.

I will illustrate this central thesis with a close analysis of vignettes of the life and works of the bishop, writer, and philosopher St. Augustine in late antiquity, and with vignettes from the life and works of the artists Alberto Giacometti and Louise Bourgeois, as well as by discussing a letter and some poems by the German poet Rainer Maria Rilke. These four examples will illustrate various ways to relate to time, demonstrating the desire and attempt to achieve eternity.

Writers such as Marcel Proust (1914–1918), William James (1890), Virginia Woolf (1925), Oscar Wilde (1891), Jorge Luis Borges (1941) and W. G. Sebald (2001), to mention a few, all tried to penetrate time's secrets as well. Proust (1914–1918) demonstrates that artistic activity always embraces the imaginary and thus is an experience of time regained. Proust addresses a new conception of temporality, "a round-trip journey from past to present and back," as Julia Kristeva explains (1996, p. 168). In Borges' short story, "The Garden of Forking Paths" (1941), he tells a suspenseful story that occurs in an absurd world where time is not singular. The narrator must imagine that he has already accomplished a difficult task in the future "as irrevocable past," even extending this duplication to space and time, "one sinuous spreading labyrinth that would encompass the past and the future" (Bal, 2003, pp. 119–130). The psychological aspects of time have been explored by philosophers such as Immanuel Kant (1781), Edmund Husserl (1905), Søren Kierkegaard (1972), Martin Heidegger (1962), Henri Bergson (1922), Maurice Merleau-Ponty (1962), Paul Ricœur (1983) and others.

One of the first thinkers to explore the intersection of artistic creation and the collapse of time into eternity was St. Augustine (354–430 A.D.), the bishop and writer from the Hippo Regius, located in today's Algeria. I would like to briefly turn to Augustine's exploration of time in order to illustrate the ways in which one ancient thinker used the art of writing as a means to overcome time and face his impending death.

Time is discussed separately as physical time and human time, but as Yuval Dolev (2007) points out there is only one time: the discussion of the same present. "The distinction between the past, present and future is merely an illusion," writes Albert Einstein (Calaprice, 2000, p. 75), addressing the metaphysical question about time posed by Kierkegaard who tells us that "the present moment is that ambiguity in which time and eternity touch each other" (1972, p. 89). Einstein's special theory of relativity denies the existence of absolute time of the present moment, as two simultaneous events would be seen occurring at different moments when viewed from different reference points. Thus time is not independent of space, but the rate of time and measure of space, is affected by the force of gravity. Therefore, each observer has his own measure of time. Time and its measure involve an interplay between subjective and objective time. Husserl (1905) sees the world necessitating an inner time-consciousness, since he believes that with every conscious experience or action, there exists a subjective time experience, a facet of the experience of the self. Kant in his *Critique of Pure Reason* (1781) suggests that space and time are not objective realities existing independently of the mind, but rather are created by the mind. The postmodern philosopher Derrida fragments the time experience of a pseudo-continuity of discrete elements. He thinks that the fragmentation of time goes hand in hand with the dismantling of the self as an entity through time (Meissner, 2007).

In Augustine's *Confessions*, as he lay on what he believed would be his deathbed, he looked back and memorialized his life. By writing down the memories of his life, Augustine captured his past in a physical book, which he hoped would survive him and both teach and influence many religious men in the future. In this process of recording his past, Augustine placed particular emphasis on Book 13, the philosophical and religious reflection of time and eternity.

"What is this time?" wrote Augustine, "If no one asks me, I know; if I want to explain it to a questioner, I do not know. But at any rate this much I dare affirm I know: that if nothing passed there would be no past time; if nothing were approaching, there would be no future time; if nothing were there, there would be no present time. . . . On the other hand, if the present were always present and never flowed away into the past, it would not be time at all, but eternity. . . . Thus we can affirm that time is only that it tends towards not being" (letter 11.14).

Augustine, a man of 43 years at the time of his writing, was confined to his bed due to debilitating inflammations. "As for my spirit," he wrote to a friend, "I am well through the Lord's good pleasure . . . pray for me, that I may not waste my days and that I may bear my nights with patience" (letter 38.1). When Augustine came close to death during this time, he wrote that he walked "in the valley of the shadow of death" (letter 38.1). In fact, however, he continued to live for another 30 years. At the time of his death, he had written a total of 93 books; *Confessions* was number 33 (Brown, 1993).

In the passage quoted above, Augustine struggles with the measurement of time, and the paradox of the being and non-being aspects of time. Later he places past and future within the present by adding the idea of memory and expectation, the idea of the fantasy of a long future and a long past.

How then does Augustine perceive eternity? He combines the mourning of the finite with the celebration of the absolute. He counteracts the fear or threat of the end of time with its images of exile, vanity, darkness and night with the opposite templates of home, living a full life, light and eternity (Ricœur, 1983).

Eternity, Augustine said, is "forever still, nothing moves into the past: all is present at once" (letter 11.13). "It is eternity which is supreme over time, because it is never ending present that you are at once before all past time and after all future time. Your years are completely present to you all at once, because they are at a permanent standstill" (letter 13.16).

Augustine's elaborations of eternity lead us to an understanding of the experience of time and timelessness in art and mourning. While absorbed with writing his autobiography at the precise period when he felt threatened by a devastating illness and close to death, Augustine counteracted the flux of time by engaging in the creative and time-extending act of writing. Through this act, he was able to reach a sense of being one with the world and to counter his fear of being abandoned through death.

I will differentiate between two different experiences of time within the artistic process. First, I will discuss the Greek concept of *chronos*, representing chronological, measured time, as a countable duration that can be perceived objectively. *Kairos*, on the other hand, is the Greek concept of time as due measure, representing fulfilled time in the timeless atmosphere of the creative encounter itself. The coexistence of these two different temporalities offers exciting insights, addressing a feeling of enlightenment, a fusion with the object and a touching of the eternal. Both of these time concepts are part of art-making and any creative process, but are especially meaningful for artists mourning the threat of death caused by illness, old age or trauma, who attempt to unconsciously overcome the limits of time and with it the fear of death. The rhythmic involvement and full absorption within the creative process can then lead to the attainment of *kairos* time, a state of fusion with the universe, allowing for an illusion of the standstill of time.

Sigmund Freud (1925) suggested the "mystic writing-pad" as a metaphor for the self and its perception of time. In his illustration, the conscious and unconscious surfaces are divided but yet are still interrelated parts of one system. "It is as though the unconscious stretches out feelers through the preconscious towards the external world and hastily withdraws them, as soon as they have sampled the excitations coming from them," wrote Freud (1925, p. 231). The unconscious links past time, the place where unconscious memories are stored in a pictorial archive, to present time, where these visual memories intermingle with thoughts in the present. The artist retrieves images linked to memories from his and her pictorial archive of the past, but she also uses material and associations to mold its content into a form in the present time. Freud (1900), in *The Interpretation of Dreams*, explored the timeless properties of the unconscious. Time in the dream and in art with its affects and wishes is always experienced in the present, even though it is often based on experiences and feelings from another time (Bonaparte, 1940). Marie Bonaparte wrote: "This flight of tyranny of time which we are able to review each night seems . . . to represent one of the greatest wish fulfillment accomplished by the dream for the benefit of human beings who remain harnessed to time's chariot while day lasts" (Bonaparte, 1940, pp. 461–462).

In artistic expression, time can unfold within a session or a working period, but the working session also allows for the storing of psychical memory for future construction.

Most likely, the Greek concept of time as *chronos* is related to the Greek god Cronus, or Kronos, in classical antiquity. Cronus is the youngest of the Titans, a divine descendent of the earth goddess Gaia and the sky god Ouranus. Cronus is the harvest deity represented by a sickle. He oversees agriculture and measures the progression of the crops, that is, time in relation to nature's cycles.

The time concept of *chronos* relates to the setting, namely the framework in which art-making can take place. It both fosters and limits time, due to the fact that it functions within the metric system. Progress in the creative activity is associated with the time concept of *chronos*, too, as the artist tries to use creatively the subjective times of the present with the past and its realm of memory, to secure a future. *Chronos* is related to Freud's concept of *Nachtraglichkeit*, translated in the Standard Edition as "deferred action" but literally translated as "afterwardsness," describing a dimension of the psyche that brings back an active transforming memory from the past, often beyond conscious recollection, addressing two directions of the temporal experience both backwards and forward (Lacan, 1975). This time concept is not necessarily linear, as it raises the possibility that what comes afterwards may give meaning and form to what came before (Freud, 1918).

This concept of time is also true for the creative, artistic process whereby we often experience time as circular or as a spiral, as we integrate experiences from different time periods into a sculpture or piece of writing in the here and now. Said differently, the writing in the here and now re-informs memories of the past as well. For Freud, the past is not only alive in the present, but the present also revives the past, through transference; thus memory is not only an inscription but also a force, constantly reconstructing the past and giving consistently new meaning to the present (Cournut, 1999).

The Greek god Kairos, on the other hand, is depicted as a young man with short hair at the back and a lock on his forehead. The lock is said to represent the opportunity to seize the appropriate moment, a way to understand the truth. Citing the art of weaving, *kairos* would explain the perfect balance and harmony of correct timing, the parting of the threads on a loom allowing for another thread to be woven in the space. This timing cannot be understood in measurable, *chronos* time, but rather in *kairos* time. *Kairos* describes the exact moment, the perfect timing of an interpretation or an insight, measuring the fulfillment of time. It seems that in the time concept of *kairos*, *chronos* is actually dissolved (Meerwein, 1988). The scholastic philosophers call it "nunc stans," the standing still of present time. In *kairos* the flux and duration of time seems suspended, and the tenses are superseded. Freud (1930), citing Romain Rolland, the French novelist, called the emotional experience going along with this sense of time, a feeling of "eternity," of something limitless and unbounded, as it were, or "oceanic" (p. 64): in 1930 Rolland had quoted the Indian philosopher Ramakrishna, who said, "the spirit is an ocean . . . boundless, dazzling, with great luminous waves" (Fisher, 1988, p. 12). In 1927, Rolland added in a letter to Freud that he always found this particular experience of time, what I refer to as *kairos* time, as a "source of vital renewal . . . a spontaneous religious sensation . . . a prolonged intuitive feeling . . . surpassing traditional categories of time, space, and causality" (Fisher, 1988, p. 10). He believed that this particular experience and the sensation of its time concept offers imaginative potential, allowing the artist to access his unconscious and creative inspiration. It is an experience of the unity of the extreme feelings of sadness and happiness or bliss and despair. *Kairos* as well as *chronos* also seems to be related to Kristeva's concept of "women's time," time from the unconscious point of view of motherhood and reproduction, which is both cyclical and eternal. This refers on the one hand to the chronological time of the cycle of menstruation, and to the cycles of generation, but it addresses also *kairos* time, the all encompassing cosmic cycles, and to the "out-of-ordinary-time-and-space sense of pregnancy and involvement with baby" (Chodorow, 2003, p. 1189).

This sense of suspended reality fosters a fusion with an idealized inner or outer object, but it can also bring forth loneliness and fear of death. Relinquishing object libido in *kairos* time can also elicit fears of dissolving into the Other and thus can bring forth the fear of killing part of oneself. Thus *kairos* is always guided by an inherent ambivalence, as fusion can lead to eternal happiness or to annihilation through death. In psychoanalysis, as well as in religious and artistic practices, we intend for such instances to happen, but only rarely do they come to full fruition. However, when they are accomplished, the feeling of a "participation mystique," a mystical reunion or reverie can develop that is particularly meaningful during the second half and at the end stage of life. Jacques Derrida (1987) called it "jouissance," a kind of feminine pleasure, "the God face," addressing the mythical sense of time. The French philosopher Emmanuel Levinas (1987) understood this movement of time in *kairos* as the "transcendence towards the Wholely Other, the infinite" (p. 31). This feeling of timelessness contains a special form of affective experience, an unconscious wish to extend time indefinitely.

The act of being completely absorbed in a creative activity, accessing both *chronos* and *kairos* time, allows for the time to be superseded. The artist who is faced with death or trauma cannot only access her pictorial and affective memories stored in her creative unconscious, but also can express universal fears of loss, fostering a fusion with the universe, and counteracting fears of separation through death.

The perception of time and timelessness in art, mourning and in the end stage of life

There are different ways to counteract the fear of death, to extend time and attain *kairos* time. The artist Alberto Giacometti employs the illusion of a double that he hoped would magically extend time and simultaneously allow him to mourn painful losses. The poet Rainer Maria Rilke expresses in some of his poems his wish to experience his own present as well as future time, and not only be viewed as having replaced somebody else's past time. In the creation and survival of his work he longed to access the infinite, expanding sense of time. Louise Bourgeois makes use of circular time, a time that never ends. Spending most of the day and night creating, even in her ninety-seventh year of life, Bourgeois was sculpting her traumatic past, informed by her mourning for the present, and thus seems able to postpone her death to what seems an indefinite future.

Despite the same chronometric time sequences, time seems to change as one ages, as one becomes terminally ill, or as one deals with trauma. In each of these circumstances, a person experiences time passing much more quickly; measured time and experienced time no longer seem identical. The perception of gaining or losing time is always related to intact ego functions and the ability to search for or resist the wanted object. The more one progresses towards the end stage of life, the less one is guided by oral, anal or genital object gratification but is rather influenced by the timeless function of the superego and the ego ideal.

We try to continually search for the availability of and the control over the flow of time, in an attempt to emotionally track our lives. If one is no longer able to do this on a constant basis, be it due to old age, terminal illness, or overwhelming mourning, then one is afraid to suffer from fear of death or fear of mental breakdown. People who live in isolation and are sick or traumatized can no longer adequately judge the flow of time, leading them to often perceive time as shorter than it is in actuality; this misperception causes them to fear for their lives (Hartocollis, 1983).

The individual threatened by death or mourning his or her own death sees in the Other the possibility of his/her own death and of time running out. To counteract the fear of one's approaching death, loss and subsequent mourning, a narcissistic transference may develop which is known as the "doppelgänger relationship" or "double relationship" (Dreifuss and Meerwein, 1984). The imago of the double is a familiar theme in Western literature as evidenced by the literature of writers Jean Paul, Heinrich von Kleist, Heinrich Hoffmann, Fyodor Dostoyevsky, Eduard Morike, Guy de Maupassant, Rilke, Wilde and others. The double, or doppelgänger, has been investigated by Rank (1914), Freud (1919), Mario Benedetti (1975), Peter Dettmering (1978), Esther Dreifuss and Fritz Meerwein (1984), and others.

For Otto Rank, the double was Narcissus who sees his own image in the reflection of the water. In the relationship with the double, one does not connect with another, but rather with one's own ego, which appears in the gestalt of one's own double. Thus the doppelgänger is actually an extension of oneself. Because one believes that the double exists outside of oneself, however, the double is simultaneously both part of oneself and not part of oneself, representing both the self and the Other. It allows for the creation of an illusionary timeless world, where the link between the awareness of time passing and the capacity to mourn the passing of time is erased. This dissolving of the link occurs because in the fantasy of the double, one of the doubles persists; but the relationship to the double also involves a split, an ambivalence that cannot be resolved. The doppelgänger, a creation of one's imagination, represents both the being and the non-being, both existing in the present time and fearing that time is running out. As a result, one may come to love one's double or come to harbor a death wish towards it. In some cultures, meeting one's double represents a magical sign that death is approaching, as well as the consoling promise of a second life. Freud (1919) in his work "The Uncanny" suggests that the double can reverse its aspect: "From having been an assurance of immortality, it becomes the uncanny harbinger of death" (p. 235). If one survives through the experience of the double, one fantasizes that one can extend time into the future.

Freud (1919) elaborated on Rank's theory in his work "The Uncanny": "the theme of the 'double' has been very thoroughly treated by Rank (1914). He has gone into the connections which the 'double' has with reflections in mirrors, with shadows, with guardian spirits, with the belief in the soul and with the fear of death; but he also lets in a flood of light to develop the art of making images of the dead in lasting materials. Such ideas, however, have sprung from the soil of unbounded self-love, from the primary narcissism that dominates the mind of the child and of primitive man. But when this stage has been surmounted, the 'double' reverses its aspect" (p. 235).

Alberto Giacometti

In the first half of the twentieth century, many Modernist artists were influenced by Egyptian art. The following artists, to name a few, created drawings modeled after Egyptian originals: Amadeo Modigliani, André Derain, Paula Modersohn-Becker and Pablo Picasso. However, unlike the artists Paul Gauguin, Franz Marc and Ernst Ludwig Kirchner, they did not leave strong Egyptian traces in their own art (Wildung, 2008).

The influence of Egyptian art on Alberto Giacometti left traces on his sculptural work from adolescence throughout his life, which is well documented in a 2009 exhibition named "Giacometti the Egyptian" in the Kunsthaus Zürich, Switzerland. I will focus on Giacometti's interest in Egyptian art as it relates to the double, death and his perception of time.

Alberto was born in 1901, the first child of Annetta Stampa, from Borgonova in the Bergell Valley, and Giovanni Giacometti. The daughter of a teacher, his mother

Annetta was very cultured and the center and stronghold of the family until her death in 1964. His father Giovanni, educated in Munich, Paris and Rome, was the most important Swiss painter of his generation after Ferdinand Hodler. He was influenced by the painter Giovanni Segantini (who painted in Switzerland though was not Swiss), from Maloja, but found his own choice of color in his art related to the theme of his family and in his art of the Engadin landscape, the Swiss high valley where he grew up.

When the artist was 10 years old, typhoid fever struck their Bregaglia Valley in Switzerland and Alberto's mother became gravely ill; she was alternatively comatose and delirious for several months during which time Alberto was not permitted to see her. Wilson (2003) describes the long-awaited emergence of Alberto's mother from the sickroom, skeletally thin, grey-haired and toothless at the age of 40. Wilson suggests that his changed mother must have frightened the little boy very much, who probably viewed her as having risen from the dead. When Alberto was 12 years old, his beloved maternal grandfather Giovanni Stampa, who came to visit their home each morning for breakfast, died unexpectedly. Alberto especially loved and adored his grandfather, who was extremely proud of his artistically talented grandson (Wilson, 2003).

Alberto was introduced to the world of art publications, and he illustrated art history books in his father's studio, where he enjoyed keeping him company. Drawing and reading were his favorite hobbies, and the first drawing he could recall was an illustration of Snow White in her glass coffin, portrayed like an Egyptian mummy, the corpse moving between life and death. In his first conscious artistic effort he drew a copy of Dürer's *Ritter, Tod and Teufel* (Knight, Death and the Devil) (Wildung, 2008). Already as a 16-year-old high school student, Alberto delivered a lecture arguing that Egyptian art and culture superseded Greek or contemporary art. In 1920, he traveled to Florence and for the very first time saw Egyptian art in the original form. He was filled with joy, as he recorded in his diary, when he viewed sculptures of Egyptian heads in life sizes.

In 1933, when Alberto was only 32 years old, his father, also a successful, very well-known artist, died suddenly of a heart attack, and Alberto did not arrive in time to say goodbye. Alberto's shock was so intense that he slept in a room in the same hotel in which his father's body was laid for viewing, and Alberto rigidly and stiffly took to bed himself. He thereby unconsciously illustrated his identification with his dead father, as a result of the guilt he felt regarding his absence immediately before his father's death (Wilson, 2003). He only arose from his bed after his father's funeral. The soul bird on his father's tombstone from 1935 in the cemetery of San Giorgio near Borgonovo is informed by the Egyptian Horus Falkon of King Neb-Re; this influence is demonstrated by the opening base of the stone through which the "ka," the double, can communicate invisibly between life and death and the here and there. Alberto's sculptures created after his father's passing *L'objet invisible* (The Invisible Object) or *Maintenant le vide* (Now the Emptiness), *Mains tenant le vide* (Hands Holding an Invisible Object) were his way to confront this important loss.

Alberto's sadness intensified a few years later when his beloved sister Ottilia died in childbirth. This event pushed him into deep mourning (Wilson, 2003).

From the late 1930s until 1945, Giacometti lived in a small apartment in Geneva and created many female miniature figurines. Nearly every day he visited his mother who educated her grandson, his nephew, Ottilia's son. Wilson (2003) traces these miniature figurines back to his interest in Egyptian "ka" sculptures, serving as spiritual doubles.

These sculptures are like amulets that were meant to protect the souls of the departed from evil on their way to eternal life. The "ka" sculptures praise and hope to magically sustain the creative power of life after death. The hieroglyph sign of ka is a pair of arms pointing upwards. By creating "ka" sculptures, it was believed that one could prolong the existence of the dead and the life of the soul, extending life to the future. In addition, the "ka" figurines could also protect the dead from a second death (Wilson, 2003). Similar to the Egyptian "ka" figurines, the double signifies the threat of death, but can also create the possibility for an imagined second life.

Wilson connects Giacometti's wish to create these small magic sculptures to his need to combat his helplessness after the death of his sister. Wilson argues that the act of carving away at these small sculptures and destroying most of them, allowed Giacometti to combat his early memories of the traumatic death and rebirth of his very sick mother, the sudden death of his grandfather when he was a boy, and the strong feelings of loss and helplessness that were revived by the new traumatic loss of his father and most of all of his beloved sister. These small sculptures thus functioned as magic doubles, with which Alberto Giacometti unconsciously hoped to secure immortality and extend the time span of his sister's soul and his own (Figure 1.1).

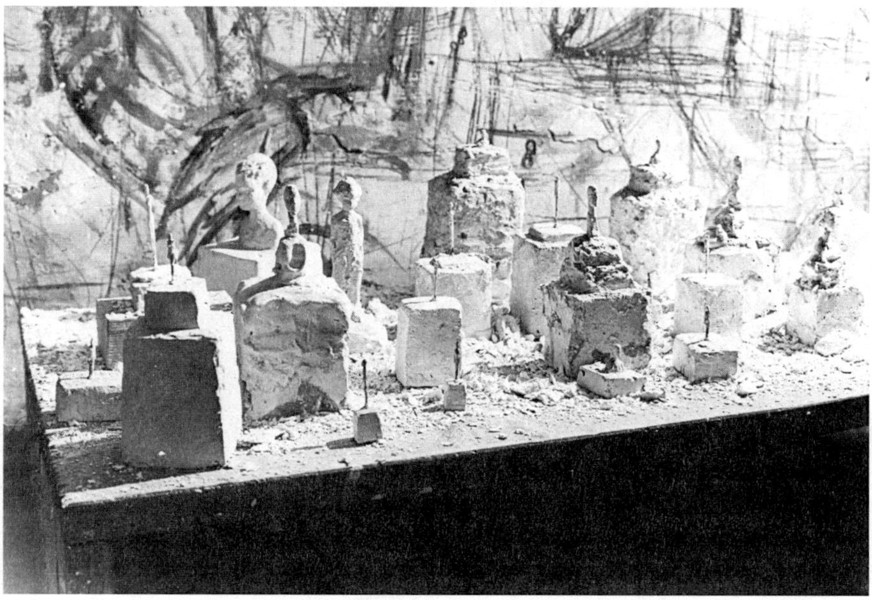

FIGURE 1.1 Brassaï. "Studio of Giacometti, October 1947." Silver gelatin print, 0.198 × 0.295 m. A234Q. Photo: R.G. Ojeda. © RMN-Grand Palais/Art Resource, NY.

Alberto relieved his guilt by immortalizing his sister in his art. By repeatedly creating and destroying these little figurines, Giacometti acted out his own internal struggle with his doppelgänger in his art. He projected not only his helplessness, but also his anger and destructive urges onto these sculpted double figurines; he came to terms with his own helplessness and fear of death and of time running out in this acute mourning period. Working through this period by creating and destroying, and creating again allowed Giacometti to re-experience the flow of time, opening up an internal space for new creativity which ultimately strengthened his identity as an artist (Wilson, 2003).

His sculpture *La main* (1947) reminds the viewer of an oversized hieroglyphic sign. This sculpture was created after the study of an arm of a "ka" of the Egyptian King Hor. Giacometti remarks to David Sylvester in an interview: ". . . and still I find that in painting that an Egyptian arm is closest to a [real] arm" (Sylvester, 1994, p. 146).

In January 1966, while hospitalized in the city Chur, Switzerland, Alberto Giacometti writes his last entry in his diary before his death: "Peaceful here in Chur, all good, becoming healthy, being healthy, I work" (Klemm, 2009, p. 61).

Agamben's (1993) idea of the coming into being through loss is not only true for Giacometti, but for many artists. With the advent of the infinite sense of *kairos* time through creating, the artist can position himself between the finite and infinite, between mortality and eternity in an attempt to illuminate the darkness of death through the process of creation. Freud summarizes it very pointedly in "Creative Writers and Day-Dreaming":

> The relation of a phantasy to time is in general very important. We may say that it hovers, as it were, between three times—the three moments of time which our ideation involves. Mental work is linked to some current impression, some provoking occasion in the present . . . from there it harks back to a memory of an earlier experience (usually an infantile one) . . . and it now creates a situation relating to the future. . . . Thus past, present and future are strung together, as it were, on the thread of the wish, which runs through them.
>
> (1908, p. 147)

How can the conflict between the wish to survive and the realization of death, between the feeling of having infinite time available and the realization that time is running out be overcome? Psychoanalytically speaking, there is a split in the mind of the dying, a splitting off of fantasy from reality, or even what seems a near suspension of reality at the end stage of life. It appears as if the person close to death is fantasizing a new beginning, counting a new type of timeline which contains a future without a deadline; he grapples with the simultaneous feeling of having infinite time available, and the realization that time is running out, as we just read in Giacometti's last diary entry (Dreifuss-Kattan, 1994).

Rainer Maria Rilke

In order to better illustrate this idea of "time split," one can study a vignette of the very end stage of life of the German poet Rainer Maria Rilke, who suffered from chronic leukemia, which at that time could not be treated effectively. Three days prior to his death, Rilke told his doctor, Dr. Hämmerli, that he planned to spend winter on the seashore. Rilke greeted his doctor as he entered the room: "You are here, my dear friend [doctor]. You will keep everything [death!] far from me." On the same day, he told Nanny Wunderly-Volkart, who attended to his terminal care at his beside, "Help me to my own death—I do not want the death of the doctors— I want to keep my freedom" (Meerwein, 1985, p. 183).

As is evident from this example, we all demonstrate unconscious defenses against death and dying, whether we are healthy, sick or terminally ill. It is as if the reality of the id with its unlimited concept of time, takes over the reality of the ego with its understanding of the finiteness of chronological time. The ego, with its ability to measure time, is suspended and its affective capability ceases. As survivors, we are then confronted with the dying person, who harbors elaborate plans for his future in spite of immediate life threats.

As a young man, Rilke composed what he called "Gebete," or personal prayers, in his "Stunden Buch" (Book of Hours). He considered these poems to be the true commencement of his poetic memory, which he wrote in the course of three intense brief periods of inspiration between the years 1899 and 1903. One of these personal prayer poems reads:

> Dying is strange and hard
> if it is not our death, but a death
> that takes us by storm, when we've ripened none within us
> We stand in your garden year after year.
> We are trees for yielding a sweet death.
> But fearful, we wither before the harvest.
>
> III, 8 (Rilke, 2005)

In this poem, Rilke explores what it might mean to experience someone else's death before one's own. Death is especially difficult, according to Rilke, when it is not one's own but rather the unexpected death of another—"dying is strange and hard if it is not our death." This line, I would like to suggest, deeply resonated with Rilke because of his childhood experience as a replacement child, born one year following the death of his older infant sister.

René Karl Wilhelm Johann Joseph Maria Rilke was born in 1875 in Prague, Bohemia, one year after the birth of his sister, who died one week after her birth. The given name "René," the "Reborn," was an obvious reference to the loss of his unknown sister. For Rilke's mother, who still grieved the loss of her baby daughter, her newborn son was to be the substitute for his dead sister. She considered him a replacement child, and dressed him as a little girl with long hair until he entered school at the age of six. In 1884, when he was nine years old, his parents' marriage fell apart. When Rilke was 11 years old, his father forced him into the military academy, away from home where he suffered from severe separation anxieties. His mother's initial denial of her son René's gender must have been very confusing for him on a psychological level, as well as on a temporal one. René had to replace his sister's past time in the present, the time of her short life and then death, in order to undo her death (Schwab, 2009). Increasingly unhappy with her own marriage and trying to find a way to mourn, Rilke's mother took little René to church to pray with her. She used to call him "Renée Marie," a female's name. When he was 22 years old, his first lover, Lou Andreas-Salomé, a married Russian-born intellectual, author and psychoanalyst who was 15 years his senior, suggested that he should change his name to the more masculine name of "Rainer." Indeed, in the poem quoted above, Rilke laments the fate of experiencing someone else's death, referencing the fact that his sister's premature death became, in a sense, his own loss even before he was born, and in his years of infancy. Because of his identification with his deceased sister, Rilke feels as though her death became his own. Before Rilke's own harvest, or birth, he already died once through his sister's death and was reborn.

Death was constantly elaborated on in his prose and poetry all through his life but particularly in the *Book of Hours*. In 1903, Rilke traveled by train through the Alpine tunnels to Italy and settled in a pension in Viareggio by the Sea, where he was to recover from physical and psychological exhaustion. In his poetry and prose, which became his transformational objects, Rilke could contain his ambivalent affects, reflect on his guilt for surviving, and express the pain that came with being a substitute for his unknown dead sister. He composed 34 poems in seven days in April. In this third book, called the book of "Poverty and Death," he writes:

> God, give us each our own death,
> The dying that proceeds
> From each of our lives:
> The way we loved,
> The meaning we made,
> Our need.[1]
>
> II, 6 (Rilke, 2005)

Rilke views death as a very intimate striving to find meaning and identity. After marrying and fathering a child, he must have identified with his own early childhood, a period that was overshadowed by death. He turned the concept of death in his poems and prose into a lifelong companion, a shadow doppelgänger. In this poem, he expresses his desire to have his own death, rather than the premature death of his sister. He also casts aside the death that his militaristic father unconsciously hoped for by forcing his son into military academies for five years at the very young age of eleven. Rilke's father hoped to force upon his son the identity of a real man, an army officer, which he, as the father, failed to become, in order to ban him from the Oedipal competition.

In his self composed epitaph, Rilke wrote:

> Rose, oh pure contradiction, desire,
> To be no one's sleep under so many lids.[2]

Rilke was diagnosed with leukemia shortly before his death. He believed that his looming death was caused by blood poisoning as the result of having been pricked by a rose thorn. The rose can be interpreted as the symbol for the primary object, the mother, with its ambivalent content of beauty and desire as well as thorny destruction (Meerwein, 1985).

"I am a stranger to myself, as though someone unknown had poisoned my mother as she carried me," he writes in the two last lines in the poem 11.2 in the *Book of Hours*. Did he identify with the corpse of his sister or was he poisoned by the toxicity of his mother's grief? These lines illustrate the poet's wish to avoid his own painful death as the German word *Schlaf* translates into "sleep," meaning death. Rilke identifies with his deceased sister and the experience of a more fragmented past related to it. The poet longs to die "nobody's" death other than his own, and he communicates his longing to experience his own present time, as well as his own future time. He expresses his wish to have a death in which he would be able to access the infinite sense of time, or *kairos* time. He told his doctor when he was actively dying that he wished to spend time at the seashore, unconsciously longing to merge with the ocean and the sky, and thereby extend time to eternity. As Meerwein (1985) points out, Rilke rather hoped that all the eyelids, *Lidern* in German, could transform themselves into the German *Liedern*, or "songs" in English, which would heighten his heavenly ascent and thus transcend time. Both German words *Lider* and *Lieder* are pronounced and sound the same. In his epitaph, Rilke expressed his wish that just as he was able to transcend personal time and ascend towards infinity in *kairos* time while writing prose and composing poetry, so too he would be able to do so in his death (Meerwein, 1985).

Louise Bourgeois

The fear of death often involves a fear of pain, both emotional and physical, which distorts the feeling of time. Emily Dickinson explains this concept very well when she writes "Pain—expands the Time . . . Pain contracts the Time" (Hartocollis, 1983).

To cope with the reality of time and its passing and the wish to transcend this finiteness, artists often employ different artistic media. Artistic narrative is the medium of temporality in Louise Bourgeois' late sculptural work that moves between memory, trauma and compulsive reenactment. Choosing the circular, rather than the sequential time in most of her sculptures created during her extreme old age, Bourgeois invokes a sense of being in the present, in spite of infusing form with personal memories from her past. When one looks at her art, trying to understand its meaning, one is placed in the present time of viewing; her sculptural narrative, as well as her narrative of memory, become her medium of temporality (Bal, 2001).

Louise Bourgeois was born in 1911 into a family of artist-restorers of tapestries. Her maternal lineage was rooted in Aubusson, in the heart of France, founded in the sixteenth century by tapestry manufacturers. Aubusson was located near the river Creuse, ideal for the washing and dyeing of wool. Her grandmother had her own workshop, and later her mother did as well. After the start of the twentieth century, her father Louis discovered the value of old, tattered tapestries found in attics and stables. Louise's parents worked together to collect, restore, and then sell ancient tapestries. Her father collected the tapestries and supplied the materials needed for their restoration. Then, Louise's mother restored, cleaned and repaired the original designs, keeping to the original design as closely as possible with new spun wool. Finally, her father later sold them through a gallery in Paris.

Louise's mother involved her in their restoration workshop at the young age of eight, after her day at school, in the reconstruction of missing patches of cloth (Kellein, 2006). After her mother became ill with the Spanish flu and later with tuberculosis, Louise's father became a philanderer. In 1922, when Louise was 10 years old, Sadie Gordon Richmond was hired as Louise's English tutor and soon became her father's mistress. Sadie lived in the family's home until the mother's death in 1932. Louise took care of her ailing mother. Bourgeois finished at the lycée (high school) and then broke off her studies in mathematics after a few years at the Sorbonne in order to study painting and sculpture with many well-known artists in Paris. She was close to the Surrealists in Paris at that time. In 1938, she

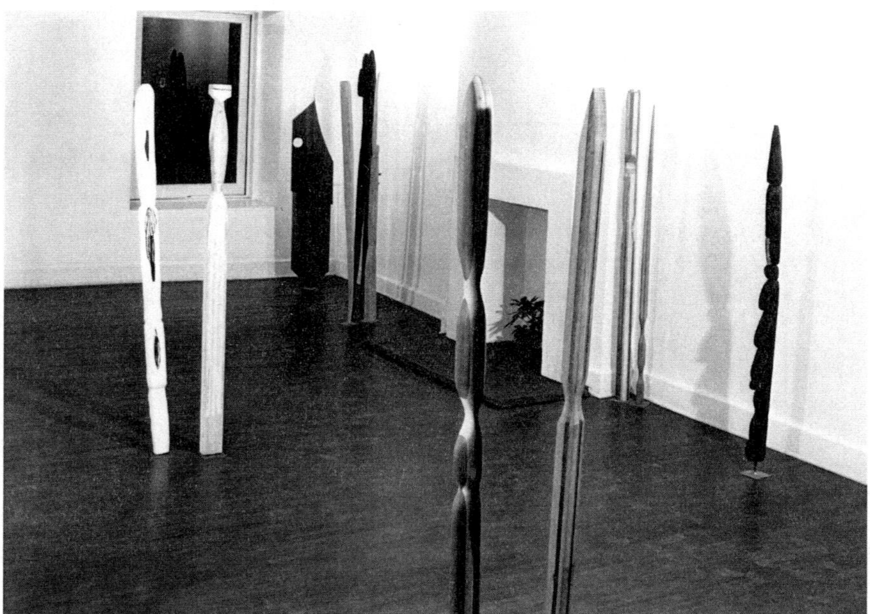

FIGURE 1.2 Louise Bourgeois. *Personages*. 1941. Wood. Art © Easton Foundation/Licensed by VAGA, New York, NY.

married the American art historian Robert Goldwater and moved with him to New York, where they raised three sons.

Bourgeois set her own rules, addressing gender and sexuality, exploring outside as well as her internal narrative and imagery. Her artistic path from the 1940s to the 1970s was recognized as a more subversive one. She was always ready for change and moved from a more Modernist tradition "towards the darkly subjective and elaborately eclectic realm of Postmodernism" (Buck, 1994, p. 16).

Some of her early sculptural works reveal the mourning she experienced for her mother, and moving away from France and leaving her family and friends behind. Bourgeois called her life-sized wood sculptures from 1941 *Personages* (Figure 1.2). The artist called these slim wood sculptures, which can stand alone or in groups, a memorial. She comments: "I was missing certain people I have left behind. It was a tangible way of recreating a missed past. The figures were presences that need the room. . . . It was the reconstruction of the past" (Nixon, 2005, p. 119). These slender posts and planks were made of balsa wood on the scale of a human body and painted black, white or red. They were set directly onto the floor without bases. These "portable brothers," as the artist called them, are set in the exhibition room, demonstrating a relationship with each other and with the viewer (Nixon, 2005, p. 124).

These sculptures remind the viewer of aboriginal "burial poles," with which Bourgeois might have been familiar through her husband's research in primitive art. The aboriginal Yolngu people of Western Australia placed their dead skeletons' bones into delicately painted, hollowed out burial poles that stood in the ground. This practice dates back 50,000 years, making it the oldest cultural tradition in the world.

Bourgeois, influenced early in her career by her Cubist and Surrealist artist friends, told her friends Pierre Matisse and Marcel Duchamp that her "Personage" sculptures were a manifestation of her homesickness. The hammering, chiseling and scraping of these totemic forms allowed the artist to exorcise her rage that was fostered by being forced to sever these attachments from her past. The act of creating these sculptures also permitted her to symbolically relive her past by re-creating her childhood memories with these sculptures. The artist considered Giacometti her spiritual mentor, evident by the similarity between these fetish-like objects and Giacometti's transition in the 1930s from the horizontal to the vertical posture, to the thin, upright sculptures for which he is most famously known (Nixon, 2005).

"Art is the Guaranty of Sanity," wrote Louise in one of her installations, addressing her need to keep creating in order to deal with her traumatic past. Bourgeois' obsession was her family, and thus this theme of family was the focal point and root of most of her creative work in her last 27 years. "Child Abuse" is an illustrated autobiographical text about the traumatic experience of her childhood that was published in *Artforum* in 1982 at the time of her first retrospective exhibition at the Museum of Modern Art in New York when the artist was 70 years old. This text describes and illustrates her archetypical childhood trauma when, as mentioned previously, Louise's father hired Sadie Gordon Richmond, an English tutor for his 10-year-old daughter Louise and her brother. Louise felt betrayed by her father, mother and especially by Sadie, who destroyed what she retrospectively perceived as the family idyll. "Everything I do is inspired by my early life," says the artist. "My name is Louise Josephine Bourgeois. My father was named Louis, my mother Josephine. All my work that I've done, and all the subjects I have ever worked on, find their source in my childhood," writes the artist (Xenakis, 2008, p. 11).

In her two sculptures *Untitled*, 1996 (Figure 1.3, see also Plate 1), made out of clothes, bone, rubber and steel, and *Spider*, 1997 (Figure 1.4), made from steel, fabric, wood, glass, silver, gold and bone, the then 85- to 86-year-old Louise Bourgeois expressed a counterforce against the chronology and the linear unfolding of time. By presenting found objects from her real and imagined past, Bourgeois forces the viewer to confront both her memory and trauma of the "once-upon-a-timeness" of her past and "now time" of her present; the viewer faces her unfinished conflict within the flow of chronological time (Bal, 2003; Pollock, 1999). The viewer becomes engaged with the three-dimensional sculptural work in a shared space of mourning in a circular viewing of time. Viewer and work are isolated and separate from one another, but do exist in close proximity to each other by being located in the same arena. The permeability of affects is intense, as the formal structure of the sculptural work allows the expression of latent, unconscious material to surface within an inter-subjective exchange of viewing. "The literalness of the object, mere objecthood, is sustained only by recourse to a highly metaphorized account of the encounter with the object, a theatrical encounter . . ." writes Briony Fer (1999, p. 31).

The sculpture *Untitled*, 1996 (Figure 1.3, see also Plate 1) presents the branches of a metal tree hung with hangers made of cow bones. Clothes from a time past, such as undergarments with lace, silk slips, and a black beaded cocktail dress are neatly draped over the cattle-bone hangers, along with children's undershirts and a silk blouse with paper-stuffed protruding breasts. Clothes are often referred to as the body's second skin, an additional protection that the artist now sheds in her old age. The clothing is a *memento mori* for the past time when the feminine, slim body was adorned with these youthful pieces of clothing. At the same time, the artist illustrates the loss of her past through her manipulation of the dissonant forms of the outsized cattle-bone hangers supporting the delicate remnants of a once young, sexy woman with a beautiful body. Now however, these once delicate pieces of clothing have aged and withered, leaving traces of the past, and presenting as objects beyond time (Schwab, 2009). This dichotomy effectively expresses Bourgeois' mourning for the time that had passed and her mourning for her own death in the near future. The oversized bone hangers also symbolize the skeleton beneath the clothing, stripped of its flesh, creating a morbid effect and a ghostly presence, both ironic and deeply moving. The tree, possibly the tree of life, is free standing, which allows the viewer to walk around it. This act of walking around the sculpture tree causes the viewer to experience no physical beginning or

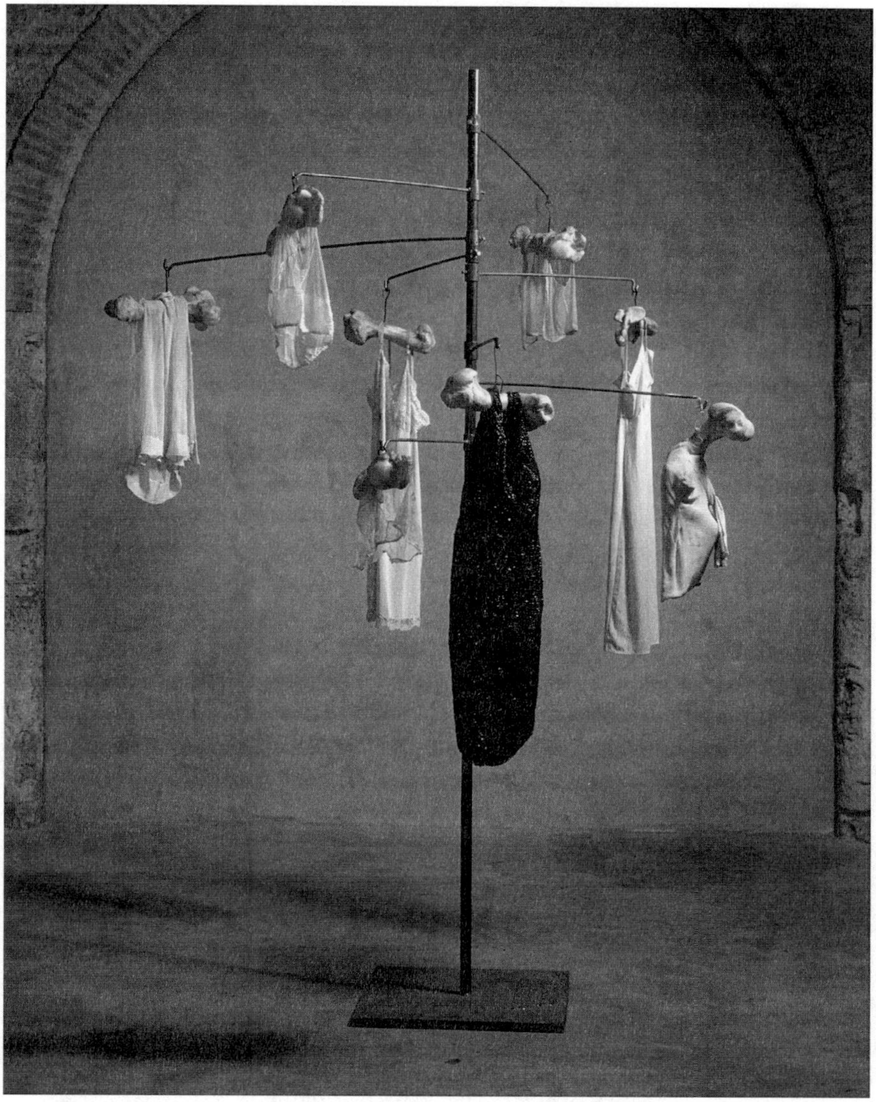

FIGURE 1.3 (see also Plate 1) Louise Bourgeois. *Untitled*. 1996. Cloth, rubber, bone and steel (118¼ × 82 × 77 in.). Art © Easton Foundation/ Licensed by VAGA, New York, NY.

ending. Bourgeois fixes her worn clothes in the "now" of chronology. The viewer is directly confronted with the psychic as well as the physical, with the uncanny effects of violence through death and tender vulnerability of the feminine and the erotic (Pollock, 1999). "Seamstress, Mistress, Distress, Stress" is inscribed into the metal stand, to help the viewer understand the biographic traumatic road map that informs so many of Louise Bourgeois' late sculptures. The sculpture also illustrates her own personal time, informed by her past losses, the trauma these losses caused, showing us her mourning of new losses in the present, such as her impending death and all of mankind's deaths in the future.

Spider, 1997 (Figure 1.4) is one of many of Louise Bourgeois' cell sculptures. The term "cell" is a play on the word for the name of the town "Choisy Le Roy," where Louise grew up in France. "Choisy" translates from French as "locus of memories," locating Bourgeois' experiences in the cell of her home. The "cell" also relates to the cells in her body, as she repeatedly addresses her childhood trauma, engaging the viewer to partake in her past with all of its psychological and physical dimensions (Qualls, 1994). By creating her own architecture, a sculptural installation, Bourgeois informs the viewer that the cell represents a prison as well as a "habitat" that goes around and around, housing physical and mental pain. It is a self-contained circular structure with the sense of circular time, attempting to integrate, merge and disintegrate (Bourgeois, in Cooke and Francis, 1991, p. 60).

In her cells, as Crone and Graf Schaesberg write, "Louise Bourgeois beguiles the viewers with an all encompassing and pervasive transparence of sculptural elements, physical form and sensuality . . ." (p. 102). The cell allows the viewer an

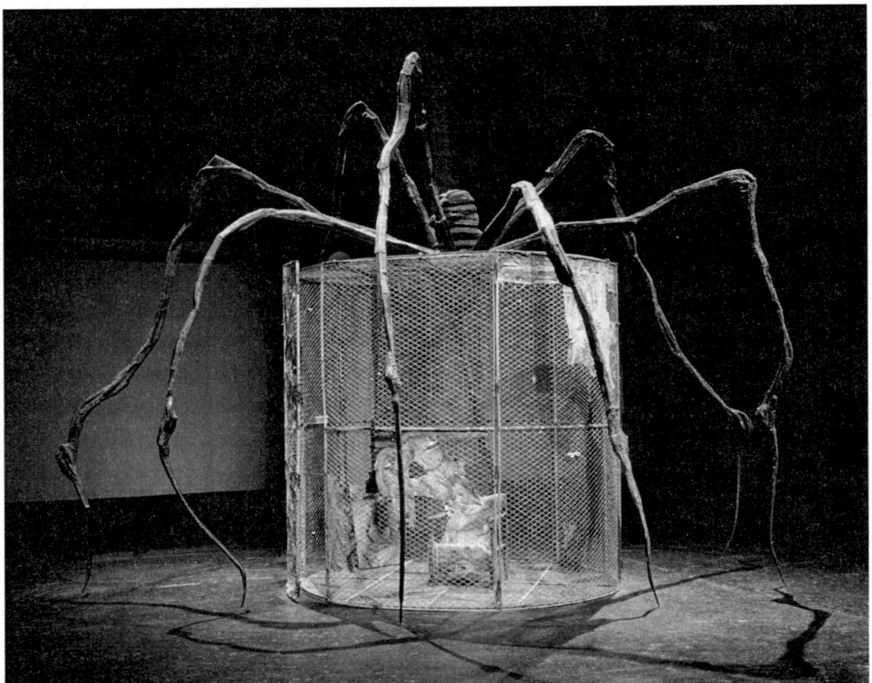

FIGURE 1.4 Louise Bourgeois. *Spider*. 1997. Steel, fabric, wood (188 × 270 × 172 in.). Art © Easton Foundation/Licensed by VAGA, New York, NY.

external view of a partially enclosed interior, and thus fosters a distinction to be made between the inside and outside space; by doing so, the artist addresses the thrill of looking and being looked at. The cell is a resting place for her mind as well as a permeable container for her childhood memories, both limiting and protecting (Bal, 2001). The giant spider that towers over the cell structure is metaphorically weaving a "web home" for old stories that are newly perceived and experienced in the "present" of extreme old age, or as Kristeva put it, "a tireless re-weaving of the maternal web" (2007, p. 249). The spider protects the cage but looms over it, threatening it as well. The cell sculpture relates to Louise's images from the past, and also facilitates the expression of childhood memories that are being newly mourned. The sculptures become a psychic inscription that is exteriorized, transforming the trauma of childhood into dreamlike associations from the past that are paradoxically set in the present. This work, which tells the viewers a story, is extremely varied, dense in meaning, visually multilayered, and addresses the concepts of "home," "body" and "memory," and of time.

In one of her descriptions of her work, Louise explains that the spider relates to her mother, who restored and repaired tapestry that little Louise then mended in her mother's workshop when she was not in school. Needles, thread, distaff and weaving are all metaphorically linked to spiders that spin webs, and relate to the thread of life, to time that unravels and to the precariousness of life hanging by a thread. This sculpture represents reparation, as spiders keep repairing their webs, as well as destruction. There is an empty chair placed in the middle of the cell that is covered with old fabric as well as fragments of old tapestries which are also placed on the steel cell walls, reminiscent of her mother's occupation. The "royal" chair is empty, suggesting that her mother is long dead and the artist's death is soon to follow, evoking a loss, as well as the missing Other. Louise's mother is idealized in her absence and the artist is identified with her mother's creative capabilities. At a young age Louise lost her father to her tutor, at the age of 21 she lost her mother due to illness, and she later lost her country by moving to the United States; all of these losses exacerbated the strong effects of her traumas in her early childhood. Like the chair that is covered with an old piece of tapestry, old fragments of tapestry are stuck to the cage's wall, with a perfume bottle from the time of the artist's youth. The cell thus houses and shelters Bourgeois' childhood memories, objects from the past but visualized in the present.

The huge spider sculpture that hovers over the cage has a belly full of glass eggs that are also wrapped in fabric. Thus the ceiling of the cell sculpture is made of eggs, projecting the future into the interiority of the steel mesh, while the spider's thick legs and extreme scale address the threat at the exteriority of the sculpture. Spiders do have an uncanny way of being suddenly present and elicit the image of being both motherly and frightening. Spiders are resilient because they have the power to survive and carry their own architecture on the outside (Pollock, 2001). Like Louise does in her sculptures, spiders also use found objects, fragments of the past when building their webs.

Inside the cell are small glass containers, called ventouses, with which Louise used to treat her mother when she was suffering from the flu and from tuberculosis. These cupping jars have been used since the seventeenth century to relieve pain and congestion by inducing suction of the bodily tissues through the glass cups. Thus, the two glass objects, the eggs and the cups, symbolically connect birth and death and function as objects of transition. The stopwatch in the cell has both the viewer and the artist wondering whether time will be running out or standing still for her. "Scraps of the past hover over the defined divide between memory and trauma, between narrative and compulsive reenactment . . .," writes Bal (2003, pp. 116–144).

By externalizing her anxiety onto the containing form of the cell, while juxtaposing very different elements, Bourgeois creates in the cell sculptures a literal embodiment of the idea of circular time, through the creation of both a spiral and a web.

In these two sculptures created in the artist's very advanced age, and in many of her other pieces created in this time period, Bourgeois focuses on the passing of time and on solitude and mourning that comes not only with the trauma of the past, but also with aging. The fragility of old age now again searches for the protection of the idealized object, the mother, represented in the overpowering, potentially destructive, but also protective spider sculpture guarding her eggs, as well as in the tapestry-covered chair in the middle of the structure, tracing her losses. In the first tree sculpture mentioned earlier, maternity and femininity merge as the artist again needs the protection of the mother and perceives herself both as mother and child.

Some of her recent soft sculptures point again to early trauma as well as to the small child's transitional object (Winnicott, 1971) in their soft, sometimes weightless form. These soft sculptures are often deformed, like human puppets with patched up bodies. Reconciled to the ultimate separation from mother, they are transitional objects of old age, easing the transition from life to death.

In Bourgeois' late sculptures, past and present time merge into "now time." While constantly creating both during the day through sculpting and at night through her *Insomnia Drawings*, she addresses the idealized and the traumatic past, merges fantasies and fear of separation with past and present mourning. In the process of creating, the artist attains a sense of *kairos* time, a wish for time to stand still and a longing to fuse with the maternal, as a defense against the fear of death. In her artistic expression, Bourgeois transcends the personal through her visual vocabulary and reaches universal themes of loss, mourning and a new perception of time. With striking discipline she was creatively weaving her own fate into the future.

Creative remembering and timelessness

The ability to employ artistic expression to work through mourning of both physical as well as mental pain due to old age, terminal illness and trauma, allows the artist to reconnect with the good internal object and the experience of time as it connects to these early affects. Artistic creation can facilitate mourning, and also produces an *Andenken*, the potential of remembrance. For the philosopher Georg Wilhelm Friedrich Hegel, to remember (*Erinnern* in German), is to transform or to interiorize, *Er-innerung*, to re-member is a way to overcome the past and to integrate one's memories as part of the Self. It allows for an *Andenken*, a lasting memorial freed from the restriction of time and space, containing in the original perception (Haverkamp and Chadwick, 1985). The act of being absorbed within one's creative activity in frequent time sequences throughout the days, weeks and years, represents the rhythmic time concept of *chronos*. Creating consistently allows the artist to deny or escape the external encroachment of time with its limits and its often traumatic memory. Creative expression allows the artist to find a more timeless world, a limitless unification of inner and outer reality or of God and Man that consists of a fantasized union with the maternal breast or a surviving double, a subjective mother time with its cyclic repetitions and cosmic sense of eternity (Kristeva, 1986). The flux of time and sense of duration then seems suspended as in *kairos* time, as the artist feels a complete absorption in being and doing, and a sense of "jouissance" (Lacan, 1999), a particular enjoyment and pleasure that fosters unity and selfhood in spite of life threat. Then the abyss of death can be bridged by filling it up with the "now" which seems outside the flow of time, a transcendence towards the Infinite that is marked by the mystery of death and the face of the "Other," so well described by Augustine. The successive moments of the creative act can then provide a sense of time standing still, with its enveloping feeling of eternity.

Notes

1 *O Herr, gib Jedem seinen eigenen Tod*
Das Sterben, da aus jedem Leben geht,
Darin er Liebe hatte, Sinn und Not.

2 *Rose, oh reiner Widerspruch, Lust*
Niemandes Schlaf zu sein
Unter so viel Lidern

References

Agamben, G. (1993) *Stanza: Word and phantasm in Western culture* (R.L. Martinez, Trans.). Minneapolis, MN: University of Minnesota Press.

Augustine. (1993) *Confessions*. Book Eleven, chs. 24–30: 211–231 (F.J. Sheed, Ed. and Trans.). Indianapolis and Cambridge: Hackett Publishing.

Bal, M. (2001) *Louise Bourgeois' Spider: The architecture of art-writing*. Chicago: The University of Chicago Press, pp. 116–131.

Bal, M. (2003) Anthropometamorphosis: Forking paths and crystals—Louise Bourgeois' philosophy of temporality. In *Louise Bourgeois: Intimate abstractions*. B. Stammer, K. Becker, A.Weitzler and V. Schulte-Fischedick (Eds.). Berlin: Akademie der Künste.

Benedetti, G. (1975) *Psychiatrische Aspekte des Schopherischen*. Göttingen, Germany: Vandenhoeck und Ruprecht.

Bergson, H. (1922) *Duration and simultaneity*. New York: Bobbs-Merrill, 1965, p. 2.

Bonaparte, M. (1940) Time and the unconscious. *International Journal of Psychoanalysis*, 21: 427–468.

Borges, J. (1941) The garden of forking paths. In *Collected fictions* (A. Hurley, Trans.). New York: Penguin, 1998, pp. 119–130.

Bourgeois, L. (2005) *Louise Bourgeois: Destruction of the father—Reconstruction of the father: Writings and interviews, 1923–1997*. Cambridge, MA: The MIT Press.

Brown, P. (1993) Introduction. In *Confessions*. Augustine. Book Eleven, chs. 24–30: 211–231 (F.J. Sheed, Ed. and Trans.). Indianapolis and Cambridge: Hackett Publishing.

Buck, R. (1994) Introduction. In *Louise Bourgeois: The locus of memory works, 1982–1993*. C. Kotik, T. Sultan and L. Leigh (Eds.). New York: The Brooklyn Museum and Harry N. Abrams, Inc, pp. 9–11.

Calaprice, A. (Ed.). (2000) *The expanded quotable Einstein*. Princeton, NJ: Princeton University Press.

Chodorow, N. (2003) "Too late": Ambivalence about motherhood, choice and time. *Journal of the American Psychoanalytic Association*, 51: 1181–1198.

Cooke, L. and Francis, M. (1991) A retrospective exhibition. Bern, Switzerland: Kunstmuseum Bern.

Cournut, J. (1999) The meanings of deferred action. In Report from France: Deferred action. *Journal of the American Psychoanalytic Association*, 47: 213–225.

Crone, R. and Graf Schaesberg P. (2008) *Louise Bourgeois: The secret of the cells*. New York: Prestel.

Derrida, J. (1987) *Memoires for Paul de Man* (A. Ronell, Trans.). New York: Columbia University Press.

Dettmering, P. (1978) *Dichtung und Psychoanalyse* (Vol. 2): *Shakespeare, Goethe, Jean Paul, Doderer*. Eschborn, Germany: Fachbuchhandlung für Psychologie, p. 179.

Dolev, Y. (2007) *Time and realism*. Cambridge, MA: The MIT Press.

Dreifuss, E. and Meerwein, F. (1984) Das Doppelgänger-Motiv. *Zeitshrift Psychomatische Medizin Psychoanalyse*, 30: 282–291.

Dreifuss-Kattan, E. (1994) *Cancer stories: Creativity and self-repair*. Hillsdale, NJ: The Analytic Press.

Emerson, R.W. (1840) Circles. In *Essays and Lectures*. New York: The Library of America, Library Classics of the United States, 1983, pp. 404, 411, 412.

Fer, B. (1999) Object beyond objecthood. *Oxford Art Journal*, 22, 2: 25–36.

Fisher, D.J. (1988) *Romain Rolland and the politics of intellectual engagement*. Berkeley, CA: University of California Press.

Freud, S. (1900) The interpretation of dreams. *The standard edition of the complete psychological works of Sigmund Freud* (Vol 9: 141–154). London: The Hogarth Press, 1959.

Freud, S. (1908) Creative writers and day-dreaming. *The standard edition of the complete psychological works of Sigmund Freud* (Vol. 9: 152–153). London: The Hogarth Press, 1959.

Freud, S. (1918) From the history of an infantile neurosis. *The standard edition of the complete psychological works of Sigmund Freud* (Vol. 17: 1–123). London: Hogarth Press, 1981.

Freud, S. (1919) The uncanny. *The standard edition of the complete psychological works of Sigmund Freud* (Vol. 24: 217–252). London: The Hogarth Press, 1981.

Freud, S. (1925) A note upon the "mystic writing-pad". *The standard edition of the complete psychological works of Sigmund Freud* (Vol. 29: 227–234). London: The Hogarth Press, 1959.

Freud, S. (1930) Civilization and its discontents. *The standard edition of the complete psychological works of Sigmund Freud* (Vol. 21: 205–214). London: The Hogarth Press, 1986.

Hartocollis, P. (1983) *Time and timelessness*. Madison, WI: International Universities Press.

Haverkamp, A. and Chadwick V. (1985) Error in mourning: A crux in Hölderlin—"dem gleich fehlt die Trauer" (Mnemosyne). In *Yale French Studies, No. 69. The lesson of Paul de Man*. Peter Brooks (Ed.). New Haven, CT: Yale University Press, pp. 236–253.
Heidegger, M. (1962) *Being and time* (J. Macquarie and E. Robinson, Trans.). New York: Harper and Row.
Husserl, E. (1905) *The phenomenology of internal time-consciousness*. Bloomington: Indiana University Press, 1964.
James, W. (1890) *Principles of psychology*, 2 vols. New York: Dover Publishing, 1950.
Kant, E. (1781) *Immanuel Kant's critique of pure reason* (N. Kemp Smith, Trans.). New York: St. Martin's Press 1964.
Kellein, T. (2006) *Louise Bourgeois: La famille*. New York: D.A.P./Distributed Art Publishers.
Kierkegaard, S. (1972) *The concept of anxiety*. Princeton, NJ: Princeton University Press.
Klemm, C. (2009) Alberto Giacometti: Ein agyptischer Lebenslauf. In *Giacometti, Der Agypter*. P.K. Schuster (Ed.). Berlin and Munich: Stadliches Museum Berlin and Deutscher Kunst Verlag München, pp. 46–61.
Kristeva, J. (1986) Women's time. In *The Kristeva reader*. T. Moi (Ed.). New York: Columbia University Press, pp. 187–213.
Kristeva, J. (1996) *Time and sense: Proust and the experience of literature* (R. Guberman, Trans.). New York: Columbia University Press.
Kristeva, J. (2007) Louise Bourgeois: From "Little Pea" to runaway girl. In *Louise Bourgeois*. F. Morris (Ed.). London: Millbank, pp. 246–252.
Lacan, J. (1975) *Le séminaire: Livre 1—Les écrits techniques de Freud, 1953–1954*. Paris: Seuil.
Lacan, J. (1999) *Écrits* (B. Fink, Trans.). New York: W.W. Norton and Company.
Levinas, E. (1987) *Time and the Other* (R.A. Cohen, Trans.). Pittsburg, PA: Duquesne University Press.
Meerwein, F. (1985) Starb Rainer Maria Rilke seinen eigen Tod? In *Psychoanalyse*. Neuchâtel, Switzerland: A. La Baconniere.
Meerwein, F. (1988) "Spute Dich, Kronos, Fort Den Rasselden Trott . . ." (November 27, 1988, unpublished first manuscript).
Meissner, W. (2007) *Time, self, and psychoanalysis*. New York: Jason Aronson.
Merleau-Ponty, M. (1962) *Phenomenology of perception*. New York: Routledge and Kegan Paul.
Nixon, M. (2005) *Fantastic reality: Louise Bourgeois and a story of modern art*. Cambridge, MA: The MIT Press.
Pollock, G. (1999) Old bones and cocktail dresses: Louis Bourgeois and the question of age. *Oxford Art Journal*, 22, 2: 73–100.
Pollock, G. (2001) Maman! Invoking the m/Other in the web of the spider. In *Louise Bourgeois: Maman*. M. Wachtmeister (Ed.). Stockholm: Atlantis, pp. 65–97.
Proust, M. (1914–18) *Remembrance of things past*, 3 vols. (C.K. Scott Moncrieff and T. Kilmartin, Trans.). New York: Vintage, 1982.
Qualls, L. (1994) Louise Bourgeois: The art of memory. *Performing Arts Journal* (September 2001).
Rank, O. (1914) Der Doppelgänger. *Imago* 3, 97: 234–236.
Ricœur, P. (1983) *Time and narrative* (Vol. 1) (K. Blaumer and D. Pellamer, Trans.). Chicago, IL: Chicago University Press.
Rilke, R.M. (2005) *Rilke's book of hours: Love poems to God* (A. Barrows and J.M. Macy, Trans.). New York: Riverhead Trade.
Schwab, G. (2009) Personal communication.
Sebald, N.G. (2001) *Austerlitz*. Munich: Carl Hanser.

Sylvester, D. (1994) *Looking at Giacometti.* London: Chatto and Windus.

Wilde, O. (1891) *The picture of Dorian Gray.* Oxford: Oxford University Press, 2006.

Wildung, D. (2008) Und immer wieder Agypten. In *Giacometti, Der Agypter.* P.K. Schuster (Ed.). Berlin and Munich: Stadliches Museum Berlin and Deutscher Kunst Verlag München.

Wilson, L. (2003) *Alberto Giacometti: Myth, magic, and the man.* New Haven, CT: Yale University Press.

Winnicott, D.W. (1971) *Playing and reality.* New York: Basic Books.

Woolf, V. (1925) *Mrs. Dalloway.* New York: Harcourt Brace and Company.

Xenakis, M. (2008) *Louise Bourgeois: The blind leading the blind.* Arles, France: Actes Sud and Galerie Lelong.

2

PAUL KLEE

Psychic improvisations in the shadow of death—some thoughts on creativity and the oceanic experience

> In the here I am utterly incomprehensible. For I dwell just as well with the dead
> As with the unborn.
> Somewhat closer to creation than most.
> But far from close enough.
>
> (Paul Klee, cited after F. Klee, 1962)

Paul Klee's late work was strongly influenced by his chronic, eventually terminal illness which caused his death in 1940. His changing style, form, content, and process are distinct expressions of Klee's awareness of his approaching death. Simultaneous threats from external reality and from his own internal world forced Klee to withdraw emotionally from public life, colleagues and family. During the last three years of his life, all of his creativity was channeled into his art. Born in 1879, he created a quarter of his entire body of work between 1937 and 1940.

Klee demonstrated that art can be conceptualized as an untouchable alternative to reality. While maintaining an active dialogue with his past, present, and future, he suspended reality with his art, creating a sense of time and life security in spite of life threat. Through his constant rhythmic acts of creating, he attained a feeling of becoming one with the universe, restoring his limitless narcissism and counteracting the horror and abandonment of death.

In the art of his final working period, Klee was able to combine his incestuous desires for his mother with pre-Oedipal cravings for the symbolic merger and body creativity of his grandmother. This combination highlighted the timeless function of the ego ideal, providing the illusion and comfort of time standing still.

Sigmund Freud was skeptical of psychoanalysis' ability to illuminate the nature of the artistic process. His works are liberally sprinkled with declarations such as,

"Where the artist gets his ability to create is no concern of psychology" (1913, p. 187). Freud also believed that the end result of the artist's endeavor cannot be judged psychoanalytically: "We have to admit also that the nature of artistic achievement is inaccessible to us psychoanalytically" (Jones, 1957, p. 114). Freud's judgments are consistently unequivocal: "[Psychoanalysis] can do nothing toward elucidating the nature of the artistic gift nor can it explain the means by which the artist works—artistic technique" (1924, p. 65).

However, Freud considered that psychoanalysis might have the ability to shed some light on an artist's motives. This more limited interpretive opportunity hinged on a rough equivalence between creative imaginings and the mechanisms of hysterical fantasy formation. In both, present perceptions are modified through fantasy to assimilate past emotional experiences (Dreifuss-Kattan, 1990). Therein lies the possibility of interpreting the artist's motives from the circumstances of the artist's present and past life.

Freud further enlarged the scope of his inquiry to question where the raw material from which creative products are shaped originate, and he found the answer to be daydreaming, the roots of which extend back to childhood (1908, p. 143). Freud described the process by which a writer creates a world of fantasy and invests it with emotion "while separating it sharply from reality" (p. 144).

> The unreality of the writer's imaginative world, however, has very important consequences for the technique of his art: for many things which, if they were real, could give no enjoyment, can do so in the play of fantasy, and many excitements which, in themselves, are actually distressing, can become a source of pleasure.

The artist is not only able to handle a sharp demarcation from reality, but manifests a curious ability to handle themes that in ordinary life are too painful to bear.

Biographical details

Paul Klee's early life and art can illuminate some aspects of his late work. His artwork, diaries, letters and biographical information will help in understanding more about the particular significance artistic expression had for him at the time he realized his death was approaching. Klee's diaries were published posthumously in 1957 and are a record of an exclusively private autobiography. Klee repeatedly rewrote and edited his diaries before 1916 and then again at later points in his life (Geelhaar, 1979). I was fortunate to visit the Klee Foundation in Bern, Switzerland several times, where I viewed most of his drawings and documents in their original form.

Paul Klee was born on December 18, 1879, in Bern, Switzerland, three years after the birth of his sister Mathilde. Paul's grandfather was an organist from Thuringia, Germany, his father Hans was a music teacher, and his Swiss mother Ida Maria was a professional singer. In 1879, the Klee family settled in Bern, where Hans Klee taught music for 52 years.

In a diary written in 1898 when he was 19 years old (first published in 1957), Klee recorded that at the age of four he received colored chalks from his maternal grandmother. Grandmother Frick, who also drew images, would expose him to colored prints of religious subjects in order to stimulate his artistic curiosity (Grohmann, 1954).

Paul's mother recognized her son's artistic talent early on and saved his childhood drawings and illustrated notebooks from school. Klee recounted in his diary that when he was four he used to rush to his mother for safety when the "evil spirits he was drawing acquired real presence." He wrote, "I ran to my mother for protection and complained to her that little devils had peeked in through the window" (*Diary*, no. 10). Outer and inner realities were confusing for the sensitive, precocious little boy. His mother's interest and understanding in cultural matters stopped, however, when it concerned the latent sexuality of her pre-adolescent son. Klee described his mother's moral outrage upon discovering his "erotic drawings," one of which pictured a "woman with a belly full of children." "I was scared to death," Klee wrote, recalling his mother's scolding (*Diary*, no. 34).

At five years old, Paul began to receive violin lessons from his father. At age 11, Klee became an associate member of the orchestra that performed subscription concerts at the Bern Music Society. After completing a classical humanistic gymnasium, including the languages of Latin and Greek, he knew that he wanted to be an artist. Unlike Klee's father, who wanted his son to follow in both his father's and grandfather's footsteps by becoming a professional musician, Paul's mother supported his wish to go to Munich to study art. His father neither understood then, nor appreciated later, his son's artistic endeavors and did not want "something that bizarre to turn into a profession" (Klee, 1988, p. 23). Klee fell in love several times during this period, and while playing in a chamber orchestra in 1901, he met an accomplished pianist three years his senior named Lily Stumpf who would later become his wife.

Paul Klee's expression of feeling in his early art

Klee's artistic progress in Munich moved slowly. He often felt discouraged and depressed, even contemplating suicide. In 1903 he wrote, "The feeling of responsibility toward my fiancée and parents and unsuccessful attempt to paint often brew a kind of suicidal mood" (*Diary*, no. 469). The following analysis of three early Klee paintings will illustrate how his depressive feelings and sense of loss early in his life motivated Klee to express himself on paper. Art allowed him to "read" his own moods, to keep up a dialogue with them and then, once fixed on paper, to distance himself from his feelings and move on.

In a self-portrait at age 25 titled *Comedian*, 1904 (Figure 2.1) Klee portrayed a man's head in profile with a mask. Both mask and man share the same cap. The mouth's wide, snarling grin exposes his large clenched teeth, conveying a menacing expression. While the man behind the mask remains passive, the mask portrays energy and aggression, representing a healthy reaction to frustration. In a letter to his fiancée he wrote, "The contrast is now coming out better. . . . Head serious, mask grotesque—humorous. Its expression flowed from my deepest soul, so that for the indeterminate future I believe myself to be healed. This Comedian is my most personal work up to now" (F. Klee, 1979, p. 370).

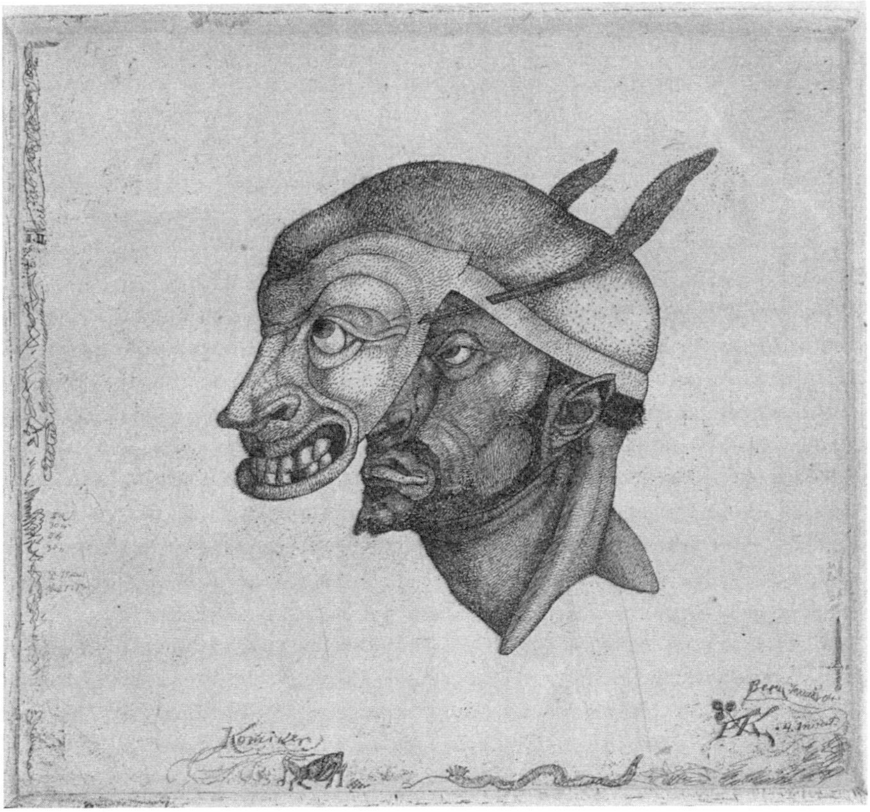

FIGURE 2.1 Paul Klee. *Komiker* [*Comedian*], 1904, 10. Etching. 14.7 × 15.8 cm. Zentrum Paul Klee, Bern.

This picture and its humor served Klee as a catharsis, neutralizing his various negative feelings such as anger and disappointment. Klee added in his diary, "one more thing may be said about 'The Comedian': the mask represents art, and behind it hides man. The lines of the mask are roads to the analysis of the work of art. The duality of the work of art and that of man is organic . . ." (F. Klee, 1964, p. 173). For Klee, the artist and his art are inseparable. Understanding the artist helps one decipher his art, and by analyzing his art one becomes familiar with the soul of the artist. But only through the mask can the artist's true feelings be expressed, which Klee demonstrates so well in his last working period.

About *Menacing Head*, 1905 (Figure 2.2) the next painting in this analysis which he completed at age 26, Klee wrote in his diary: "[It] is a gloomy conclusion. . . . A thought more destructive than action. Pure negation as demon" (*Diary*, no. 510). Vishny (1985) viewed this etching as another self-portrait, pointing to its physical resemblance to Klee. She believes that in this work Klee succeeded in "exorcising his demons" and moved on toward a new artistic expression. In a letter to Lily we read, *Ich schaffe pour ne pas pleure, das ist der lezte und erste Grund* (F. Klee, 1979, p. 492). This phrase combines German and French, the two official

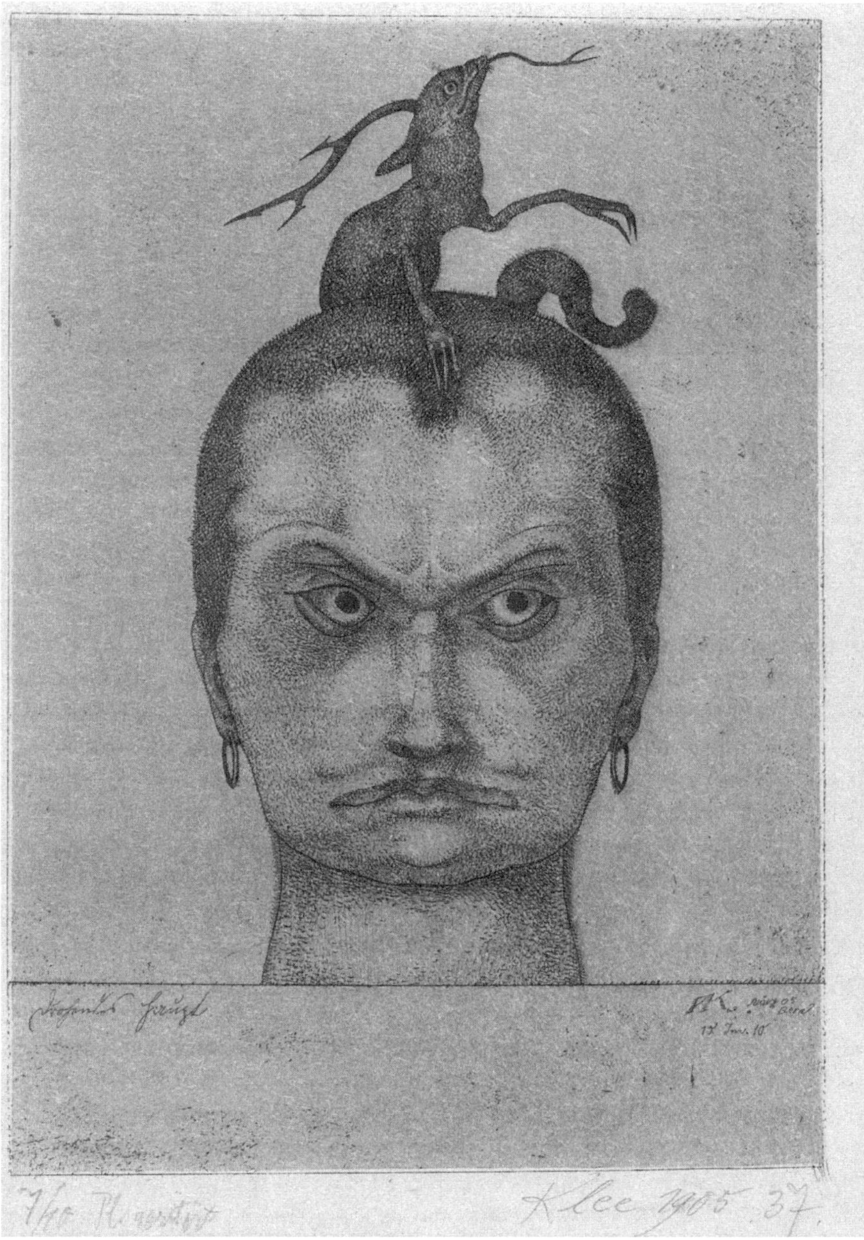

FIGURE 2.2 Paul Klee. *Drohendes Haupt* [*Menacing Head*], 1905, 37. Etching. 19.5 × 14.3 cm. Zentrum Paul Klee, Bern.

languages of his native city Bern. It translates: "I create in order not to cry, this is the last and first reason" (F. Klee, 1979, p. 492). Thus Klee consciously used his art to wrestle with depressive feelings and to overcome them. This ability became immensely important to him in the final part of his life.

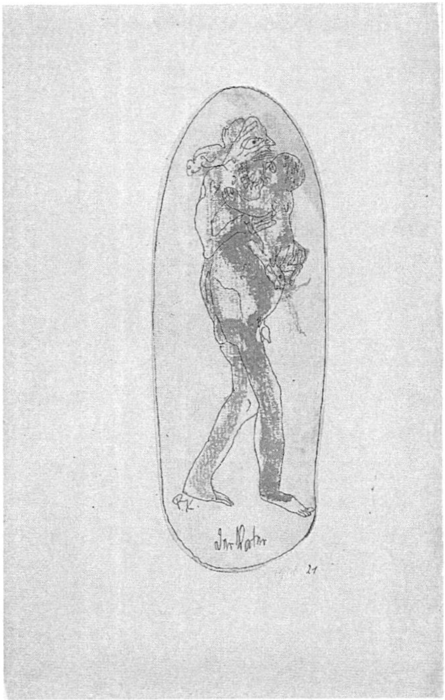

FIGURE 2.3 Paul Klee. *The Father (Two Nudes)*. 1908. Ink and wash on laid paper mounted on cardboard, comp. 6¼ × 2⅜ in. (15.9 × 6.0 cm); mount 9½ × 5⅞ in. (24.1 × 14.9 cm). © Norton Simon Museum, The Blue Four Galka Scheyer Collection.

In 1907, when Klee was 28 years old, he and his wife Lily were blessed with the birth of their only child, Felix. At the time of Felix's birth, Lily was the main breadwinner of the family. An active concert pianist, she was absent most of the day teaching, causing Paul to assume the responsibility of his son's upbringing.

Klee's new role as "mother" is captured in the ink drawing of 1908, titled *The Father (Two Nudes)* (Figure 2.3). In this unusual drawing, Klee depicted himself and the newborn naked, clinging to one another, and thus emphasizing the helpless state of both figures (Vishny, 1985). This picture has particular significance since, towards the end of his life, Klee often compared the process of drawing and painting to "giving birth to children," perceiving his works of art as children, as life's continuation. When Klee was 12 years old, as was mentioned above, he had completed a drawing of a woman with many children in her belly, already identifying with women's ability to procreate and fantasizing about a symbiotic union with his mother. While the androgynous "Father" drawing conveys nearly symbiotic closeness between father and son, the father's movement and facial expression focuses away from the child, towards the future.

During these years in Munich, Klee continued to experiment with colors and also emphasized form. He viewed a Van Gogh exhibition at this time that impressed him immensely. Fascinated by the healing power of Van Gogh's art with which he could easily identify, Klee wrote in his journal of Van Gogh, "Here one sees a mind consumed by a cosmic conflagration. On the eve of the catastrophe, he liberates himself through his work" (F. Klee, 1964, p. 224).

During his first years in Munich, most of Klee's drawings and paintings were inspired by nature. He later began to remove himself from nature, emphasizing the more familiar tonalities in his more childlike drawings and paintings.

In spite of the outbreak of World War I, Klee was extremely productive artistically. In 1914, Klee discovered that his German artist friend August Macke (1887–1914) was killed fighting in France at the young age of 27. Klee's grief was great, as he noted in his diary, "In order to work my way out of my dreams, I had to learn to fly. And so I flew. Now, I dally in that shattered world only in occasional memories—the way one recollects things now and again. Thus I deal abstractly with my memories" (Grohmann, 1954, p. 57). As he described it, art gave him the opportunity to escape the reality of war and death: this abstract way of the arts was a less threatening manner of mourning for his lost friend, or of struggling with his fears about the future (Grohmann, 1954, p. 57). His friend Franz Marc (1880–1916), another artist colleague, was also killed in action just one day before Klee himself was drafted into the German army. This second death prompted Klee's further reflection: "One of Marc's traits was a feminine urge to give everyone some of his treasure . . . My fire is more like that of the dead or the unborn. No wonder that he found more love . . . Art is like Creation: it holds good on the last day as on the first" (*Diary*, no. 1008).

The threat of death reawakened Klee's early symbiotic needs and his wish to fuse with the universe. "I only try to relate myself to God, and if I am in harmony with God, I don't fancy that my brothers are not also in harmony with me . . . I tend rather to dissolve into the whole creation . . . My love is distant and religious. In my work I do not belong to the species, but am a cosmic point of reference" (*Diary*, no. 1008, p. 343). The loss of his two friends fostered his escape from the world of temporal reality into an experience of eternity as a defense against anxiety (Loewald, 1972). After the death of these two German artists, Klee was taken from the front to an air base where he painted planes; he spent most of his time doing office work, however, and was able to paint and draw many pictures reflecting on the horrors of the war. Once again, depressive times stimulated Klee's creativity.

In 1920, Klee was invited to become a teacher and artist in residence at the Staatliches Bauhaus in Weimar. A close friendship developed between Klee and the older Russian artist Wassily Kandinsky, who had come to teach at the Bauhaus a few years earlier. Klee first met Kandinsky in 1911. When the Bauhaus moved to Dessau, they decided to share a townhouse, fostering a closer relationship; this friendship lasted until the end of Klee's life.

Although Klee's life was full of art and teaching, music still remained a very important activity for him. He played his violin daily for hours, often with his wife Lily. Through his music, Klee could lose himself completely in what became for him a spiritual experience. When he played the violin it appeared as though he lost awareness of his surroundings, to an even greater degree with music than with art (Grohmann, 1954). Music allowed him to completely immerse himself in being.

In 1933, Klee was violently attacked by the Nazis, who degradingly called him a Jew and foreigner: he was in fact neither. Klee painted yet another self-portrait at this time, *Struck from the List*, 1933 (Figure 2.4, see also Plate 2), a broken surface which communicated his feelings of uncertainty and dejection. In this small oil painting daubed with brown and black shades of color, the individual's eyes are closed and the mouth appears tightly shut and turned down. The dark colors and the facial expression with its turned down mouth and chin portray grief, despair and anger that was never expressed by Klee in words. A large "X" on the left side of the head, crossing the forehead and cheek, gives it the title *Struck from the List (Von der Liste geschtrichen)*. With the rise of the Nazis, Klee lost his professorial chair at the Art Academy and his place as one of the most significant artists in Germany. Even though Klee was born in Switzerland to a Swiss mother, he was considered German because of his father's German origins, for at this time in Switzerland, one's paternal nationality was the one that counted for citizenship.

His reaction to his dismissal and the personal attacks by the Nazis was not conveyed through outspoken revolt, but rather in withdrawal and in intense artistic communication. As in the past, and as we will see in the future (especially in the final phase of his life), despair, depression and anger stimulated his creativity, protecting him to a certain degree from this grave narcissistic injury. His art was rejected by his fatherland (and its Nazi government) as it had been 36 years earlier by his father. Disgusted, he returned to Switzerland in 1934.

After 13 years of teaching in a creative, stimulating atmosphere, it was challenging for Klee to adapt to the isolation of Bern. This abrupt change in his surroundings prevented Klee from painting for some time. After six months passed, he wrote to his friend and biographer Will Grohmann that he had started to paint again "with reduced orchestra" (Grohmann, 1954, p. 90). Having been rejected by Germany, and having not been fully accepted in Switzerland, his only reliable partner was his own creativity. Even Klee's father, despite his son's world fame as an artist, refused to accept his art, causing old tensions between father and son to resurface.

The outbreak of Paul Klee's disease must also be considered in the context of his hopeless situation. In 1935, Klee fell sick with measles, which eventually led to the diagnosis of scleroderma, a rare, chronic, and ultimately fatal rheumatic disease better known today by the name of Progressive Systemic Sclerosis (PSS). This generalized disorder of connective tissues is characterized by inflammatory fibrotic and degenerative changes of the vascular lesions in the skin, which becomes taut and hidebound, affecting the hands, forearms and face. It can also affect internal organs such as the heart, lungs, intestinal tract and esophagus (Spiegel, 1983).

Klee was forced to give up his beloved violin due to the weakening of his heart. After losing his friends, colleagues, job, and fatherland, he now had to forego his

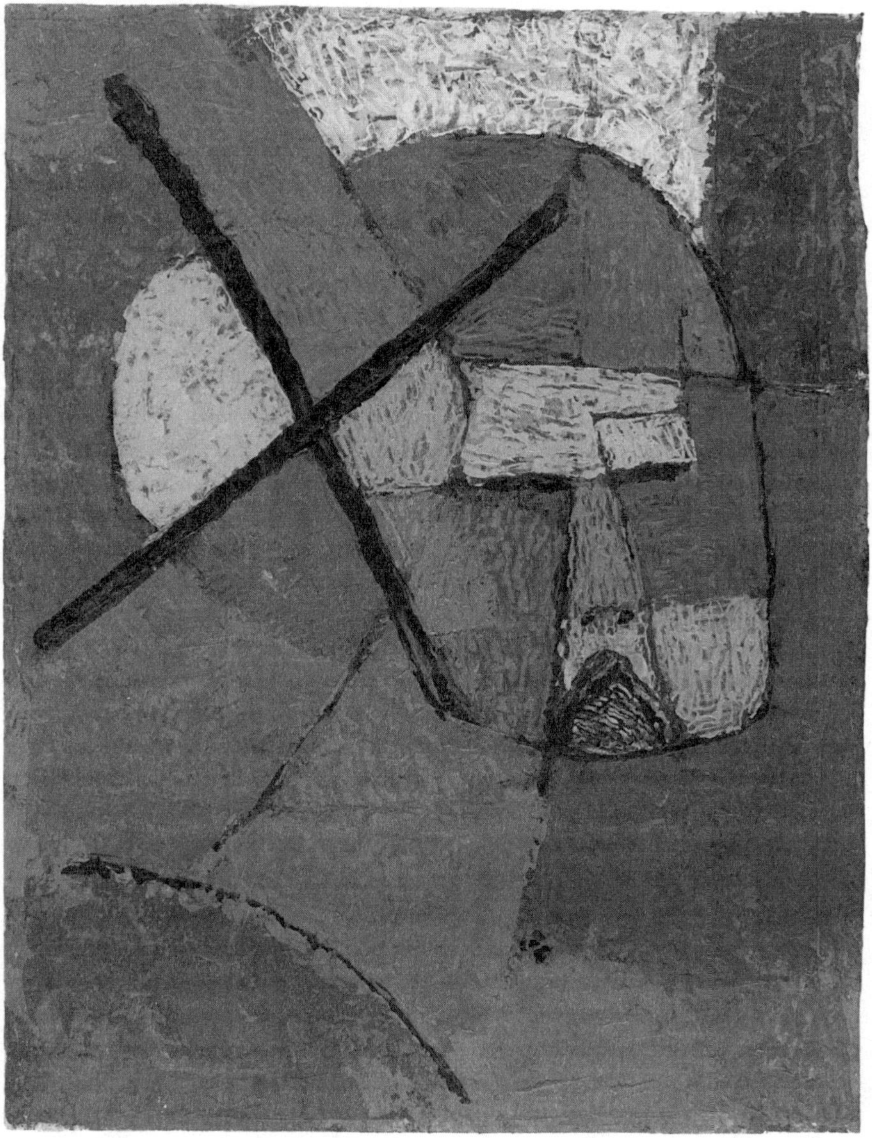

FIGURE 2.4 (see also Plate 2) Paul Klee. *Von der Liste gestrichen* [*Struck from the List*], 1933, 424. Oil on paper on cardboard. 31.5 × 24 cm. Zentrum Paul Klee, Bern, Livia Klee Donation.

daily ritual of playing music, a ritual that provided security and a harmony of spirit and sensuality, a blending of Eros and Logos, the spiritual with the rational. It was only through music that Klee could still connect emotionally with his wife and his father (Kagan, 1983). In addition to losing his ability to partake in music, he could now no longer stand and paint at an easel, but instead had to sit down and paint on a large drawing board. For most of the year of 1936 he was ill, able to only draw and paint 25 works.

Paul Klee's last working phase

Driven by his terminal illness and the knowledge of his approaching death, Klee's autobiographical artistic work gained a universal dimension. In his "psychic improvisation," as he referred to his drawings, he successfully integrated lines as a gestalt of form, which informs the viewer of its content. Although Klee painted many pictures during this late phase, my research will focus on a select group of Klee's drawings. As Paul Klee became increasingly solitary, he concentrated entirely on his work. His work increased not only in number but also in intensity, becoming an obsession protecting him from the fear of his terminal illness and from the external, extremely troubled times. His future seemed more and more hopeless. His late work often illustrates a transitional world between dream and reality, between past memories and future vision, between childhood and death. Klee's "unconscious automatization" (as he referred to it) was inspired by the Surrealists, and with his intuitive associative playfulness it allowed him to integrate form and content, and allowed him his own self-repair in spite of life threat.

Beginning in 1938, at a time when his physical symptoms worsened, Klee demonstrated an astonishing surge in his artistic output. He must have realized that his health was unremittingly deteriorating and that his time remaining to paint was limited. In 1939, the final year of his life, and the year that marked the beginning of World War II, Klee created 1,253 works. In the last five months of his life during 1940, he produced 366 pictures. Interestingly, 1940 was a leap year, which consists of 366 days (Glaesemer, 1979). In other words, in the last five months of his life, Klee created the equivalent of a picture a day for an entire year. Through his constant art-making, Klee experienced these five months as a much longer period, counteracting the split between the threatening reality of his impending death and the fantasy of immortality. Insofar as Klee maintained his constant creating, he secured timelessness and suspended the perception of limited reality. In 1938, the artist began a continuous dialogue with himself, similar to the one in his earlier diary (Glaesemer, 2005). He noted in his work catalogue, after the number 365, *nulla dies sine linea*, "no day without a line," a quote taken from Pliny's *Historia naturalis* (Glaesemer, 1979).

Under immense time pressure, Klee realized that the time had come for him to condense his works rather than to expand; he would have to be more precise, more direct, and more concise in the expression of his thoughts and feelings. He reflected not only on his own death, but also on death in general. This confrontation with death led Klee to momentous inner changes. On a narcissistic level, Klee mourned the lost integrity of his own body, which was continually changing. Since the earliest development of the ego is closely connected with the image of an intact body ego, Klee must have felt threatened by a feeling of diminished self-worth as his body disintegrated, fostering strong emotions of shame and anger. Forced to withdraw all libidinal cathexis from his body and thus from most of his drives, the artist was able to cathect much more strongly with his inner experiences and fantasies.

In a letter to his son Felix and daughter-in-law Efrossina Klee, written on December 29, 1939 just six months prior to his death, Klee wrote: "My production is taken over with increasing speed, and I can hardly catch up with these children" (F. Klee, 1979, p. 1295). In a theoretical text published in 1928 by the journal *Bauhaus*, Klee had already written, "Genius is Genius, a blessing, without beginning and end, procreation" (Geelhaar, 1979). He expresses a wish to suspend the flux of time and thereby experience eternity. Or, as he wrote earlier in his diary, possibly inspired by Henri Bergson and Albert Einstein, "The time element must be eliminated. Yesterday and tomorrow as simultaneous" (*Diary*, no. 1081, p. 374).

Well aware of his approaching "deadline," Klee's need for production increased immensely. He felt as if he were being overtaken by his own creative force. In his last letter to Felix, Klee wrote about an impending loss of conscious control: "I am myself amazed and look at my pen as it dips, even though it seems to belong to a fountain pen and how it runs over the beautiful paper and does that in common understandable writing and not in the usual secret signs . . ." (F. Klee, 1979, p. 1282). Glaesemer (1979) explains that a reversal occurred between writing and drawing. Even though drawing, with its "secret signs," is not a universal comprehensible script as is writing, it became Klee's only possible mode of communication at this most difficult time. The actual process of documentation through writing, which he had utilized throughout his life in the form of his written diary entries, poetry and theoretical writings on art became in the last period of his life an unaccustomed form of communication. This reversal from writing to drawing is even portrayed in Klee's choice of paper for his drawings: he selected crisp white writing paper in a standard size, he drew in linear lines, and abstained from any color or shading. It was as though he "wrote" his drawings (Glaesemer, 1979). His wife recounted in a letter to Will Grohmann: "Klee drew until 11 p.m., dropping one piece of paper after the other on the floor after finishing them" (Grohmann, 1954). The art of drawing served as the bookends to Klee's method of communication in his lifetime; at the young age of three years old, Klee had begun his artistic career with drawing and he ended it with drawing as well.

He wrote in his diary in 1908, "I may dare to enter my prime realm of psychic improvisation again . . . I may again dare to give form to what burdens the soul. To note experiences that can turn themselves into linear compositions even in the blackest night . . ." (*Diary*, no. 842, p. 232). This comment seems appropriate for his late work. The line, often drawn in pencil, becomes part of a particular kind of self-reflection on the artist's psychic situation. Fantasies expressed in his pictures, similar to dreams, helped Klee maintain the integrity of his self and thus mitigated unbearable loneliness and terror.

One of the best-known cycles of Klee's last working phase is the "Eidola," a series of 24 drawings executed in 1940, Klee's final year of life. *Eidola*, stemming from the ancient Greek word *eidolon*, first found in two episodes of Homer's

Iliad and *Odyssey*, describes the soul of the dead (Werckmeister, 1999). Klee used "Eidola" in the sense of "ghost." All drawings in this cycle of works are figurative, with defined individual characteristics documented through specific attributes. Glaesemer (1979) suggests that the Greek work *eidola*, sometimes also written as *idol*, not only represents a prototype but also defines "shadow creatures" who move in the land between life and death, neither here any longer nor yet there. The repeating title *Weiland*, "erstwhile," appears in a group of pictures that also points in this direction. All these creatures seem to be in the process of physical and psychological transformation, as was Klee himself in his chronic illness.

Interestingly, Klee would often write "Eidola" with Greek letters, and he was evidently influenced by Greek tragedies. In his last letters to Grohmann, in January 1940 (Gutbrod, 1968), Klee explained that he was reading the classical tragedies. He wrote, "I indulged myself reading tragedies. I read of Orestes finally, three translations one after the other, part after part, scenes after scenes, with the intention to find the real meaning within them all. Naturally, I do not by accident find myself on tragic tracks. Many of my pictures point to it and say: it is time. Will I ever produce a Pallas?" Pallas is the Goddess of Wisdom, which relates to the Greek myth of Athena's birth from Zeus (Werckmeister, 1999). "Pallas," as with "The German Art" of Klee's time, embodies the domination of contemporary culture. Contemporary artists such as Pablo Picasso, Max Ernst, and John Mason lived up to the Pallas task, but Klee's emotional precondition due to illness and exile in Switzerland stood in his way. Then, just as Pallas matures in Zeus' body and was finally born out of his head, so too did Klee's immense production blossom, a non-reflective but a deliberate process (Werckmeister, 1999). "The year was pictorially very rich," he wrote, "so much I never drew and never as intensively" (cited after Glaesemer, 1979).

The Greek tragedies provided Klee with a mirror of his own tragedies, particularly the beginning of World War II and losing his German "fatherland," losing his renowned professional career, as well as being faced with a life-threatening disease and his own process of dying. There is great ambivalence in this statement. One finds the wish to synthesize dualism in all of Klee's late work—a dialogic play of movement and countermovement, a synthesis of the defined and undefined. The definiteness of the drawn line often contrasts with the instability of the whole composition. Klee's inner wish for integration is not denied, but is instead made the central theme. His early diaries stated, "The demoniacal shall be melted into simultaneity with the celestial, the dualism shall not be treated as such, but in its complementary oneness" (*Diary*, no. 1079, p. 372). Elsewhere he wrote, ". . . as an entity down here, with connections to what is up there . . . To be anchored in cosmos" (*Diary*, no. 421, p. 123). Klee seems to say that when he is able to find a symbolic gestalt for a troubling feeling, it can lose its destructive power and can drop back into his unconscious.

In the following drawings the strong, sharp edges communicate a different type of affective state, such as aggression, disappointment, or disillusionment, and they also illustrate the progression of Klee's disease, which made fine motor control less easy to accomplish.

Analyzing the titles of selected works of this cycle—*Erstwhile Musician*, 1940 (Figure 2.5), *Erstwhile Pianist* (Figure 2.6), 1940 and *Erstwhile Harp Player* (1940)—reveals that all three have biographical significance. *Weiland*, a late German medieval word meaning "erstwhile," has been used since the nineteenth century to also mean "deceased." Klee utilized the word as an adjective before a profession or a quality. Understanding the combination of the ancient Greek *eidola* with *Weiland*, Klee determined its meaning as "deceased" to refer to a group of dead people who have all lost their profession and status. Most are artists, including these musicians depicted, who after having lost their instruments continued to play music using their bodies (Werckmeister, 1999). The *Erstwhile Harp Player* still plucks the strings of his invisible instrument, reminding the viewer of Klee's own painful loss of his violin playing to which he was so vitally connected. The *Erstwhile Musician* faces his left, towards the past. Instead of drawing eyes, Klee chooses to draw skull-like circles, as he also did in the *Harp Player* and the *Erstwhile Kettledrummer*, 1940 (Figure 2.7); all four of these works of art depict images of death. The subject of the *Erstwhile Pianist*, who carries the keyboard as part of his body, is perhaps an

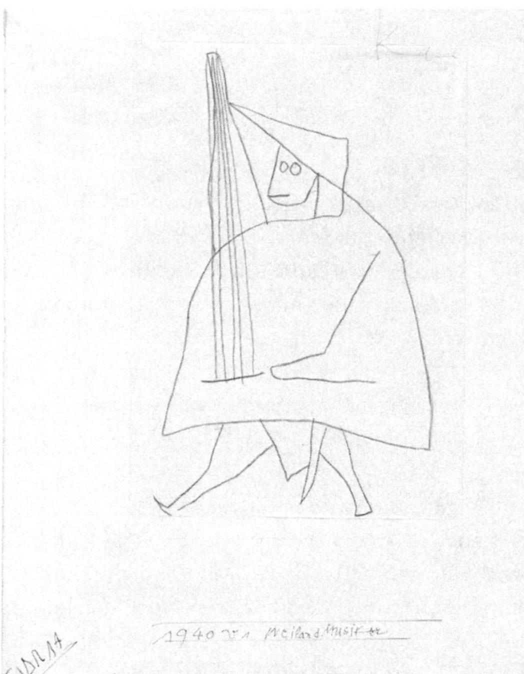

FIGURE 2.5 Paul Klee. *EIDOLA: weiland Musiker* [*Eidola, Erstwhile Musician*], 1940, 81. Chalk on paper on cardboard. 29.7 × 21 cm. Zentrum Paul Klee, Bern.

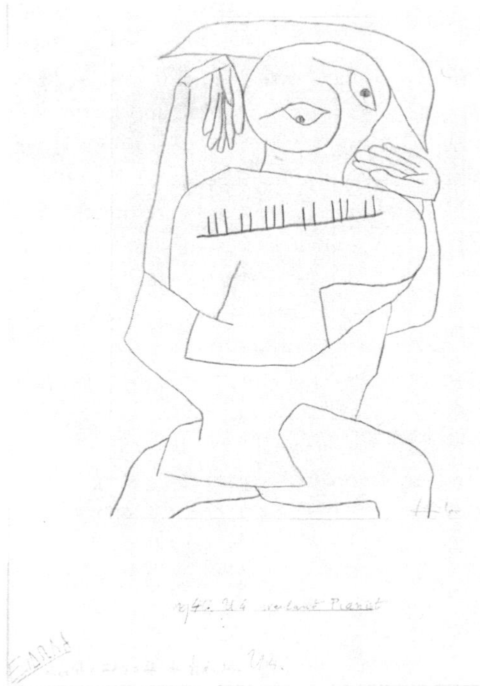

FIGURE 2.6 Paul Klee. *EIDOLA: weiland Pianist* [*Eidola: Erstwhile Pianist*], 1940, 104. Chalk on paper on cardboard. 29.7 × 21 cm. Zentrum Paul Klee, Bern.

illustration of himself as well as his wife Lily, the pianist with whom he connected, as in a spiritual act, through playing music together.

These automatic drawings or psychic improvisations not only express deep content but also illustrate great rhythmic intensity, as demonstrated by the image of the *Erstwhile Kettledrummer.*

Grohmann writes, "I remember [Klee] saying that one evening in the excitement of drawing he had the feeling that he was striking a kettle drum" (1954). The kettledrum association reminds the viewer of Klee's beloved idol Mozart and his last *Requiem.*

Klee considered Wolfgang Amadeus Mozart a perfect artist and felt connected to him because of their shared happy playfulness and childlike charm. He felt a deep affinity with the eternal child in Mozart, who started as a *Wunderkind* and would continue as an un-selfconscious genius. The humor often expressed in Klee's drawings and even in the titles of his works is an expression of this lightness, similar to the charm and humor of Mozart's instrumental pieces and of *The Magic Flute*. Admiring *The Magic Flute*'s beauty and charm, Klee stated that Mozart's death would have been illogical had he died before writing it (White, 1964). Klee mirrored Mozart's self-expression not only through playing the violin but also through art-making. Klee's art process allowed him to share in the joyful,

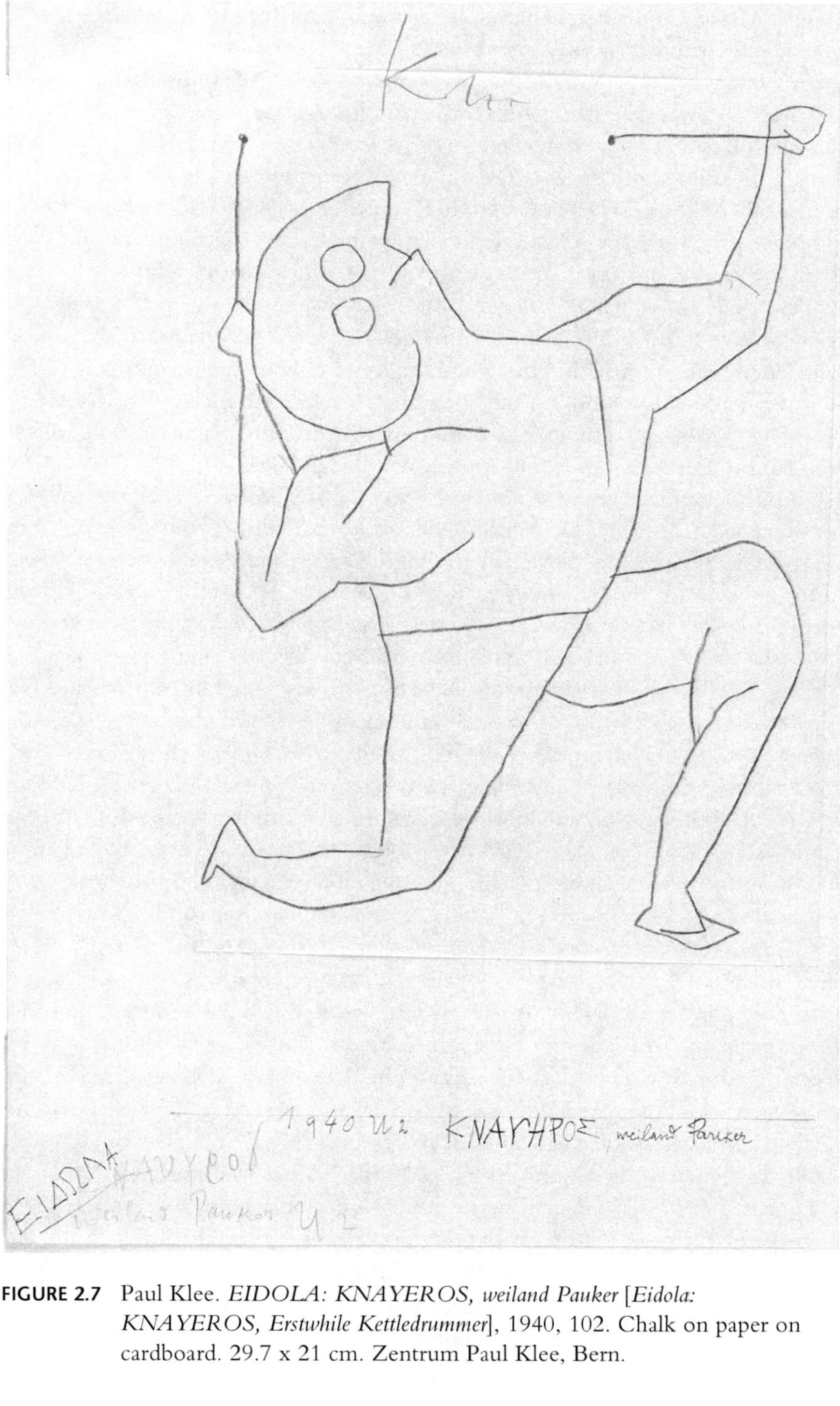

FIGURE 2.7 Paul Klee. *EIDOLA: KNAYEROS, weiland Pauker* [*Eidola: KNAYEROS, Erstwhile Kettledrummer*], 1940, 102. Chalk on paper on cardboard. 29.7 x 21 cm. Zentrum Paul Klee, Bern.

expressive aspect of Mozart's music, an openness that Klee was unable to express in life directly with others, but only through his art.

Mozart was Klee's favorite composer and he played many of Mozart's pieces by heart. He was described by his fellow musicians as a *Mozartspieler*, or "Mozart player" (Kagan, 1983). At the age of 19, Klee described Mozart as a "youthful king"; his admiration for Mozart continued throughout his life, and he even elevated Mozart to the status of God in his lectures at the Bauhaus (Geelhaar, 1985).

Not only did Klee and Mozart share a joyful, youthful playfulness but they also shared a common view of death. On April 14, 1787, Mozart wrote to his sick father, "A death, when we come to consider it closely, is the true goal of our existence. I have formed during the last few years such a close relation with this best and truest friend of mankind that his image is not only no longer terrifying to me, but it is indeed very soothing and consoling! And I thank my God graciously for granting me the opportunity . . . of learning that death is the key which unlocks the door to our true happiness" (Anderson, 1985, p. 907).

Possibly inspired by these thoughts, Klee similarly wrote in Dessau, "Death is nothing bad; I long ago reconciled myself to it. How do we know what is more important, our present life or what comes after? I won't mind dying if I have done a few more good paintings" (Klee, F., 1962, p. 90). And earlier, as a young man, Paul Klee had already written in his diary, "Then I philosophize about death that perfects what could not be completed in life. The longing for death, not as destruction, but as striving towards perfection" (*Diary*, no. 143).We can also recognize Klee's longing for death as a defense against fear of death. As Kagan (1983), observes, Klee and Mozart were the most similar at the time of their deaths.

According to Mozart's sister-in-law, the last movement of the great composer before his death was his attempt to vocalize the kettledrum passes in his *Requiem* (Anderson, 1989). Following in Mozart's footsteps, Klee drew his own requiem in the form of these rhythmic psychic improvisations, exemplified particularly well by his drum images.

Kagan (1983) writes that Klee had also found in the image of the kettle drummer an abstract poetic metaphor for his own dying. One of Klee's most famous late paintings, *Erstwhile Kettledrummer* (1940), created with colored paste on handmade paper, is an innovative, daring expression. The strongly defined lines are potent, reduced to abstract essence, as are the three colors: red, black and brown. Glaesemer (1979) sees in it the Greek god Chronos, who beats the passing of time for the terminally sick Klee, while Werckmeister (1999) defines the work as a symbolic expression of the swastika shape of Nazis and their war drums of 1940. The fragmented kettle drummer—wearing the Nazi colors brown, black and red—engages in energetic self-destructive performance. I suggest that the political and personal tragedies are merged together in this strong artistic expression.

Similar to the "Eidola" series, Klee's group of "Angels" illustrates a transitional phase between life and death, an intermediate realm. In his collection of at least 35 works depicting angels, Klee seems to depict the good souls who become angels after their resurrection, imagining in detail the transformation of the human shape

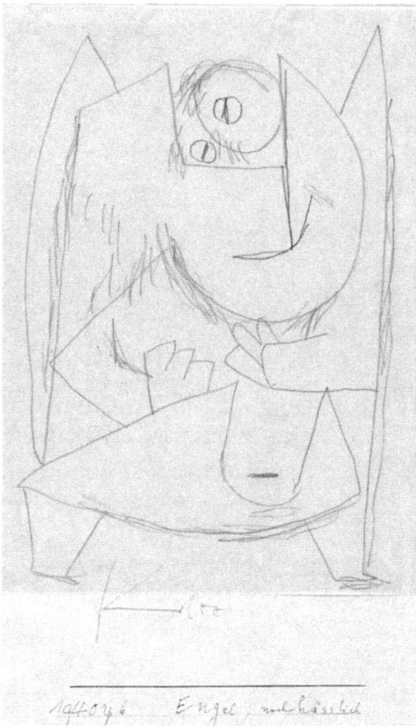

FIGURE 2.8 Paul Klee. *Engel, noch hässlich* [*Angel, Still Ugly*], 1940, 26. Pencil on paper on cardboard. 29.6 × 20.9 cm. Zentrum Paul Klee, Bern.

into an angelic one. According to Klee's interpretation, angels retain their sexes but cease to interact amorously, as they attain a spiritual state beyond sexual differentiation (Schiff, 1987). In this last period of his life, Klee was able to attain spiritual satisfaction in lieu of physical gratification. Klee's angels possess human attributes, colored by the artist's own experience with his illness, and are not yet purely heavenly figures, as can be seen in *Angel, Still Ugly*, 1940 (Figure 2.8).

Fostered by Klee's terminal illness, these angels stir human emotions such as joy, hope, shame or fear. But they have not yet reached heaven, as illustrated in *Unfinished Angel* (1939) or *In the Antechamber of Angelhood* (1939). The angel in these images explores the growth of his wings and Klee depicts this transformation with fine humor. He examines the angel's organic metamorphosis, reminiscent of his own terrifying physical change, and thus gains a necessary distance.

In the *Old Musician Behaves Angel-like* (1939), Klee most likely depicts himself as the old musician. He not only mocks his emotional control and distance from his immediate environment—namely his wife and son, colleagues and friends—but reflecting on it he considers this effort more angelic than human-like. He wrote a first title for this drawing, "Would like to be part of," on its cardboard base, which supports this idea. Although he still wanted to be part of earthly life, physical limitations and his inability to share his strong emotions (such as fear, anger,

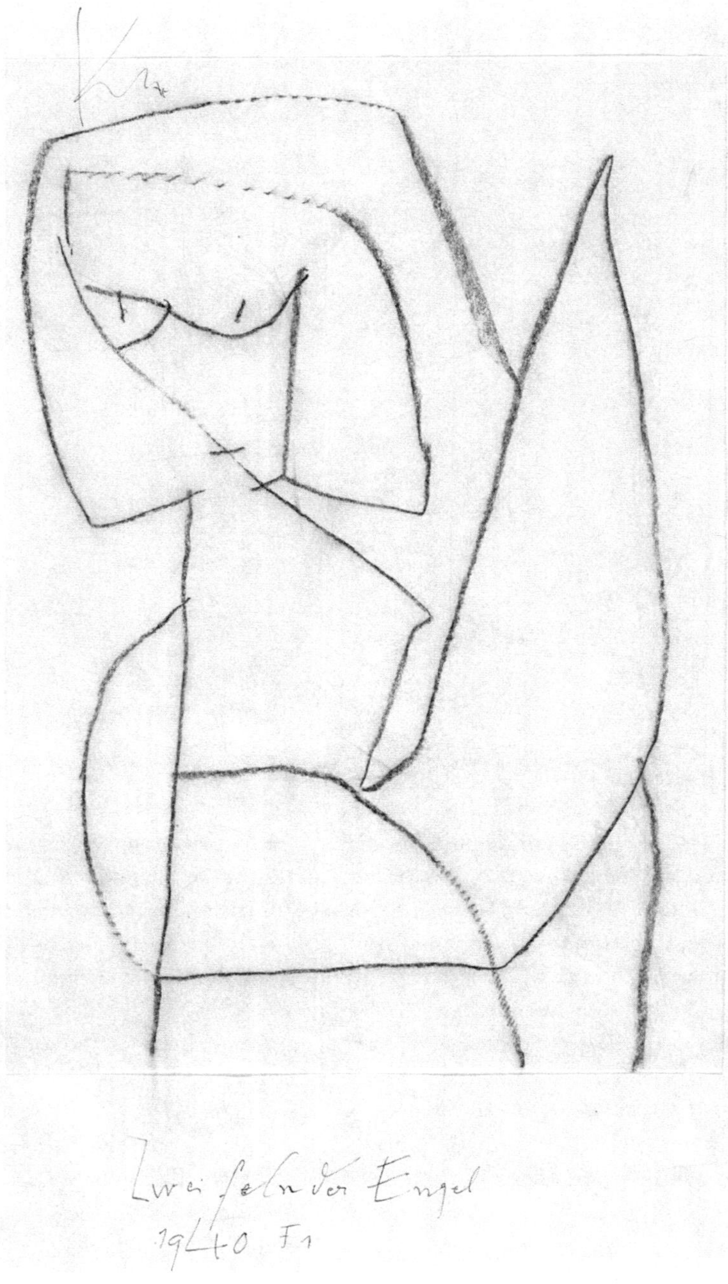

FIGURE 2.9 Paul Klee. *Zweifelnder Engel* [*Doubting Angel*], 1940, 341. Pastel on paper on cardboard. 29.7 × 20.9 cm. Zentrum Paul Klee, Bern.

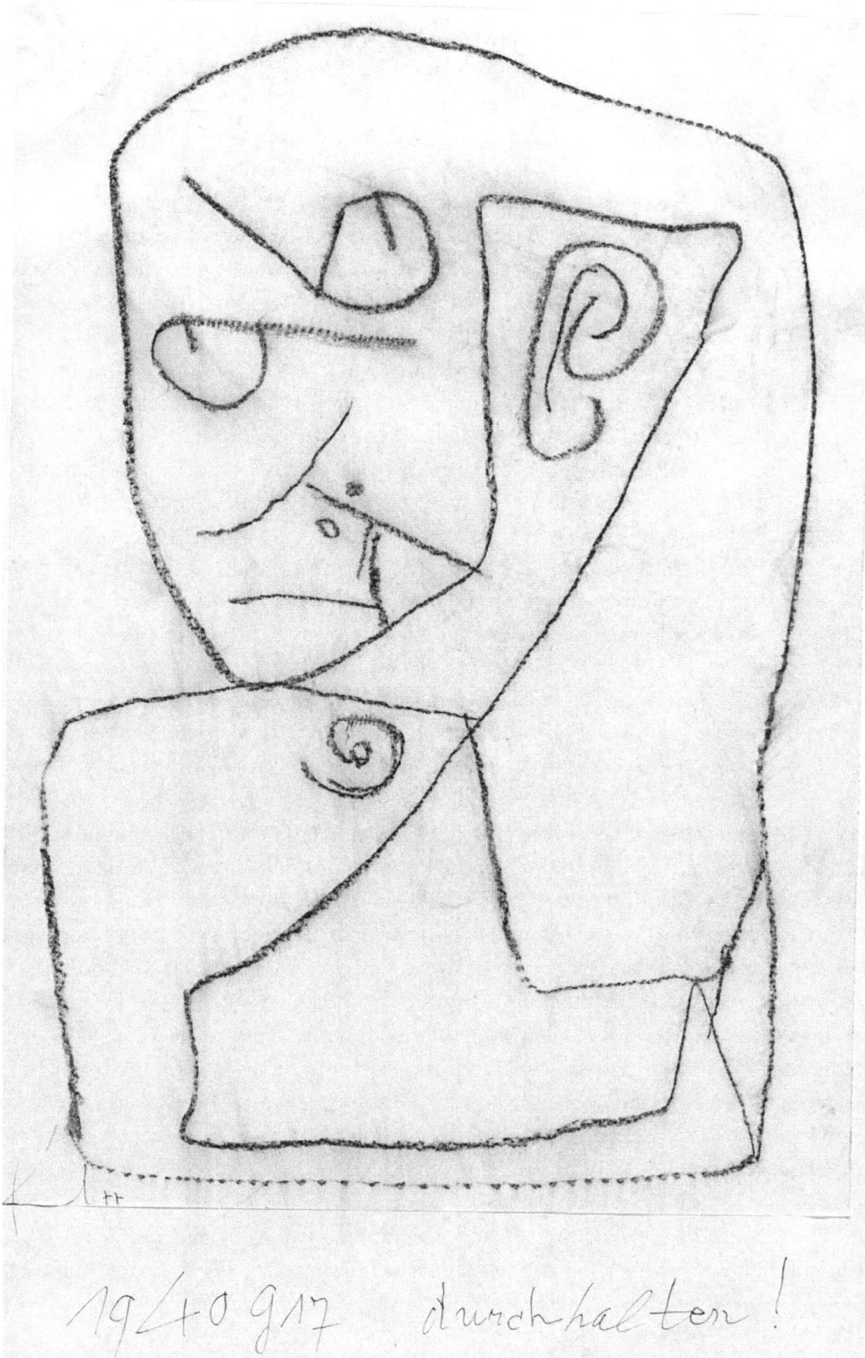

FIGURE 2.10 Paul Klee. *Durchhalten!* [*Stick It Out!*], 1940, 337. Pastel on paper on cardboard. 29.6 × 20.9 cm. Zentrum Paul Klee, Bern.

disappointment, and hope) directly with the ones closest to him kept him isolated and alone. Although still alive and productive physically, drawing all the time, emotionally he was no longer part of the living environment, as evidenced by his wife Lily's reference to Klee as "Him" in her letters and memories. She placed her husband onto a superhuman pedestal, idealizing him. In a letter to Will Grohman, asking him to visit Klee again, she wrote, "He is spiritually a completely lonely person and his life is lonely and renunciatory" (Glaesemer, 1979). Felix Klee, Paul's only son, remembers that on his numerous visits to Bern he was instructed not to talk about his father's work or illness. Klee could not share the two most important topics in his life at that time with the ones closest to him, he could only express those strong needs through his art (Glaesemer, 1979).

Doubting Angel, 1940 (Figure 2.9), drawn only a few days before Klee entered the sanatorium where he later died, portrays a state of utmost despair. The word *Zweifeln*, "doubting," is closely related in German to *Verzweifeln*, meaning "despairing," giving the viewer a precise insight into Klee's extreme state of despair at this time.

Most interesting in Klee's late work is the discrepancy between the spontaneity of the lines, content, style and title of his creations, and the obsessive manner in which he documented his entire pictorial production. First, Klee matted each drawing on a cardboard mat. Then he signed it with his full name. He often sketched a title in pencil before deciding on a definitive one. In reference to the titles of his late works, Klee "spoke" freely about what moved him, fostering not only dialogue with a possible audience but also one with himself, as he had done earlier in his life in his diaries and pedagogical writings. On one of his last drawings, executed before he left for the hospital in southern Switzerland, Klee inscribed the title *Durchhalten!* (1940), "endure" or "Stick it out!" (Figure 2.10). In a corner he noted with pencil, as though in a dialogue with himself, "Should all of this have been known? Oh, I don't think so!" (Glaesemer, 1979, p. 50).

The last step in the recording process was entering each work in the catalogue with striatum, adding a description of the technique, the background and the type of work. Even as the number of his produced works exploded, Klee did not slack in his discipline. Before his last trip to the hospital, from which he was never to return, Klee spent the time and effort to document his last finished works. It brought Klee great satisfaction to count the number of pictures he had created in one month, and to observe his rapidly growing production, "Twelve hundred numbers in the year 1939 are indeed a record," he wrote proudly to his son in December 1939 (Glaesemer, 1979).

Glaesemer (1979) is convinced that this bookkeeping pleased the artist. With this strict order and systematizing, Klee could incorporate his dreamlike, spontaneous images back into the reality of his daily artistic life. It allowed him to take full control of the short time he still had remaining. Klee's tight control kept his life seasons in balance, thereby avoiding a sense of lost time, which would have paralleled his loss of life security and could have produced an overwhelming fear of breakdown (Winnicott, 1974). This exact methodology of bookkeeping might have counterbalanced Klee's continuous sense of losing time (of life). He could thus maintain a connection between past, present and future with this self-imposed structure. With death, time is abolished, connectedness disappears, and for Klee eternity would have ceased to exist (Loewald, 1972).

Unlike all of his previous works, Klee never signed or documented what is called the *Last Still Life*, 1940 (Figure 2.11, see also Plate 3). Perhaps he did not consider it complete. In the foreground on an orange tabletop strewn with flowers

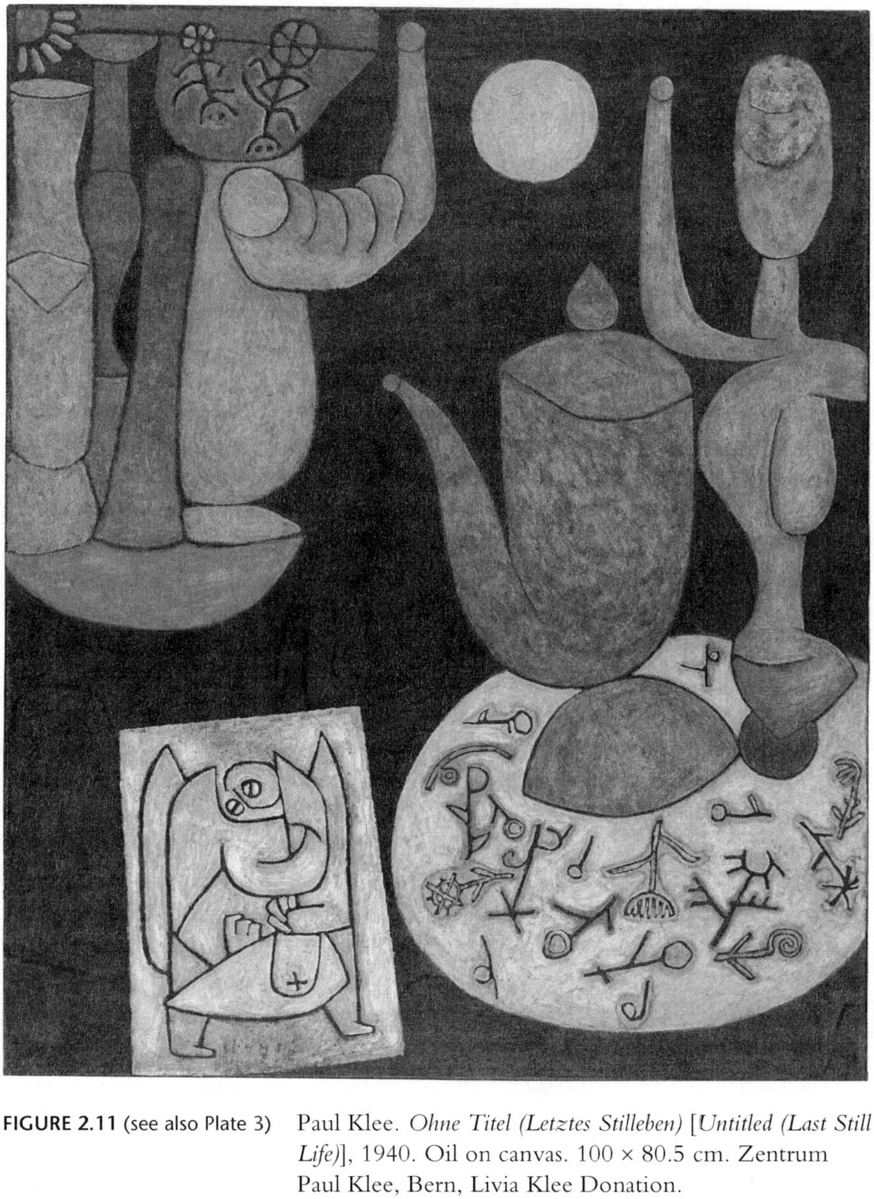

FIGURE 2.11 (see also Plate 3) Paul Klee. *Ohne Titel (Letztes Stilleben)* [*Untitled (Last Still Life)*], 1940. Oil on canvas. 100 × 80.5 cm. Zentrum Paul Klee, Bern, Livia Klee Donation.

stand a green coffee pot and a lilac statuette. Four vases in the colors purple, brown, olive and sienna are squeezed on a bright red table into the top left corner. Two red objects, which appear to be flowers, float out of the vase. All of the elements sit against a dark brown background lit up by a yellow full moon. A red sun is painted in the left corner. It seems as though all elements are capable of transformation. The tabletops move into dark infinity. The flowers are broken and lie strewn on the table. A card with a drawing on the lower left corner is based on Klee's picture *Angel, Still Ugly*, which he documented in his catalogue in January 1940. The minus mark in the earlier picture has transformed in this version into a plus sign, a cross, perhaps an affirmation not only of approaching death and spirituality, but also of his still active creative powers. The rose colored phallic object paralleling the shape of the statuette's raised arm and the coffee pot's spout drifts unconnected in space. There seems to be an erotic encounter taking place between the statuette and the vessels (Werckmeister, 1990). In an earlier picture, Klee described the Chinese vases and containers he painted as "ceramic-erotic-religious" (Werckmeister, 1990). This erotic encounter is repeated in the two red-black flower figures in the upper left corner. If one turns the picture 180 degrees, one can distinguish stick figures of a man and woman cycling towards each other on a unicycle.

The angel in the painting, caught in the process of change, is smiling. The artist seems to say, "In spite of my progressive, debilitating disease, profound emotional isolation, and fast approaching death, I still remain the spiritual and physical father of my own creations." Klee's drawings and paintings exist in an imaginative, almost hallucinatory world, sharply separated from reality. For Klee, art was the safe means to express the anger, disappointment, fear, disillusionment, and even hope fostered by his terminal illness, all of which were verbally inexpressible for him. Art's ability to allow the artist to communicate his overwhelming emotions is related to D.W. Winnicott's (1971) concept of the transitional object, representing both a foothold in reality and a guarantor of continuity; it becomes the talisman par excellence for warding off fear and anxiety (Dreifuss-Kattan, 1990). According to Winnicott's (1971) logic, creativity first arises out of transitional phenomena, and therefore has a unique link to theories of loss and mourning. Through play, the special form of a child's own creativity, the child first learns to be alone. It is through creative, symbolic play that the artist learns to survive his own rages and fear of death, all while maintaining a belief in his basic goodness and the goodness of his internal objects. Creativity, loss, mourning and reparation are thus all intertwined (Dreifuss-Kattan, 1990).

For Melanie Klein (1977) and her followers, the establishment of the depressive position is directly connected to the establishment of a reality-oriented ego. The intense feelings of loss that the child experiences as a result of his own attacks on his mother, whether fantasized or not, give rise to a wish to repair the lost, loved object and instill it with new life and wholeness (Segal, 1973). These reparative activities—which are essential in the process of working through the depressive position and thus in the formation of the ego and sense of reality—are animated by the wish to restore, preserve, and recreate the lost happiness of symbiosis, and thereby give the internal object external life.

Creating when faced with death is a powerful alternative to more primitive responses, such as denial or projective identification. The fear of dying is often a fear of being overtaken by evil internal objects; the race against a slow process of destruction can thus only be successful if the ego ideal, represented by the good internal object, can be preserved and the ego can still identify with it (Meerwein, 1989).

Klee's consistent creating satisfied his omnipotent and narcissistic wishes so badly damaged by his terminal disease. While creating, he gained psychic pleasure and a diminution of his fears, counteracting the internal malignant process experienced in his progressive systemic disease. The created pictures thus became for the artist a way to say goodbye, while at the same time they ensured the artist's immortality by enduring after the artist's death. At the moment of creation on the brink of death, the concepts of an end and endlessness seem identical, and the threatening reality is somehow suspended.

Klee's late work contains two kinds of experiences of time, defined as *chronos* and *kairos* in the previous chapter. *Chronos* describes intentional time, measured time still available in one's life, properly measured with stable ego functions, time not yet lived (Meerwein, 1989). *Chronos*' sequence of measurable times is well illustrated in the sequence of the many drawings Klee created each day. *Chronos* can also be found in the content of Klee's "Kettledrummer" pictures, where Klee drums the passing of time through his rigorous methods of daily documentation of his creative output.

Kairos describes a generalized, religious feeling which develops out of a sense of fusion with the other world, a mutual permeability which Sigmund Freud (1930), after Romain Rolland, refers to as the "oceanic feeling." It is a feeling of something limitless and unbound, expressed so well in Klee's *Last Still Life*. Freud (1930) calls it a "oneness with the universe . . . a restoration of the limitless narcissism." Marie Bonaparte (1940) describes it as the "paradise of our childhood and dreams" and Chasseguet-Smirgel (1984a) creates for it the term "Mother-prior to the loss of fusion state" (p. 217). In *kairos*, time is recognized as eternity and *chronos* actually appears to be eliminated as the flux of time is suspended. This echoes Klee's diary entries: "Today is a transition from yesterday" (*Diary*, no. 951) and "The time element must be eliminated, yesterday and tomorrow as simultaneous" (*Diary*, no. 1081).

Through his constant art-making, Klee was able to counteract his horror of abandonment through death and his fear of being left alone. The process of constant creation fostered for him the sensation of living in an oceanic womb to which he longed unconsciously to return, as he did many times throughout his life when life-threatening dangers surrounded him. His desire to merge with the universe helped him to integrate and synthesize that which he felt further and further removed from, such as his healthy family and his successful colleagues. Due to his disabilities and the progression of his illness, he feared he would psychologically disintegrate and would fall more and more into disconnected parts, described so well in Winnicott's essay "Fear of Breakdown" (1976). Through an exclusive absorption in his art, Klee could reinstate, as Freud calls it, "a feeling of an indissoluble bond of being one with the external world as a whole" (Freud, 1930). In his early diary Klee was already in search of what he called a "Divine Ego" (*Diary*, no. 961). "Art imitates creation," he wrote (*Diary*, no. 1008). The merging with God and God's universe, indeed a virtuous union, constitutes not only a defensive attempt to transcend the painful limitation of his emotional isolation in the face of death, but also a restorative act that robbed the bad internal objects of their powers, symbolized by Klee's progressive illness of scleroderma. Chasseguet-Smirgel (1984a) suggests that the creative act is prompted by a strong narcissistic desire to rediscover a lost sense of unity, a bringing together of the ego and its ideal.

Childhood was always an important theme for Paul Klee. He created his famous childlike pictures of 1914–1920 and also took on the role of a devoted mother in raising his own child. Early in his life, he recognized the power of children's art and therefore started an oeuvre catalogue with 18 of his own childhood drawings, executed between the ages of 3 and 10. He also began his famous diaries with 36 early childhood memories.

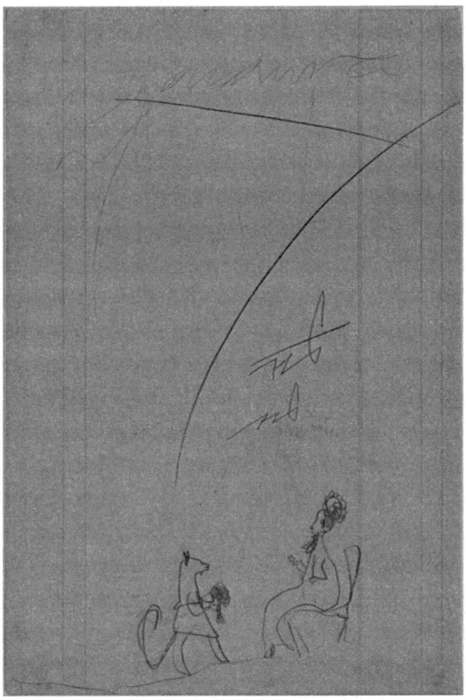

FIGURE 2.12 Paul Klee. *Ohne Titel (Mimi überreicht Madame Grenouillet Blumen)* [*Untitled (Mimi presents flowers to Madame Grenouillet)*], 1883–1885. Pencil on paper. 28.3 × 18.8 cm. Privatbesitz Schweiz, Depositum im Zentrum Paul Klee, Bern.

At the age of eight, Klee recalled that despite his extreme excitement, he pretended to sleep, delaying the celebration of his mother's homecoming after a three-week absence until the following morning (*Diary*, no. 28). He demonstrated the strength and intensity of his longings as well as his ability to suspend gratification. As a three year old, he remembered his fear of watching his mother cry hysterically when she returned home and found her favorite lamp broken (*Diary*, no. 4, p. 3). In *Ohne Titel (Mimi überreicht Madame Grenouillet Blumen)* [Mimi presents flowers to Mrs. Grenouillet] (Figure 2.12), a drawing from around age four, we recognize a physical and emotional distance between the child and his mother to whom he presents the flowers, so unlike the comic illustration that had inspired his drawing, a picture-story page in the magazine *Epinal* from around the year 1861 (Eckstaedt, 1984). His picture shows us rather stiff postures of the child-figure and mother-figure and the mother's short arms point to the fact that the four-year-old Klee unconsciously knew not to expect emotional or physical closeness from his "mother figure" explains Eckstaedt (1984).

While both Klee's father and mother had provided Paul with a home supportive of and conducive to creative expression and intellectual growth, the only real affectionate memory Klee recalled in his diary was that of his maternal grandmother. She was the one who taught him how to draw, gave him colored crayons, and showed him religious pictures. When he was three, his grandmother affectionately cleaned him with particularly soft toilet paper, a memory sufficiently worthy for Klee to record in his diary many years later after the incident (*Diary*, no. 5, p. 4).

Paul was five years old when his grandmother died, and he later described himself as an "orphan-artist." In contrast to his competitive father, or his interested but more narcissistic mother, to whom he was drawn but also feared, his grandmother must have filled him with warm, artistic and religious feelings. "The dead body of my grandmother made a deep impression on me," he described in his first memory of death when he was only five years old (*Diary*, no. 12, p. 5). In the mind of the precocious little Paul, anality, art, affection, religion and death were fused parts of a beloved grandmother.

For Klee, art was thus very much connected to early childhood, apparent in his entire artistic opus. In art, we could speculate he could combine his incestuous desires of the Oedipal stage towards his mother with pre-Oedipal cravings for the symbiotic merger and "body creativity" (Shengold, 1988) he had experienced from his grandmother. The following dream, which he noted in his diary, describes this wish for synthesis: "I flew home, where the beginning lies. I started with brooding and chewing of fingers. Then I smelled or tasted something . . . If a delegation were to come to me now and bow solemnly before the artist gratefully pointing to his works, I wouldn't be surprised much. For I was there where the beginning lies. I was with my adored Madame Monad [unit], which means, so to speak, being fruitful" (*Diary*, no. 748, p. 169).

In the end of life, oral, anal, and genital needs are pushed further into the background as are the ego functions which are directed towards object gratification. It is the timeless function of the ego ideal which provides comfort and allows one to create the fantasy that time actually stands still. In merging with creation and the universe, Klee was able to undo the previous unconscious withdrawal from his ambivalently experienced love object. While constantly creating, he could escape infinite parental control and felt empowered to control the universe himself. Klee wrote to his friend Grohmann, before his death, "Even though there are obstacles to experience joy of life, maybe I am able to reconstruct it through the detour of my work. Since I am working well, I am experiencing a kind of happiness. New paths—an image of creation" (Gutbrod, 1968, pp. 83–84). Through his trancelike creating he was able to satisfy his regressive wishes for fusion, which protected him from pain and fear of separation by death and brought him happiness until the last few days of his life.

References

Anderson, E. (1989) *The letters of Mozart*. New York: Macmillan.

Bonaparte, M. (1940) Time and the unconscious. *International Journal of Psychoanalysis*, 21: 427–468.

Chasseguet-Smirgel, J. (1984a) *Creativity and perversion*. London: Free Association Books.

Chasseguet-Smirgel, J. (1984b) *The ego ideal*. New York: Watson and Company.

Dreifuss-Kattan, E. (1990) *Cancer stories: Creativity and self repair*. Hillsdale, NJ: The Analytic Press.

Eckstaedt, A. (1984) Mimi überreicht Madame Grenouillet einen Blumenstrauss: Eine psychoanalytische Studie über den Weg der Phantasie des vierjährigen Paul Klee anhand einer Kinderzeichung. In *Psychoanalyse, Kunst und Kreaativität heute*. H. Kraft (Ed.) Cologne, Germany: Dumont Verlag, pp. 254–279.

Freud, S. (1908) Creative writers and day-dreaming, *The standard edition of the complete psychological works of Sigmund Freud* (Vol. 9: 141–154). London: Hogarth Press, 1986.

Freud, S. (1913) The claims of psychoanalysis to scientific interests, *The standard edition of the complete psychological works of Sigmund Freud* (Vol. 13: 165–189). London: Hogarth Press, 1953.

Freud, S. (1924) The resistance to psychoanalysis, *The standard edition of the complete psychological works of Sigmund Freud* (Vol. 19: 213–222). London: Hogarth Press, 1961.

Freud, S. (1930) Civilization and its discontents, *The standard edition of the complete psychological works of Sigmund Freud* (Vol. 21: 175–196). London: Hogarth Press, 1961.

Geelhaar, C. (1979) Paul Klee: Biographische Chronologie. In *Paul Klee: Das Frühwerk, 1883–1922*. Catalog. A. Zwite (Ed.). Munich: Städtische Galerie im Lenbachhaus München, pp. 29–42.

Geelhaar, C. (1985) Vom Klang der Bilder. In *Musik in der Kunst*. Munich: Prestel, pp. 422–429.

Glaesemer, J. (1979) *Paul Klee: Handzeichnungen III 1937–1940*. Bern, Switzerland: Kunstmuseum Bern.

Glaesemer, J. (2005) Nulla dies sine linea. In *Paul Klee, Kein Tag ohne Linie*. T. Osterwald (Ed.). Bern, Switzerland: Hatje Cantz, pp. 75–79.

Grohmann, W. (1954) *Paul Klee*. New York: Harry N. Abrams, Inc.

Gutbrod, K. (1968) *Künstler schreiben an Will Grohmann*. Cologne, Germany: M. DuMont, Schauberg.

Jones, E. (1957) *The life and work of Sigmund Freud*. New York: Basic Books.

Kagan, A. (1983) *Paul Klee: Art and music.* Ithaca, NY, and London: Cornell University Press.

Klee, F. (1962) *Paul Klee.* New York: George Braziller.

Klee, F. (1964) *The diaries of Paul Klee 1898–1918.* Berkeley: University of California Press.

Klee, F. (Ed.) (1979) *Paul Klee: Briefe an die Familie, 1893–1940* (Vol. 1) and *1907–1940* (Vol. 2). Cologne, Germany: DuMont Verlag.

Klee, P. (1988) *Paul Klee (1879–1940) (The Pitman Gallery).* New York: Pitman Publishing Corporation.

Klein, M. (1977) *Love, guilt and reparation: And other works, 1921–1945.* New York: Delacorte Press.

Loewald, H. (1972) The experience of time. *Psychoanalytic Study of the Child,* 27: 405–510.

Meerwein, F. (1989) Zeiterleben im psychoanalytischen Prozess. *Zeitschrift für Psychosomatische Medizin und Psychoanalyse,* 2, 35: 156–174.

Schiff, G. (1987) Klee's array of angels. *Artforum,* 25, 9: 126–133.

Segal, H. (1973) *Introduction to the work of Melanie Klein.* New York: Basic Books.

Shengold, L. (1988) *Halo in the sky: Observation on anality and defense.* New York: The Guilford Press.

Spiegel, T. (Ed.) (1983) *Practical rheumatology.* New York: John Wiley & Sons.

Vishny, M. (1985) Paul Klee's self-image. In *Psychoanalytic perspectives in art.* M. Gedo (Ed.). Hillsdale, NJ: The Analytic Press, pp. 133–168.

Werckmeister, O.K. (1990) Die Portraitphotographie der Zürcher Agentur Photopress zum Anlass des Sechzigsten Geburtstages von Paul Klee am 18. Dezember 1939 Paul Klee. *Das Schaffen im Todesjahr.* Stuttgart, Germany: Verlag Hatje.

Werckmeister, O. K. (1999) Will I ever bring forth a pallas? *Paul Klee: In the mask of myth.* P. Kort (Ed.). Cologne, Germany: DuMont, pp. 136–159.

White, J. (1964) Eine Kleine Kleemusik. *Arts in Virginia,* 4, 3.

Winnicott, D.W. (1971) *Playing and reality.* New York: Basic Books.

Winnicott, D.W. (1974) Fear of breakdown. *International Review of Psycho-Analysis,* 1: 103–107.

3

DINA GOTTLIEBOVA BABBITT

Painting trauma, painting history—Gypsy portraits in Auschwitz

Ordered to create art for her German oppressors, the young adult artist Dina Gottliebova Babbitt bonded not only with her fellow victims at the concentration camp but also forged a unique relationship with her tormentors. Her distinctive watercolor portraits of the Roma people became silent testimonies of their fate, and forced the young artist to confront her own death.

By weaving together publications of Dina's testimony collected at the Shoah Foundation, as well as conversations I had with her in her home a few years before her death, this chapter will attempt to explicate her experience at Auschwitz, in particular her encounter with the Roma inmates, in both personal and historical context. The artist was able to utilize her identity as an artist and her exceptional artistic talent in her struggle to survive the concentration camp, and even succeeded to create a new productive life as a survivor. Gottliebova Babbitt's personal struggle continued for many years afterwards, however, reflected in her strong desire to recover her seven original watercolors from the Polish Government, the portraits of the Gypsies she was forced to paint in Auschwitz.

Although a biography is never a case study and a biographer is not an analyst, psychoanalysis might provide some deeper insights into Dina Gottliebova Babbitt's trauma as it relates to her identity as an artist and her ability to create art both in her past and after World War II. The extreme horror of her wartime memories caused Gottliebova Babbitt to use defenses such as denial, splitting, and disassociation, which consequently prevented the artist from conducting the work of mourning necessary to revive any genuine artistic expression.

The readers of survivors' stories bear witness, and as Dori Laub (Felman and Laub, 1992), the director of the Video Archive for Holocaust Testimonies at Yale University, points out, "trauma's impact on the hearer leaves no hiding place intact" (p. 72) because Holocaust testimonies raise existential questions for everyone. One is confronted with the realization of time's passing, the meaning and purpose of life, the necessity to face death, ultimate loneliness, evil, and the limits and potentials of one's own omnipotence (Felman and Laub, 1992). Listening to a testimony is an encounter for which one cannot be prepared. It is an encounter with "strangeness," challenging one's intellectual and affective understanding. Recording, listening to, and researching Holocaust testimony not only chronicles overwhelming events, but also, one hopes, memorializes the injustices inflicted (Felman and Laub, 1992).

Witness reports about the incomparable atrocities are impossible for the outsider to fully grasp: the arrests, the rounding up, the overcrowded "transports" with their over-powering stench, thirst, hunger, deception, and violence; the horrific routines of the camps, the haunting of the ever present gas chambers, the unpredictability of survival and death, with its pain, exhaustion, and cold. Prisoners did not only respond to their own trauma, but were constantly re-traumatized by the trauma of others (Lanzman, 2012). That is why Aaron Appelfeld, the famous Israeli author and Holocaust survivor, states in his book *Beyond Despair* (1994) "that testimonies often contain repressions in chronological order, as the survivors attempt to veil their inner truth. One could refer to it as an adaptive defense to protect the inner pain and suffering of the actual trauma" (p. 14). Prisoners faced horrors beyond human capacities, and they were given choices that were inhuman. The forces were too overwhelming, unable to be processed by one's unconscious, like a "mortal illness," continues Appelfeld (p. 72). Appelfeld also aptly describes the prisoner's inner need, even in the camps, to ritualize this inner pain and suffering into an artistic expression in an attempt to "banish fear and fortify 'courage' and to escape the surrounding darkness" (p. 27). But once the prisoners survived these horrors, for years many could not bear to be reminded of their past before the Holocaust, not even with artistic productions they loved before. Being moved by artistic expression punctured their constructive defenses, as their trauma had blocked any enjoyment of the past.

Biographical details

Dina Gottliebova Babbitt was born in 1923 in Brno, then the capital of Moravia in Czechoslovakia. In 1930, Brno held a Jewish population of 10,202, which made up 6.9 percent of the total population of the city (*Encyclopaedia Judaica*).

Dina grew up without a father in a household of seven women. When she was five months old, her parents decided to separate, and her father, an artist who made hand-painted dolls, moved away from the family to another city. He completely disappeared from Dina's life from that moment until she was six years old, at which time he came to visit her. She recalled her fear of her father, remembering her mother's fit of rage when his child support money did not arrive in time, and thus Dina felt she could not really trust him.

Her mother, a very attractive and popular woman, played the role of the breadwinner by becoming a bookkeeper. She was a very talented woman who played the piano and sang with a beautiful voice. Dina's grandmother, a social and witty woman, raised Dina until she was eight years old, at which point her mother hired a nanny to care for her. In addition to the nanny, the household was taken care of by a housekeeper. They all lived together in a house in an impoverished middle-class neighborhood, along with Dina's maternal aunt and cousin.

Dina enjoyed playing imaginatively with her cousin using self-made dolls, making up life stories for these dolls and creating endless picture stories with text about their families. The stories recreated the ideal family romance, illustrating her unconscious need to repair the loss of her father and get rid of her financial deprivation. Due to her great artistic talent in high school, Dina won a scholarship to a prestigious art school in Prague, and moved there from Brno when she was 16 years old.

In 1939, when Hitler invaded Bohemia and Moravia and installed his rule from Prague Castle, Dina Gottliebova Babbitt and her fellow Jewish students and teachers were expelled from art school. Finding herself unable to attend school and in dire financial need, especially given the harsh rationing of food, she searched out her father and asked him for financial support. At this time, he was working as a cabinetmaker, and was remarried with two children. He gave Dina a few coins, suggested that she request financial assistance from the Central Agency for Jewish Emigration, and advised her to remain a virgin until she was 20 years old. This meeting with her father left Dina feeling rejected and disheartened; she did not seek him out again, though their families would meet in the devastating circumstance of the concentration camp Theresienstadt a few years later. Dina found work as a commercial artist, and always remembered her family back at home by sending them money to help support her mother and grandmother.

This was the beginning of a life-long pattern of love and a feeling of responsibility toward her close family members, in particular towards her mother. She identified with her mother, who was charming, capable, and in charge of supporting the family. Realizing death was lurking as World War II approached, Dina Gottliebova Babbitt decided to immigrate to Palestine, following in the footsteps of many of her young friends. At the last minute, however, she could not separate from her mother and instead volunteered to join her in the train car to Theresienstadt.

Theresienstadt (or Terezin in Czech) was a town that served as a ghetto between 1941 and 1945 where approximately 150,000 Jews from Central and Western Europe were deported by the Nazis. The Nazis planned to concentrate most of the Jewish population of Bohemia and Moravia in Terezin, together with elderly, famous, or privileged Jews from Germany and other Western European countries, and from there to gradually transfer the inhabitants to the extermination camps. Theresienstadt was portrayed as a "model settlement" in an attempt to conceal from the world the fact that European Jewry was being exterminated. Even as a "model settlement," the overcrowded conditions, malnutrition, lack of sanitation and German cruelty caused the death rate in Theresienstadt to rise to over 50 percent in 1942 (*Encyclopaedia Judaica*).

When Dina Gottliebova Babbitt arrived, pioneer Zionist leaders and teachers imprisoned in Theresienstadt took charge of the children's and adolescents' schooling and living arrangements in an attempt to shield them, as best as they could, from the ghetto's threatening and depressing atmosphere. Despite the horrid conditions of the ghetto, it was also well known for its underground artistic and intellectual life because many leading European artists and intellectuals were imprisoned there.

While Dina Gottliebova Babbitt remembered the constant disappearance of people, the shootings and public hangings, she also recalled fond memories of participating in stage plays and the living quarters she shared with teenagers her own age. Her mother became the housemother for all of the young girls, and thus avoided separation from her teenage daughter again. Gottliebova Babbitt was named the "resident artist" of the teen group, as she would create fantastic body paintings on her friends. This group of adolescents became close friends; as they sang together their lives became intertwined. Gottliebova Babbitt also fell in love with a young man, K., who would become her fiancé.

Dina Gottliebova Babbitt was assigned to the *Zeichenstube*, the drawing studio where she had to copy and enlarge postcards into full-sized oil paintings. Each picture needed to be completed in two to three days in order for it to be shipped to Germany. She remembered the method she used, starting a painting in one corner and finishing it in the other, like a coloring book, in an attempt to diminish its artistic value—her silent protest.

In September 1943, Dina Gottliebova Babbitt's mother was deported to the concentration camp Auschwitz-Birkenau; once again, Dina volunteered to join her on the train in an effort to remain in close proximity to her mother. Gottliebova Babbitt's most painful memory of this period was her separation from K., whom she loved very much. The journey to Auschwitz was horrible: she remembered sitting on her suitcase in the horrible, cramped cattle-car and crying for three consecutive days. Their arrival was also traumatic and frightening, as everybody in their group was sent with 5,000 other inmates to the family camp. Three months later, Dina's aunt, cousin and grandmother joined them along with another 5,000 prisoners. Soon after their arrival, Dina's grandmother died of pneumonia in her daughters' arms. Gottliebova Babbitt long remembered her grandmother's funeral, listening to the *Kaddish*, the Jewish mourning prayer.

Later, Dina Gottliebova Babbitt was introduced to a *Kapo* named Walter. A *Kapo*—possibly from the Italian word *capo* for "boss" or from *Kameradtschaftspolizei*—was a German prisoner, often a Jew, who was placed in charge of a group of Jewish inmates. It was a *Kapo*'s task to carry out the orders for the *Schutzstaffel* (S.S.) and to ensure absolute control over the prisoners. When Walter began to like Dina, he appointed her as his cook, offering her better protection and granting her more privileges, such as taking leftover food to her starving mother. She came to love and respect him as her protector.

At Auschwitz, Dina Gottliebova Babbitt was once again asked to work at the studio where she and other artists were ordered to paint pictures by numbers and to paint signs, such as the famous one above the entrance to the death camp, *Arbeit macht frei* or "work makes you free." It was during this time that Gottliebova Babbitt was asked by a Jewish educator from Berlin, whom she had met in Theresienstadt, to paint a mural on the walls of one of the children's barracks in the family camp. She happily painted an idyllic "Swiss" landscape—drawn in a cartoon-like fashion—with flowers, cows and sheep, adding Snow White and some dwarfs from her favorite new Disney movie. She remembered how she drew Dopey dancing with Snow White and another little dwarf playing music. The kids in the camp loved her mural and it even inspired them to perform *Snow White* as a play with the help of an inmate who had been a professional theater director.

The mural was admired by everyone in the camp; one of the S.S. officers, who loved Dina Gottliebova Babbitt's art, talked about her to the infamous Dr. Mengele, the "Angel of Death." Joseph Mengele had studied medicine and philosophy in Germany before the war, but had been declared unfit to practice medicine at the front. Upon his own request, he was appointed doctor of the Auschwitz camp from 1943 to 1945. There he initiated the cruel "medical" experiments for his "scientific investigations," and was known to the inmates as "The Auschwitz Monster." The S.S. officer brought Dina Gottliebova Babbitt to meet the doctor, who was taking colored photos of subjects he was studying. Five months later, she was ordered to paint for Dr. Mengele.

A few months after Dina Gottliebova Babbitt began working for Dr. Mengele, drawing x-rays and body parts, rumors spread that her own camp was being liquidated. When Dr. Mengele arrived for selection, to decide who would live and who would die, Dina Gottliebova Babbitt and her mother were on his list of 27 people to be saved. The others, 20,000 people, marched into the gas chambers singing the *Hatikvah*, a Zionist song that would later become the national anthem of Israel. As she and her *Kapo* friend Walter stood by crying, Dina watched as her mother's hair turned grey in this one night.

The Roma in Auschwitz: the Roma portraits

In May 1942, the S.S. shot 11 artists in Auschwitz for not completing their works in time for Himmler's visit to the camp, although a report indicates that the artists were never informed of the existence of a deadline. This was the atmosphere of fear in which Dina Gottliebova Babbitt was ordered to produce her assigned art. Some of her assignments came from individual requests, such as painting horses for a foreman or creating copies of masters for S.S. officers, works that Gottliebova Babbitt remembered she produced with an "ape-like speed." "This earned me status and more lucrative jobs like fruit picking or herding sheep," she recalled (Gottliebova Babbitt, 1998).

However, the new assignment that Dr. Mengele had in mind for Dina Gottliebova Babbitt was of a different kind; he wanted her help to document the Roma in the camp. The Roma people have been the victims of prejudice and repression in Europe from their arrival out of India in the Middle Ages until the present day, similar to the experience of European Jews: their darker skin, strange language and unfamiliar customs set them apart and made them unwelcome. They were regarded by their hosts with a mixture of envy, fear, nostalgia and contempt (Tyrnauer, 1997). A 1905 German census of the Roma describes them as "a pest against which society must unflaggingly defend itself" (Fisher, 1999). Jews and Gypsies were the only people marked by the Nazis for total extermination, as they believed these groups were of "different blood and exhibit innate feeblemindness"; Goebbels asserted that the "Jews and the Gypsies should be exterminated unconditionally" (Fisher, 1999). The Roma were defined as vagabonds, anti-social criminals and racially inferior aliens (Milton, 1992). In 1933, the Nazis arrested them, and intended to make them *Zukunftlos*, "futureless," by ordering their forced sterilization (Fisher, 1999).

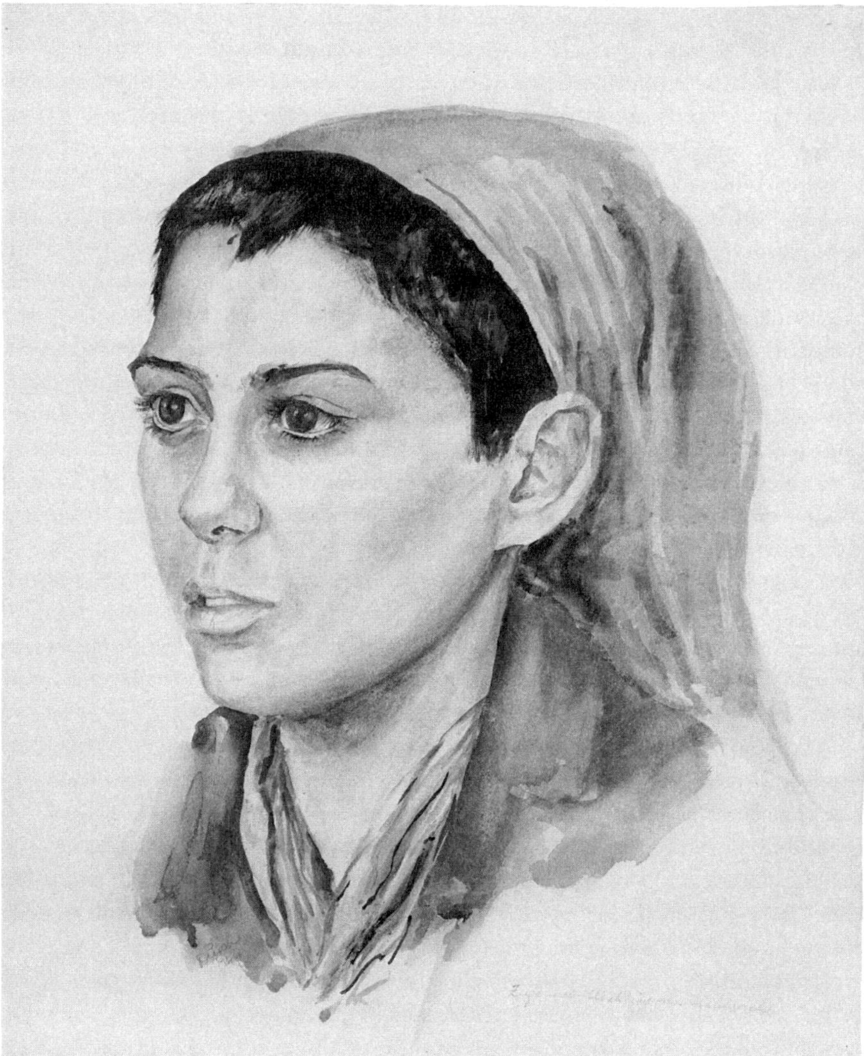

FIGURE 3.1 (see also Plate 4) Dina Gottliebova Babbitt. *Zigeuner-Mischling aus Frankreich*. 1944. Watercolor. 38.5 × 31.1 cm. © KL Auschwitz.

Dr. Mengele was particularly interested in documenting the Roma peoples' facial characteristics as he conducted his measurements and horrific experiments, and he asked Gottliebova Babbitt to help him illustrate his "medical studies." She was driven to the Gypsy camp where he supplied her with paper and watercolors. She worked in a room next to his office and was instructed to make portraits of the Gypsies. Initially, she was free to choose her own subjects but, dissatisfied with her choices, Dr. Mengele later selected the models for her and gave her specific instructions as to the method to use to paint them. Gottliebova Babbitt was given two to three days to complete one watercolor portrait.

Zigeuner-Mischling aus Frankreich, 1944 (Figure 3.1, see also Plate 4) is the portrait of a young Roma woman, Celine, who was beautiful despite her sad eyes. She revealed to Gottliebova Babbitt that she had very recently lost her little baby in the camp due to starvation. As the two women became friends, the artist tried to prolong their time together in order to bring her better bread to help heal her stomach ailments. Gottliebova Babbitt remembered Celine as being as delicate as a porcelain doll, and she titled her portrait *The Gypsy Madonna with Ear*. The Madonna picture is beautiful, painted in near transparency. In spite of Celine's intense hunger and the loss of her child, she faces the artist directly with her straight gaze, giving her an air of hope and confidence. Her matching scarf covering her cropped hair grants her dignity. It appears as though the respect and love Gottliebova Babbitt extended to her model is reflected back to the viewer in the picture. The viewer recognizes how Gottliebova Babbitt could easily identify with this sad but confident young female prisoner.

The girl with the red scarf (Figure 3.2) looks into an uncertain future with longing and sad eyes. She seems more distracted, and her contact with the artist is different. "Can you help?" she might ask.

The piercing look of this middle-aged woman with a white head-covering (Figure 3.3) seems to communicate a strength prepared to face the threatening future. While she appears worried—her forehead is furrowed and her eyebrows are defined and full—she also seems to project her confidence to Gottliebova Babbitt, to express pride in her Roma traditions.

This young boy with dark hair seems very distraught, sad and angry (Figure 3.4). He seems to know more than the women painted before him; his eyes have seen too much already. He is afraid to exhibit his fear and vulnerability to the young artist, and needs to hold on in order to prevent himself from falling apart.

The subject looks over the artist's eyes, exhibiting a confident and somewhat content expression (Figure 3.5). The slightly curved line of his lush lips indicate that he is charmed by the young beautiful painter.

Dina Gottliebova's job as an artist in the Gypsy camp lasted about four weeks. All of these Roma in Auschwitz were dressed in their traditional clothes, unlike the Jewish prisoners who were given striped prison uniforms. Their hair had not been shaved, and their dignity was still somewhat intact. Looking at these paintings, the viewer develops the impression that the subjects did not perceive any imminent threat to their lives. It is for this reason that the events that followed were so traumatic to everybody who witnessed them.

On the night of August 2–3, 1944, referred to as *Zigeunernacht* or 'Gypsy Night,' the Gypsy family camp section B-11 of Birkenau, which had existed for 17 months, was liquidated. Although many Gypsies had died earlier of malnutrition and brutal medical experiments, in this one night alone 20,000–30,000 Gypsies were gassed. The entire Gypsy camp had ceased to exist in one night; only 1,500 survived (Milton, 1992).

In his book *Unfree Associations* (1999), Dr. Alfred Bloch, a psychoanalyst and survivor of Auschwitz, writes: "Trucks from the Gypsy camp came to the gas chambers—there was chaotic turmoil. Although I can recall that it was terrible, I have no recollection of the scene. There is a rare blank in my memory of that night." But

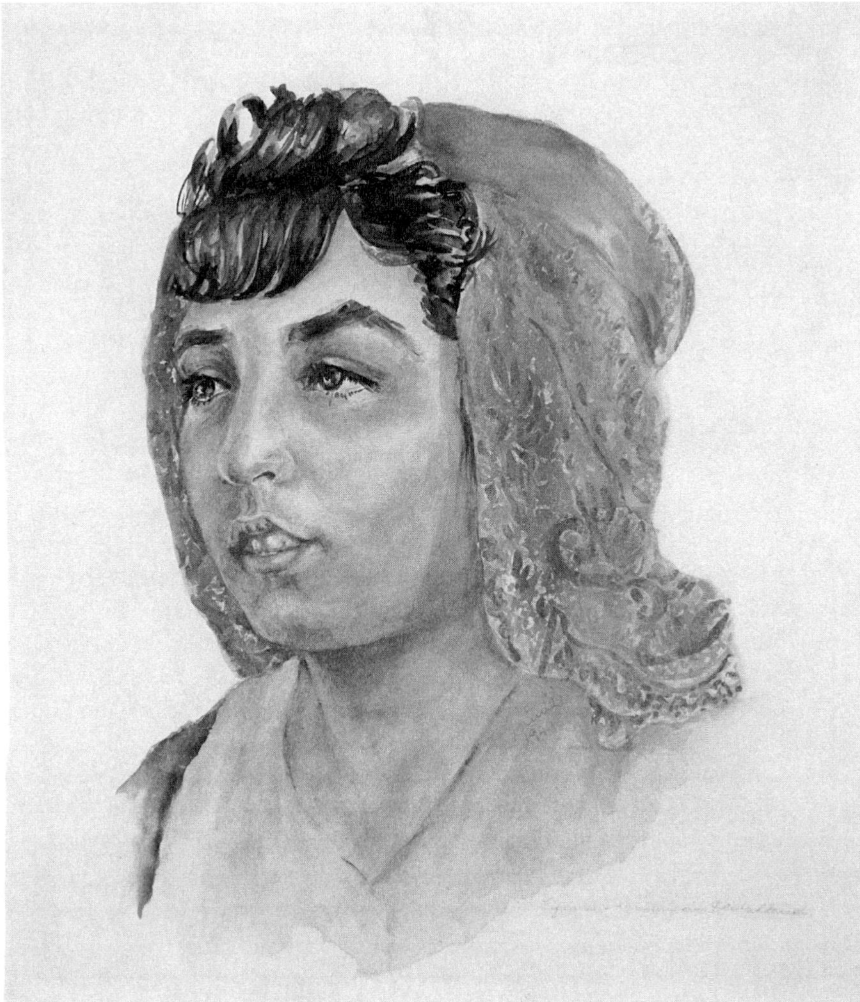

FIGURE 3.2 Dina Gottliebova Babbitt. *Zigeuner-Mischling aus Deutschland*. 1944. Watercolor. 38.4 × 32.8 cm. © KL Auschwitz.

just a few lines later he continues, "The Queen of the gypsies, knowing that it was her end . . . The sound of her voice piercing the air, echoed in my mind for years." He later goes on, "The whimpering out of the neighboring Gypsy camp had taken my last protective apathy, an excruciating feeling of emptiness replaced it" (p. 159).

Dr. Bloch may not have had the same personal relationships to the Gypsies as our artist did. However, the trauma of that night, though partly repressed, still haunted Dr. Bloch 50 years later. As Dina Gottliebova Babbitt remembered this night, so full of emotion, she began to cry. In her testimony, she revealed that one morning it was rumored that the Gypsy camp had been liquidated. The 19-year-old artist had established personal friendships with her eleven models, leaving her completely devastated by the realization that they had all been murdered.

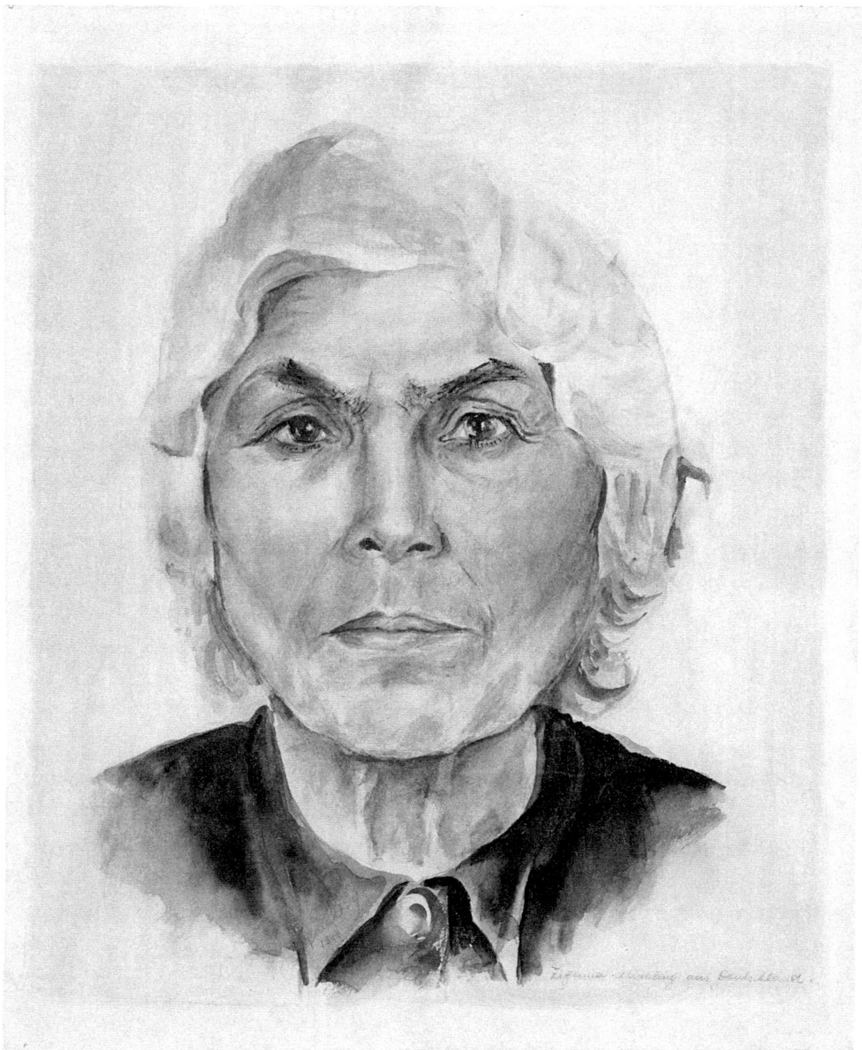

FIGURE 3.3 Dina Gottliebova Babbitt. *Zigeuner-Mischling aus Deutschland*. 1944. Watercolor. 38.5 × 31 cm. © KL Auschwitz.

Dina Gottliebova Babbitt also recognized that she had only been saved in order to document their history. She was forced to continue to work for Dr. Mengele, who ordered her to draw further medical subjects, such as the hands of dwarfs. He acted in a friendly and reserved manner towards Gottliebova Babbitt; he ensured that she received better shoes and clothes, and sometimes he even brought her cigarettes and cookies. One day he ordered her to paint his own portrait. She remembers joking with him on that occasion. As perverse as it sounds, the "Angel of Death," the murderer of her Roma friends and her Jewish family, also became the missing father Dina never had, simultaneously her victimizer and her protector.

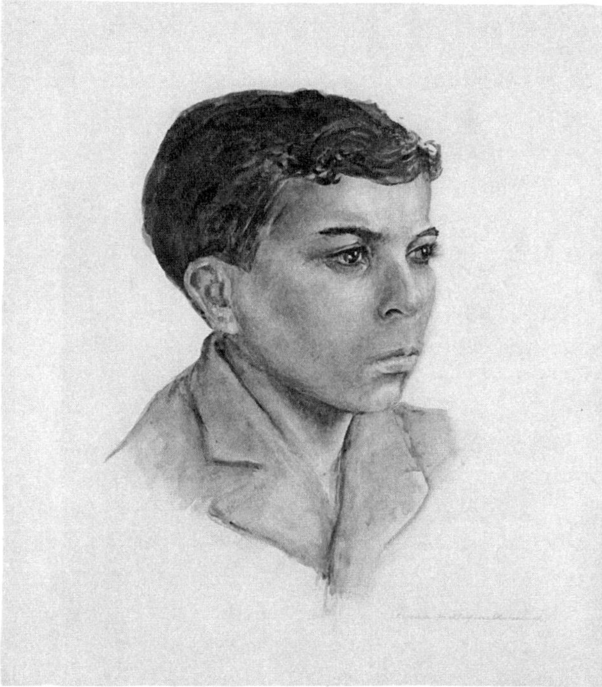

FIGURE 3.4 Dina Gottliebova Babbitt. *Zigeuner-Mischling aus Deutschland*. 1944. Watercolor. 43 × 37.8 cm. © KL Auschwitz.

Dina Gottliebova Babbitt and her mother survived Auschwitz despite many more horrendous instances of death selection processes. On several occasions, Dina actively saved her mother in these selections. She was forced to watch horrific experiments, took part in the devastating death march, and endured weeks of starvation and exhaustion. It was always Dina's talent at art-making that brought her and her mother some food and relief in desperate situations. When asked about the whereabouts of her Roma portraits many years later, Gottliebova Babbitt said, "It never occurred to me to smuggle anything out of Auschwitz. I didn't think anybody cared what happened to us. I just used my ability to draw to save my life" (Gottliebova Babbitt, 1998). Seven of Dina's portraits were given to a Polish family by a prisoner for safekeeping after the Russian troops liberated Auschwitz. Later, the family passed the pictures on to the Auschwitz Memorial Museum, where they still hang today.

After the war, Dina Gottliebova Babbitt met a man in Prague who brought her a moving, handwritten note from her fiancé K., whom she had left behind in Theresienstadt. The note was written to her before his death. In the letter, he acknowledged his impending death and informed Dina that he considered her his legal wife and wanted her to claim the assets he had left. She was unable to receive anything from his estate, however, and her mother suggested that she move on and live with relatives in Paris, where she eventually found a job as an assistant cartoonist for Disney-Paris. Dina fell in love with one of the main creators of the movie *Snow*

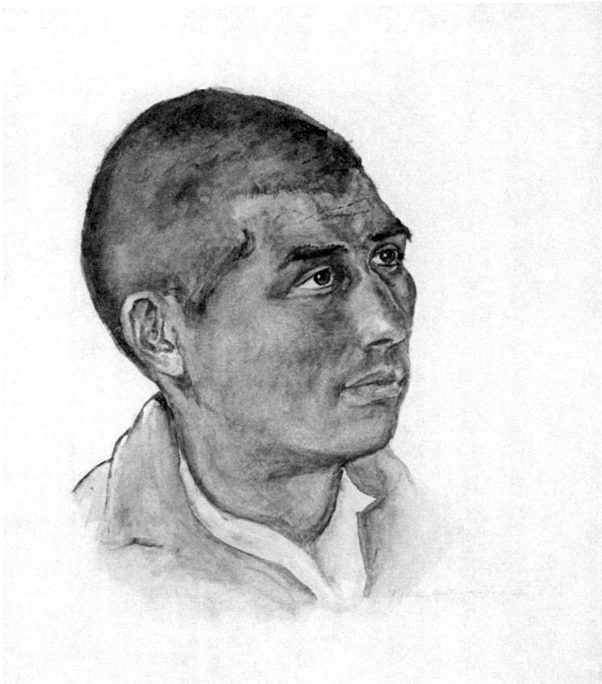

FIGURE 3.5 Dina Gottliebova Babbitt. *Zigeuner-Mischling aus Frankreich*. 1944. Watercolor. 45 × 39.5 cm. © KL Auschwitz.

White and the Seven Dwarfs, and eventually moved with him to Hollywood. Once established in the United States, Dina Gottliebova Babbitt invited her mother, who lived in Paris, to come live with her and her husband in Los Angeles.

Holocaust trauma

When an adult faces severe trauma, earlier infantile primary traumatizations can be reactivated. Dina Gottliebova Babbitt's earliest trauma was the loss of her father, when she was just a few months old, and his subsequent rejections when she was 6 and 16. These memories, which she drew in picture stories as a child, expressed her wish for a complete family in a secure place, and for a loving father who could have provided her with the ability to distance herself from her mother. When she voluntarily accompanied her mother to the death camp in Auschwitz, her choice to separate from her beloved fiancé in Theresienstadt reactivated this early loss—a loss complicated by her fear for her mother's life as well as her own.

In the overwhelming situation of the concentration camp, many individuals resorted to primitive defenses to ward off fragmentation of the self. While one part of the ego perceives the threatening reality, for the other the threatening scenes do not really take place. Many years later, this acknowledgment and disavowal can continue simultaneously. The worst of what prisoners dared to imagine had actually occurred, so reality and fantasy became blurred. The prisoners' experiences were so traumatic that they could not be communicated any longer, neither to their fellow inmates nor to themselves. There was no imagined 'other' present to be heard, and so the victims often felt that they no longer existed as real individuals. "During massive trauma," say Laub and Auerhahn (1993), "fiction, fantasy and demonic art can become historical fact." This blurring of boundaries between reality and fantasy can conjure up affects so violent that it can exceed the ego's capacity for regulation. "To protect ourselves from affects," Laub continues, "we must, at times avoid knowledge. We defend against intense feelings of rage, cynicism, shame and fear by not knowing them consciously" (p. 288).

Speaking and listening to Dina Gottliebova Babbitt revealed the deep truth of this formulation. While Gottliebova Babbitt's report of her overwhelming experiences are horrifying, her manner of report itself is often devoid of real affects. When she remembered the loss of her Roma friends, however, her defenses broke down and she became very sad. Part of Gottliebova Babbitt's idealization of her past—her happy, carefree female-centered household of music and song—stemmed from her wish to preserve what existed before, untainted by her later traumatic experiences (Auerhahn and Perlinger, 1983). Her past needed to be protectively sealed off. The boundary between what was possible and what actually occurred became traumatic in itself.

Life theme: *Snow White and the Seven Dwarfs*

Laub and Auerhahn (1993) discuss the process of forming a narrative, a life theme that can become an organizing and unifying principle to help one cope with massive trauma. This process is unconscious, in particular the linkages to the survivor's underlying memories. The message of this theme and its symbolizations can be acted out on any level of object relations. This life theme allows for a much greater differentiation and distance from the actuality of the traumatic experience itself by becoming the center of an individual's personality for a particular time.

The major theme in Gottliebova Babbitt's life narrative was the animated film *Snow White and the Seven Dwarfs*, Disney's first full-length movie released in 1937, when Gottliebova Babbitt was 14 years old. This movie, adapted from the Brothers Grimm fairy tale, was a pioneering classic in film history, featuring color animation and sound, and figures modeled on live actors. Fairy tales can act as early screens for one's projections, and their structure is familiar to the thinking minds of children (Kast, 1996). With fairy tales, children can project their own psychic situations, their wishes and their longings. Fairy tales demonstrate that problems can be resolved, or that one can actually grow out of them. They employ magical thinking and their motifs often point to the future. As Freud (1911) said, "In a few people, recollection of their favorite fairy tale takes the place of memories of their own childhood, they have made the fairy tales into screen memories . . . then fairy tales are used as associations" (p. 281).

Looking at the symbolism in *Snow White*'s narrative may help us to understand its impact on Dina Gottliebova Babbitt. Snow White is faced with dangerous people and situations, and a near-death experience. Gottliebova Babbitt was first exiled from her home in Brno to Prague, and later from art school into the concentration camps, where she was surrounded by murder and death; she succeeded in surviving these horrific episodes in her life and escaped from the dangers she faced, much like Snow White did. *Snow White* is also the story of an adolescent—initially white, pure, and untouchable as snow—a pregenital little girl who awakens and physically matures. The huntsman (hunting for her budding sexuality) is ordered to kill her but sends her into the forest instead, not unlike Dina's own estranged father, who did not protect her early on from poverty, nor later from her horrific experiences in the camps. It is no coincidence that Snow White found herself in the forest, a place filled with wild animals, nightmares, id-like monsters, attractions and seductions.

Dina Gottliebova Babbitt's childhood was not a particularly happy one. She lived in a fatherless household in harsh economic times and in adolescence was thrown into camps by Hitler. Because Gottliebova Babbitt was not fortunate enough to experience a secure early childhood bond and attachment to two parents, and she was not given the opportunity for a slow adolescent separation in this historical period where separation could translate into eternal separation through death. Gottliebova Babbitt had a complex relationship with her mother, from whom she had a very hard time separating during this terrible period. Gottliebova Babbitt chose to stay by her mother's side, refusing to leave her mother when she moved to Prague. Later, Gottliebova Babbitt chose to accompany her to Theresienstadt, the bleak, deadly concentration camp that ultimately saved both their lives, rather than immigrate to Palestine. Even when faced with a harsh, bitter life in the concentration camp, Dina clung to her mother's side; she decided not to stay with her fiancé in Theresienstadt, but again followed her mother voluntarily to Auschwitz, not knowing what would await them at the death camp.

Unlike Snow White, Dina Gottliebova Babbitt was not saved or redeemed by the men in her life: not by her father, who had not shown interest in her as a little child or later as a teenager and perished in the camp, nor by her first love K., who also died in the camp and most significantly of all, not by God the father. Though Gottliebova Babbitt was not killed in the camps and survived Auschwitz she was not protected from the horrendous trauma of the Holocaust. Still, in this time of overwhelming deprivation and fear of death, but also a time of her budding sexuality in a horrific world dominated by powerful, controlling, frightening men, Gottliebova Babbitt wished unconsciously for an idealized fairy tale image, highlighting her own life passage.

"Dream symbolism extends far beyond dreams . . . but exercises a similar dominating influence on representation in fairy tales, myth and legends . . . [it is] a characteristic of the unconscious thinking which provides the dream work with the material for condensation, displacement and dramatization," wrote Freud in his *Interpretation of Dreams* (1900). Seven became a magical number for Dina Gottliebova Babbitt. She reported that she viewed the Disney movie *Snow White* seven times. There are seven dwarfs in the story, there were seven women in Gottliebova Babbitt's household when she was growing up, and seven of her pictures survived the Holocaust. She reported, "My career as a survivor began in Auschwitz-Birkenau by decorating the children's barracks to the children's specifications with Disney's *Snow White* in giant size on the inner walls . . ." (Gottliebova Babbitt, 1998). Dina painted the beautiful mural of Snow White on the sad barrack walls of the children marked for death in Auschwitz-Birkenau, and later she moved to Hollywood's "fairyland" with her husband after the war. Fifty years later when I visited Gottliebova Babbitt, she lived in a small house in the middle of a forest, quite like Snow White and her seven dwarfs.

Because of her unique artistic talents Dina Gottliebova Babbitt was spared by the "Angel of Death." Her identity as an artist not only gave her special privileges in the concentration and death camps, saving her and her mother's lives, it also strengthened her ego and feeling of self in a situation where machinery was used to dehumanize each and every prisoner. Fisher (2001) points out that Gottliebova Babbitt must have projected her romantic notion of Snow White's seven dwarfs onto the Gypsies. The cruel annihilation of the Roma on *Zigeunernacht* was overwhelming and traumatizing for everybody involved, but particularly for Gottliebova Babbitt. This event not only marked the killing of naive, innocent people, among them many children and adolescents, but more significantly it included the killing of people with whom Gottliebova Babbitt identified, people who represented happiness, creativity and positive childhood memories.

Trauma and art

Dina Gottliebova Babbitt's ability to create first the fairy tale murals and then the Gypsy portraits, even when faced with death, provided a powerful alternative to more primitive responses such as denial, projective identification and overwhelming depression. The race against destruction can be counter-acted psychologically by creating something new, as happened when Gottliebova Babbitt was ordered to paint the Gypsy portraits, thereby fostering an ego ideal based on good internal objects. D.W. Winnicott's concept of the transitional object plays an important role here (1971). Since the transitional object as described in Chapter 2, p. 58 can be lost and rediscovered therein, the child's first acceptable meaningful experience of the "not me" can be transformed by creating and making it "mine." The same is true of Gottliebova Babbitt's paintings, as they represent both a foothold in reality and a guarantor of continuity, and as they become the talisman par excellence for warding off fear and anxiety (Dreifuss-Kattan, 1994).

Depressive reactions in the child are not based on loss alone, but are also ushered in by aggressive and destructive urges (Klein, 1975). For Melanie Klein and her followers, the establishment of the depressive position goes hand in hand with the establishment of a reality-oriented ego. The intense feelings of loss that the child experiences as a result of his or her own attacks on the mother and primary objects, whether fantasized or real, give rise to a wish to repair the lost, loved object and instill it with new life and wholeness (Segal, 1973). These reparative activities, which are essential in the working through of the depressive position, and thus in the formation of the ego and the sense of reality, are animated throughout by the wish to restore, preserve, and recreate the lost happiness of symbiosis, and so give the internal object external life. If one accepts Winnicott's (1971) logic that creativity first arises out of transitional phenomena, then it certainly has a special relation to the trauma of loss and mourning.

Dina Gottliebova Babbitt's art-making—first as a small child drawing picture stories of idealized, wholesome families, and later as a young artist in Prague, Theresienstadt, and eventually in Auschwitz—satisfied her omnipotent and narcissistic needs which were being attacked in a destructive environment of constant deprivation and fear of death. Gottliebova Babbitt was able to utilize her creativity in order to mediate and master her trauma. Through her artistic assignments in the camps, she succeeded in finding some meaning in a life overwhelmed by trauma. The artistic expressions that defined her as an artist and kept her in touch with her ability to imagine acted as a vital shield against overwhelming pain, suffering, dehumanization and deprivation (Auerbach, 1989). Art-making allowed Gottliebova Babbitt to better tolerate her losses and to stave off, if only for a time, the approach of death.

Thus, the Roma portraits have a dual aspect. For Gottliebova Babbitt, they represented something like a goodbye present, while at the same time they endure after the artist's death and thereby ensure immortality for both the artist and for the perished Roma people portrayed. While the artist is painting and creating, the feeling of the end and the feeling of endlessness seem identical, and the threatening reality seems to somehow be suspended.

Having to create—even though it was assigned art—enabled Dina Gottliebova Babbitt to infuse meaning into what was otherwise a life devoid of any meaning. While in the process of painting, however, she also became a silent witness to a death machine, and thus unconsciously stored a wealth of overwhelming traumatic memories.

The closeness she developed as an artist to her Roma models forged a strong and powerful bond. Painting them as they posed for her for hours and days fostered an attunement; inquiry into their fate and lives sustained an empathy that fostered a bond and a sense of responsibility for her subjects. Equally vulnerable, she easily identified with their fate and believed death would soon be her fate as well.

Dina Gottliebova Babbitt's highly ambivalent relationship to the "Angel of Death," Dr. Mengele, who was at the end the protector of both Gottliebova Babbitt and her mother, but also the horrific tormentor of others, must have left her completely isolated and emotionally strained. This situation thus forced her to recognize the nightmare around her and simultaneously split it off from her awareness. When a conflict arises between knowing and not knowing, between facing memories and resisting them, traumatic memory develops (Laub and Podell, 1995). In these portraits, Dina Gottliebova Babbitt not only became the silent witness of someone else's death, namely her Roma friends, but she was also forced to contemplate her own death with each new selection process headed by Dr. Mengele.

The wish to regain her original Gypsy paintings

Unlike Snow White, Dina Gottliebova Babbitt was able to develop a transitional space with her good mother and thus could better handle the threatening outside world. Gottliebova Babbitt had a good enough mother, but unlike Snow White who was rescued by her prince, Gottliebova Babbitt was never really unambivilently supported or loved by a father. During her internment at the camps, she could only fully rely on her own creativity to provide her with a transitional space, and this also caused her to identify with her lost artist father. After the war, however, with the memory of overwhelming trauma, Gottliebova Babbitt lost the capacity to access her transitional creative space in order to create original art. Her inability to freely associate, symbolize and fantasize after the liquidation of the Roma people might be responsible for this inability to create a safe transitional space. Gottliebova Babbitt worked as an assistant animator first in Paris and later in Los Angeles Disney and never really succeeded in creating satisfying original art work in her own studio.

This situation also explains Dina Gottliebova Babbitt's nearly 30-year legal and public quest to regain and own her seven surviving original watercolor portraits, which now belong to the Polish Government and hang in the Auschwitz Museum. Her quest represents a yearning and searching for the dead, a half-belief that the dead could be found and recovered. Even though her mourning was much delayed, and it seems that her search was futile, it served a vital function for the artist. It enabled her to believe that she could have made peace with the dead, which would have allowed her to find a much needed transitional space. In order for her to complete her work of mourning and regain her original artistic impulse, she would have needed to transform her ties with her internal dead mother, her dead Roma friends, and her former Holocaust self. The artist believed that she might be better able to attain peace if she could have obtained her lost "children," in the form of the original Roma portraits, so they could have "lived" with her and memorialized by her forever, thus also relieving her survivor's guilt. Having the pictures by her side could have, I suggest, aided her in connecting to her vanishing internal past and in re-linking her with her fantasy life and the lost people in it. Then Gottliebova Babbitt could have reconnected to her traumatic memory in order to create associative links, and most importantly revive split-off affects.

Auerhahn and Laub (1984) have said that the Holocaust survivor attempts to bring the past to life in an effort to recapture it, to rebuild trust and foster coherence and substance in one's new life. As the reader learns from Dina Gottliebova Babbitt's story, however, she had to complete a complicated mourning, not for her real mother, but for the mother she had internalized. While she was successful in mourning the death of her mother—whose life she saved, and with whom she lived after their liberation from the camp and before Dina's marriage—she had not yet been able to work through her ambivalence towards the internal mother whom she had, in a certain sense, frozen in idealization, and from whom she was never able to separate in a mature way.

Successful mourning would have entailed giving up this idealized internal mother; the incompleteness of that mourning expressed itself in her obsessive, almost manic wish to acquire and possess the original Roma portraits. Could it be that these portraits, in their idealized originality, became a substitute for

Gottliebova Babbitt's idealized mother? The enduring pain of this depressive position (Klein, 1971), mourning the loss of these idealized objects, might have been necessary to open up a transitional space for the original creative productivity of her new post-war life (Schwab, 2015). The immense psychic damage caused by the trauma of her Holocaust experience, however, also aggravated her ability to access anew her true, creative self.

References

Appelfeld, A. (1994) *Beyond despair.* New York: Fromm International.

Auerbach, D. (1989) Creativity and the survivor: The struggle for mastery. *International Review of Psycho-Analysis*, 16: 273–286.

Auerhahn, N. and Laub, D. (1984) Annihilation and restoration: Post-traumatic memory as pathway and obstacle to recovery. *International Review of Psycho-Analysis*, 11: 227–344.

Auerhahn, N. and Perlinger, E. (1983) Repetition in the concentration camp survivor and her child. *International Review of Psycho-Analysis*, 10, 1: 31–46.

Bloch, G. (1999) *Unfree associations: A psychoanalyst recollects the Holocaust.* Palmdale, CA: Red Hen Press.

Dreifuss-Kattan, E. (1994) *Cancer stories: Creativity and self-repair.* Hillsdale, NJ: The Analytic Press.

Encyclopaedia Judaica. Jerusalem: Keter Publishing House.

Felman, S. and Laub, M. (1992) *Testimony.* New York: Routledge.

Fisher, B. (1999) No roads lead to Rom: The fate of the Romani people under the Nazis and in post-war restitution. In *Symposium on Nazi gold, and assets of the Holocaust, 15th Annual International Law Symposium*, 20 Whittier L. Rev. 513.

Fisher, B. (2001) Verbal communication.

Freud, S. (1900). The interpretation of dreams. *The standard edition of the complete psychological works of Sigmund Freud* (Vol. 5: 339–686), London: Hogarth Press, 1981.

Freud, S. (1911) The occurrence in dreams of material from fairy tales. In Papers on techniques. *The standard edition of the complete psychological works of Sigmund Freud* (Vol. 12: 281–287). London: Hogarth Press, 1982.

Gottliebova Babbitt, Dina. (1998) Personal interview.

Kast, V. (1996) The clinical use of fairy tales by a "classical" Jungian analyst. *Psychoanalytic Review,* 83, 4: 509–524.

Klein, M. (1975) *Love, guilt and reparation: And other works, 1921–1945.* New York: Delacorte.

Lanzman, C. (2012) *The Patagonian hare.* New York: Farrar, Straus and Giroux.

Laub, D. and Auerhahn, C. (1993) Knowing and not knowing: Massive psychic trauma: forms of traumatic memory. *International Journal of Psychoanalysi*, 74: 297–302.

Laub, D. and Podell, D. (1995) Art and trauma. *International Journal of Psychoanalysis*, 76: 991–1006.

Milton, S. (1992) Nazi policies toward Roma and Sinti, 1933–1945. *Journal of the Gypsy Lore Society* 5, 2, 1: 1–18.

Schwab, Gabriele (2015). Personal correspondence.

Segal, H. (1973) *Introduction to the work of Melanie Klein.* New York: Basic Books.

Tyrnauer, G. (1997) The Gypsies of Europe: From persecution to genocide. In *Ethnicity, immigration, and psychology.* I. Al-Issa and M. Tousignant (Eds.). New York: Plenum.

Winnicott, D.W. (1971) *Playing and reality.* New York: Basic Books.

4

FERDINAND HODLER

From the vertical of life to the horizontal of death—Ferdinand Hodler and Valentine Godé-Dorel, 1908–1915

Ferdinand Hodler lived in Switzerland from 1853 to 1918 and is considered to be the most prominent Swiss artist of the turn of the century. Hodler was one of the most important figures to introduce Europe to Symbolism and was, together with his colleagues Paul Gauguin and Edvard Munch, committed to the spiritual content of life. These three artists utilized a formal symbolic language to express their cosmic ideas and spiritual content, specifically the meaning of life in the presence of death. This chapter will review the cycle of works Hodler created between 1908 and 1915, in which he drew, painted, and sculpted his model and lover Valentine Godé-Darel—who eventually died from breast cancer—as she transformed from a beautiful woman into a sick and suffering patient.

One unconscious motive of Hodler's active artistic involvement with death, particularly in the cycle of pictures of Godé-Darel's death process, may have been his loss-filled childhood. By creating this cycle of pictures, the artist was able to cope with the feelings of love, aggression and guilt that are components of every mourning process. He not only portrayed Godé-Darel's end of life, but captured the universal experience of death and dying. He created immortal works that have survived Godé-Darel and the artist himself. Feelings of loss are followed by longing, a longing for the transitional space, the early space between mother and the playing child and the sense of time and feeling of reverie which is part of that space. Through his art-making, Hodler may have hoped to regain his once loved and now lost inner objects. The artist allows the viewer to join him in mourning not only the transience of beauty with its loss of sexual, physical gratifications, but at the very end Hodler also invites the viewer to mourn the ultimate loss, that of life itself. Together with the artist, the viewer can mourn the illusionary timelessness that he considered life to be.

Biographical details

Ferdinand Hodler was internationally celebrated as one of the fathers of modern art outside of the French school, together with Edvard Munch, James Ensor, Vincent Van Gogh and Gustav Klimt. Hodler met Auguste Rodin and Edgar Degas in Paris, and was endorsed by the well-known artist Gustav Klimt in Vienna. In 1913, after many years of struggling with poverty in his apprenticeship, Ferdinand Hodler was finally recognized and decorated by the French President Raymond Poincaré and the German Kaiser Wilhelm II. An exponent of *Jugendstil* and a precursor of the Expressionists, Hodler is credited with introducing the concept of Symbolism to Europe and also focused on modern monumental paintings (Vaughan, 1993). Like the poets Stéphane Mallarmé and Arthur Rimbaud, or the composers Claude Debussy, Gustav Mahler and Erik Satie, Hodler and his colleagues Paul Gauguin and Edvard Munch emphasized the consistent presence of death in their work.

Leaning on the traditions of the Swiss Romantic philosopher Jean-Jacques Rousseau, who in the eighteenth century was inspired by the natural beauty of the Swiss Alpine landscape and linked man's spiritual origins to the universe, Hodler introduced Swiss landscapes like the Alps as a motif into visual art—heroic forms of nature that not only inspired visions of divine intensity, but also reflected emotional states (Vaughan, 1993). This approach, which he called Parallelism, is a distinctly humanistic creation in which figures or scenes from nature are arranged symbolically as repetitions of one basic image, and through this linkage attain a cumulative effect. Viewed together, the figures or imagery of nature simultaneously express a variety of feelings, and show the viewer a fundamental harmony, or Parallelism, as well as communality and formal unification (Honisch, 1983). Hodler said, "A landscape you know touches you more, you understand it better when you know it. You had to live in it, to understand it [the landscape], how one suffered in it, to be able to communicate the pain. The landscape you lived in becomes part of yourself, like a relative" (Brüschweiler, 2004).

Hodler's idealism expressed his belief that human beings were equal to nature and had a common destiny, thus illustrating the unity of all matter with nature. His idealism was summed up well in the following statement, which he wrote in his early notebooks: "*Das Herz ist mein Auge* [The heart is my eye]." He later expanded on this by saying, "Real art is the kind that sprouts in the brain and in the heart" (Brüschweiler, 2004, p. 7, my translation).

His 1890 painting entitled *Night* (Figure 4.1) granted him his first international recognition. In this painting, Hodler implements the human figure, as well as color and light, to create a symbolic parallelism, evoking a feeling of night and suggesting a fusion of Eros, sleep and death. Six of the eight figures are asleep. The central figure is recognizably the artist, who had known death since his early childhood. He seems suddenly awakened and terrified by a black, hooded, cloaked figure who represents death. This death figure also seems like a seducer, crouching on the artist's genitals, thus portraying death as the castrator.

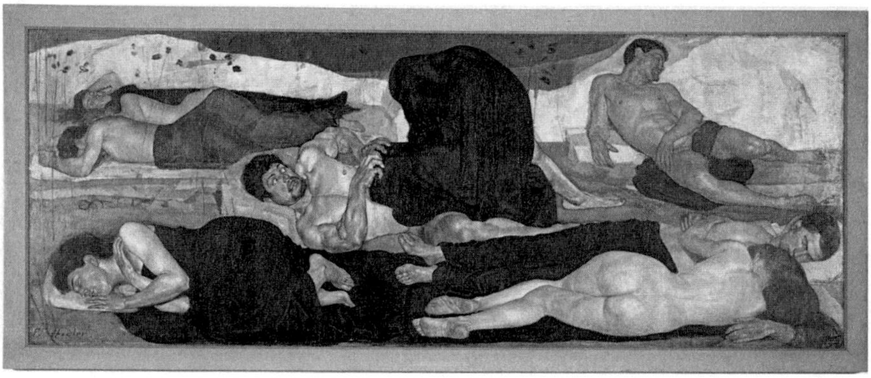

FIGURE 4.1 Ferdinand Hodler. *Die Nacht* [*Night*]. 1889–1890. Oil on Canvas. 116 × 299 cm. © Kunstmuseum Bern, Stadt Bern.

Hodler wrote on the frame of this picture: *"Plus d'un qui s'est couché tranquillement le soir, ne reveillera pas le lendemain* [when one goes to sleep quietly in the evening, one might not wake up in the morning]" (Hodler after Selz, 1972, p. 30, my translation).

The woman who sleeps alone in the lower left corner of the painting rests in a position of closure, with her body covered and her knees, feet and elbows crossed. Interestingly, the model is Hodler's lover Augustine Dupin, the mother of his only son, Hector. The sensuous, seductive nude embracing a young man on the lower right of the painting is his new wife Berta Stucki, with whom he lived only while he was working on this painting. Hodler had relationships with several women in his lifetime. His first marriage to Stucki lasted only a couple of months. His second marriage to Berthe Jacques in 1898 was initially stable, but not for long; despite the instability of his marriage, he remained married to her until the end of his life.

In 1909, Hodler heard from his son Hector that Dupin was dying. Upon hearing this news, Hector and Ferdinand Hodler kept a vigil at her deathbed for several months (Hirsh, 1982). Five years after Augustine's death, when he could already foresee the pain of his lover Valentine Godé-Darel's death, he wrote: "If you accept death with all your conscience and all your will, this will give birth to great works. One has only one life to realize this. This concept orders all our existence and imprints on it an entirely different rhythm: to have an awareness of transformation, the idea of death into an enormous power" (Hirsh, 1982, p. 50).

The content in Ferdinand Hodler's paintings thus focuses on questions of existence, such as life and death, or content that dealt more with the realities of emotions, with inner thought and imagination in a spiritual symmetry of sorts, than to representations of a more mundane external reality. Love was also a very important aim and focus in Hodler's work. "*Aimer c'est le principal* [love is what counts]," he writes in one of his notebooks, and later, "*Le présent c'est la vie* [the present is what life is]." We will understand these statements better once we look at his childhood (Brüschweiler, 2004, p. 10).

Hodler's past, paved with many losses, may have been one unconscious motive for his active artistic involvement with death, particularly the cycle of pictures on Godé-Darel's death journey discussed below. When he was five years old, Ferdinand Hodler lost his father to tuberculosis. His misfortunes continued when, at the age of 14, he had to carry his dead mother home from their farm's pasture. "The funeral was as paltry as possible. The rough-hewn coffin was taken to the cemetery on a worn pushcart, and the funeral procession consisted of us children, I and my brother and sister, stumbling along in the rear." Between the ages of 6 and 31, Hodler lost five brothers, his only sister, and his half-brother to tuberculosis. "In the family there was constant dying, I felt as if there was always someone dead in our house and as if that's how it had to be," Holder later recalled (Kraft, 1984, p. 318).

Ferdinand Hodler and Valentine Godé-Darel, 1908–1915

When Ferdinand Hodler was 55 years old and at the height of his artistic expression, he met a French woman named Valentine Godé-Darel who influenced not only his personal life but also his late work. Godé-Darel was born in Paris in 1873, and was thus 20 years younger than Hodler. Brought up in an intellectual, middle-class household, she attended drama school and later became a porcelain painter. She was an elegant, cultivated woman who divorced Monsieur Darel in 1907. When she was 35, she went to live with her mother in Geneva, and there met Hodler.

From 1908 to the end of 1910, Hodler painted numerous works for which Godé-Darel posed as his model. In over 50 oil paintings, 130 drawings, 200 sketches, and one work of sculpture, Hodler illustrated how, in his words, he observed his lover "move from the vertical of life to the horizontal of death" (Kraft, 1984, p. 312). This cycle of pictures has been compared by art historians to the series of self-portraits by Rembrandt and Van Gogh because of their emotional immediacy and intensity (Brüschweiler, 1976). Hodler's very beautiful and powerful works in this series are a testimony to the significance of this particularly close, loving relationship.

The picture *Portrait of Valentine Godé-Darel* (*La Parisienne II*), 1909 (Figure 4.2, see also Plate 5), illustrates a seductive Godé-Darel looking back over her shoulder. She seems to look at the artist, a man who was enthralled with her, with both self-assurance and playfulness *Portrait of Valentine Godé-Darel*, frontal view, 1909 (Figure 4.3), is the most modern, free and emotionally expressive piece in this entire cycle. The subject's open look expresses a dreamlike state and communicates intense sensuality. The red lips exposing a divine smile portray to the viewer a very feminine side of Godé-Darel, which the artist himself seems to be discovering. Jura Brueschweiler (1976) believes that this painting is Hodler's first love

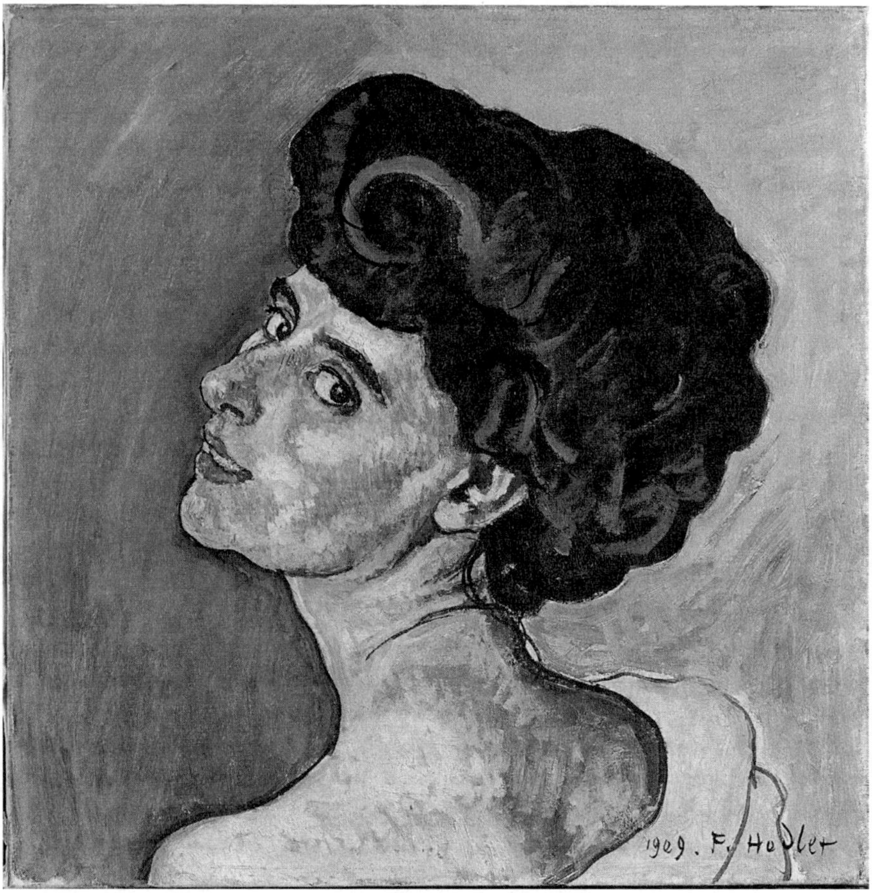

FIGURE 4.2 (see also Plate 5) Ferdinand Hodler. *Bildnis Valentine Godé-Darel (La Parisienne II)* [*Portrait of Valentine Godé-Darel (La Parisienne II)*]. 1909. Oil on canvas. 41.5 × 40.5 cm. © Private Collection, SIK-ISEA, Zürich.

letter to Godé-Darel. In "*Red*" *Portrait of Valentine Godé-Darel*, frontal view, 1910 (Figure 4.4, see also Plate 6), the red color of the lips extends to her sweater and further to the model's entire face, which blushes right up to her eyelids and nose. The red tone is even continued again in the background. While the lips express a more contained emotion, it appears that the painter and model are wrapped in a transparent shawl of love. The year 1910 seems to be the height of their happiness together in their new-found love, which was also well documented in several drawings.

Like all of Ferdinand Hodler's love relationships, this one was threatened by tensions. Valentine Godé-Darel was 20 years his junior and seductive to other men, provoking extreme jealousy in the artist; furthermore, Godé-Darel was

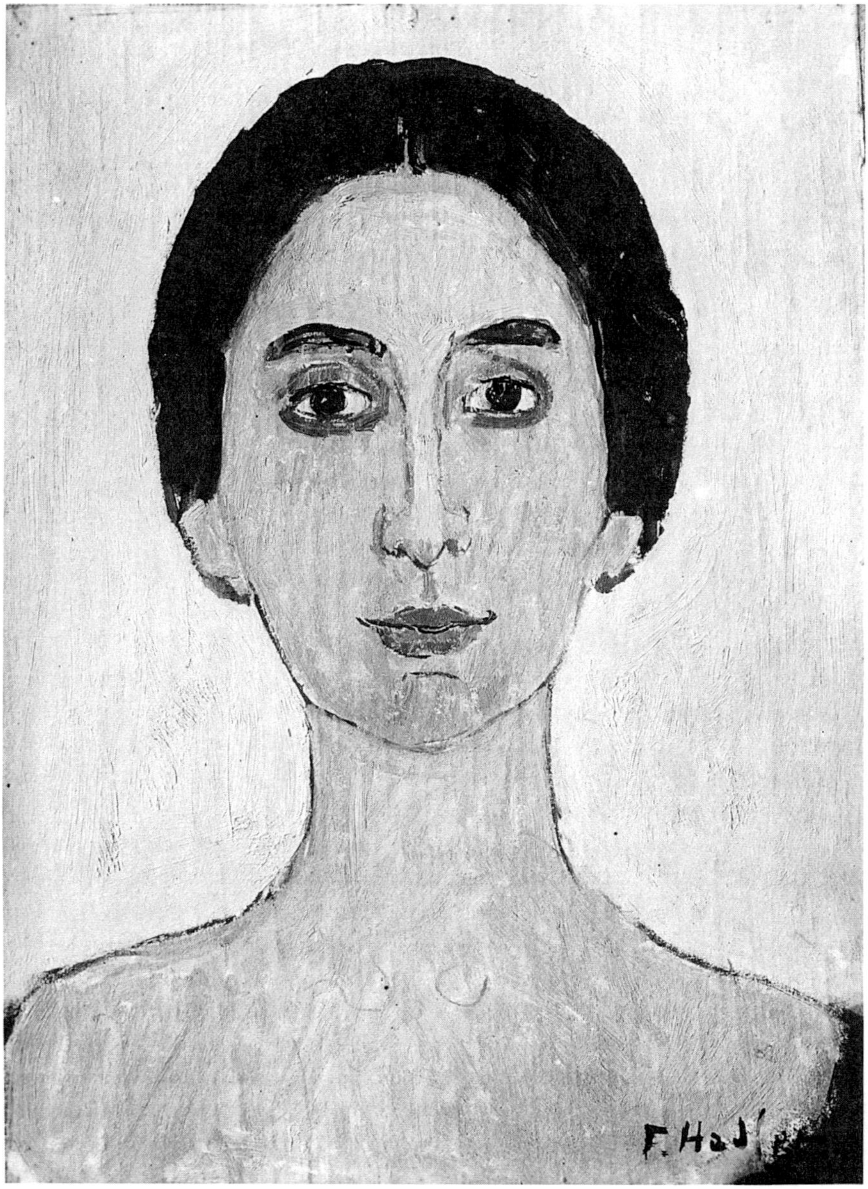

FIGURE 4.3 Ferdinand Hodler. *Bildnis Valentine Godé-Darel* [*Portrait of Valentine Godé-Darel*]. 1909. Oil on canvas. 36 × 28 cm. Private collection © SIK-ISEA, Zürich.

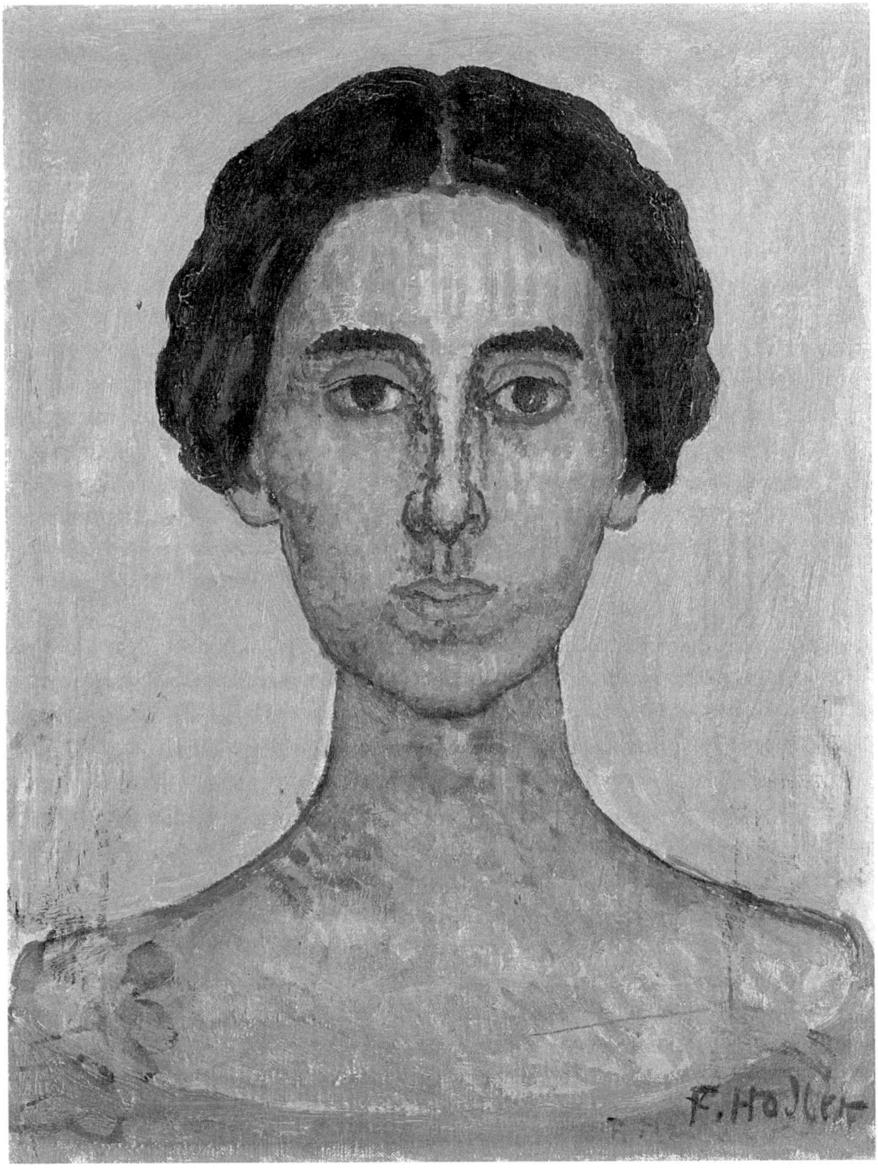

FIGURE 4.4 (see also Plate 6) Ferdinand Hodler. *"Rotes" Bildnis Valentine Godé-Darel* [*"Red" Portrait of Valentine Godé-Darel*]. c. 1910. Oil on canvas. 43 × 33 cm. © Kunsthaus Zürich, Vereinigung Züricher Kunstfreunde.

financially dependent on Hodler, who remained married during the course of this relationship. In November 1910, Godé-Darel and her mother thus decided to move away from Hodler to Vevey, a town on Lake Geneva. The lovers' relationship resumed in 1911, as the two portraits of 1912 celebrate their reconciliation. The picture *Portrait of Valentine Godé-Darel Surrounded by Roses, Left Profile*, 1912 (Figure 4.5, see also Plate 7), again uses the color red to demonstrate Hodler's love for her and shows the viewer the more romantic side of love. Hodler implements the decorative style of Art Deco and utilizes the imagery of roses, the favorite flower of both Hodler and Godé-Darel, which appear repeatedly in his paintings. "What is the most beautiful aspect of life?" wrote Hodler, "Women and roses" (Brüschweiler, 1998, p. 15).

In February 1912, Valentine Godé-Darel's mother died, a very painful loss for Valentine as she had always been accompanied by her mother during the previous years living in Switzerland. It seems that Hodler's drawing of 1912 (Figure 4.6) indicates a much closer relationship between the artist and Godé-Darel, perhaps due to the loss of her mother as a constant companion. This special picture of himself and Godé-Darel in profile, her cheek tenderly touching his forehead, represents a kind of unity that shows great intimacy and softness. This is the only picture or drawing in which the artist draws himself with any woman, indicating a sign of great closeness developing between the two. She seems to both protectively watch over the artist and seductively empower him, engendering a feeling of great love and intimacy, and resulting in an astonished expression in Hodler's face as he glances outside of the picture's frame.

Between 1912 and 1913, Godé-Darel felt weak and went to a sanitarium to recover, where the artist visited her frequently. But in May 1913, Hodler had to fetch Godé-Darel with an ambulance. Not only was the 40-year-old Godé-Darel sick, but she also was pregnant with Hodler's child. On October 13, 1913, Godé-Darel gave birth to their daughter Pauline. Hodler's great joy was expressed in his letter written on October 15, 1913 to Godé-Darel, ending with the words: "Thousands and thousands of kisses, tenderness and beauty for you and your little Tintine [Pauline's nickname]" (Brüschweiler, 1976, p. 32).

Hodler never divorced his second wife, even after Godé-Darel gave birth to their daughter. While his relationship with Godé-Darel was initially stable as she served as his muse, model and partner, it changed as she became pregnant and sick. The more Godé-Darel needed Hodler's presence, the more it engendered his fears of loss, transforming their relationship into one that was tense, aggressive and confrontational. They separated from each other often, only to be reunited again. Hodler's more distant relationship to his wife must have served as a counterbalance to his very intimate—and consequently highly ambivalent—relationship to Godé-Darel, which was marked by deep love and passion, but also by a fear of loss, and a fear of and wish for fusion in death.

The portrait titled *Valentine Godé-Darel with Loose Hair* 1913 (see book cover) was created shortly before or after the birth of little Pauline. Godé-Darel's loose hair

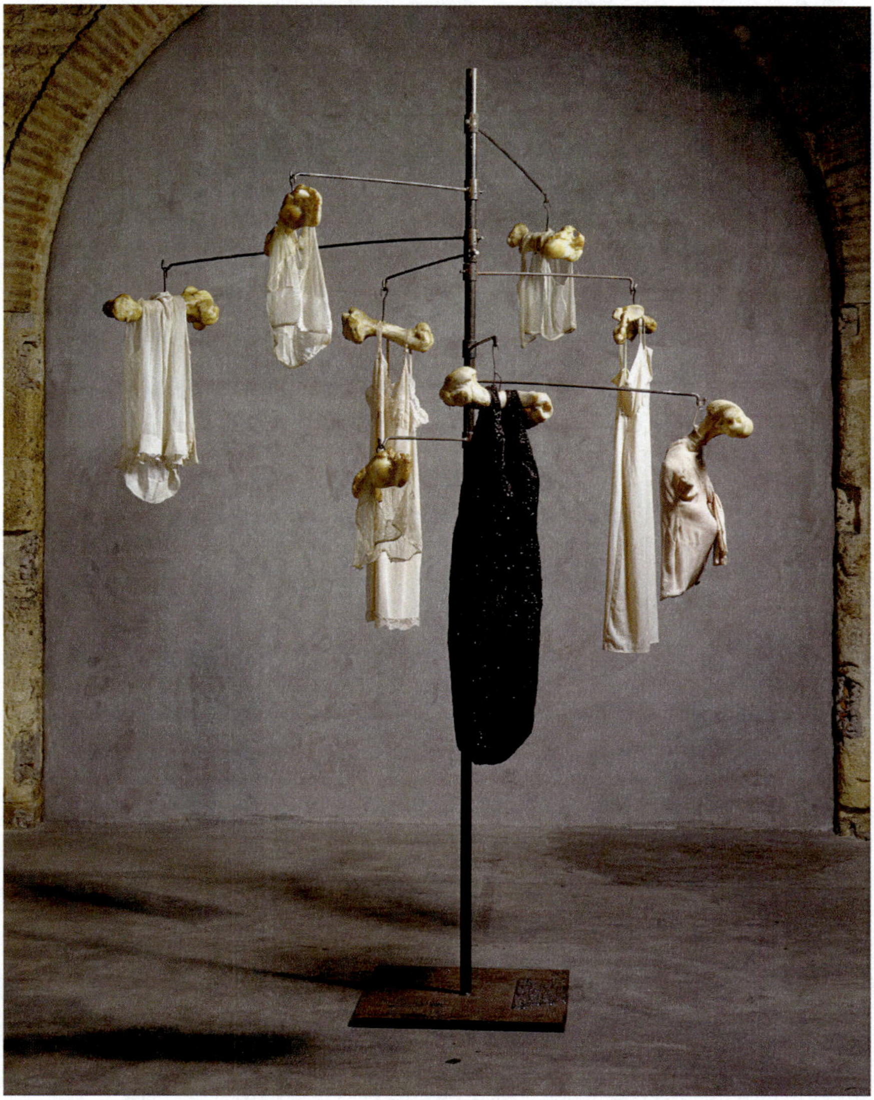

PLATE 1 (see also Figure 1.3) Louise Bourgeois. *Untitled*. 1996. Cloth, rubber, bone and steel (118¼ × 82 × 77 in.). Art © Easton Foundation/ Licensed by VAGA, New York, NY.

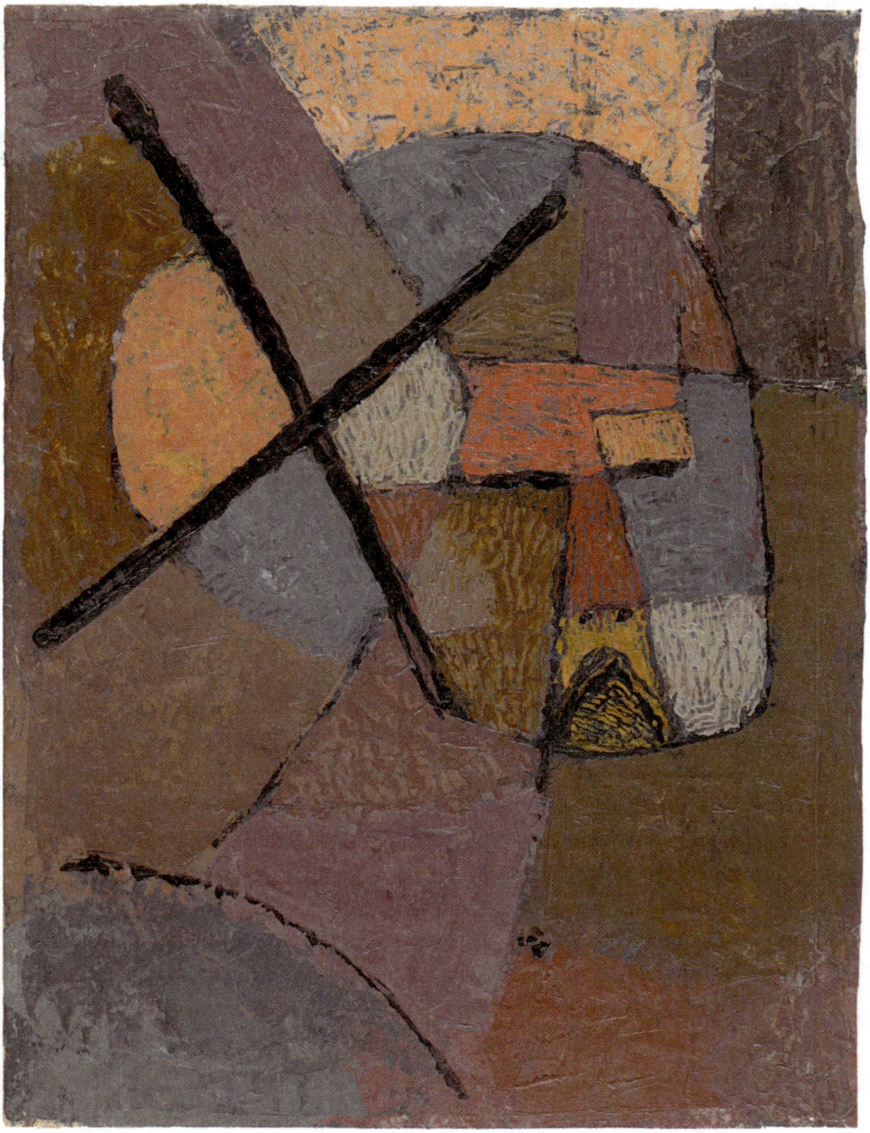

PLATE 2 (see also Figure 2.4) Paul Klee. *Von der Liste gestrichen* [*Struck from the List*]. 1933, 424. Oil on paper on cardboard. 31.5 × 24 cm. Zentrum Paul Klee, Bern, Livia Klee Donation.

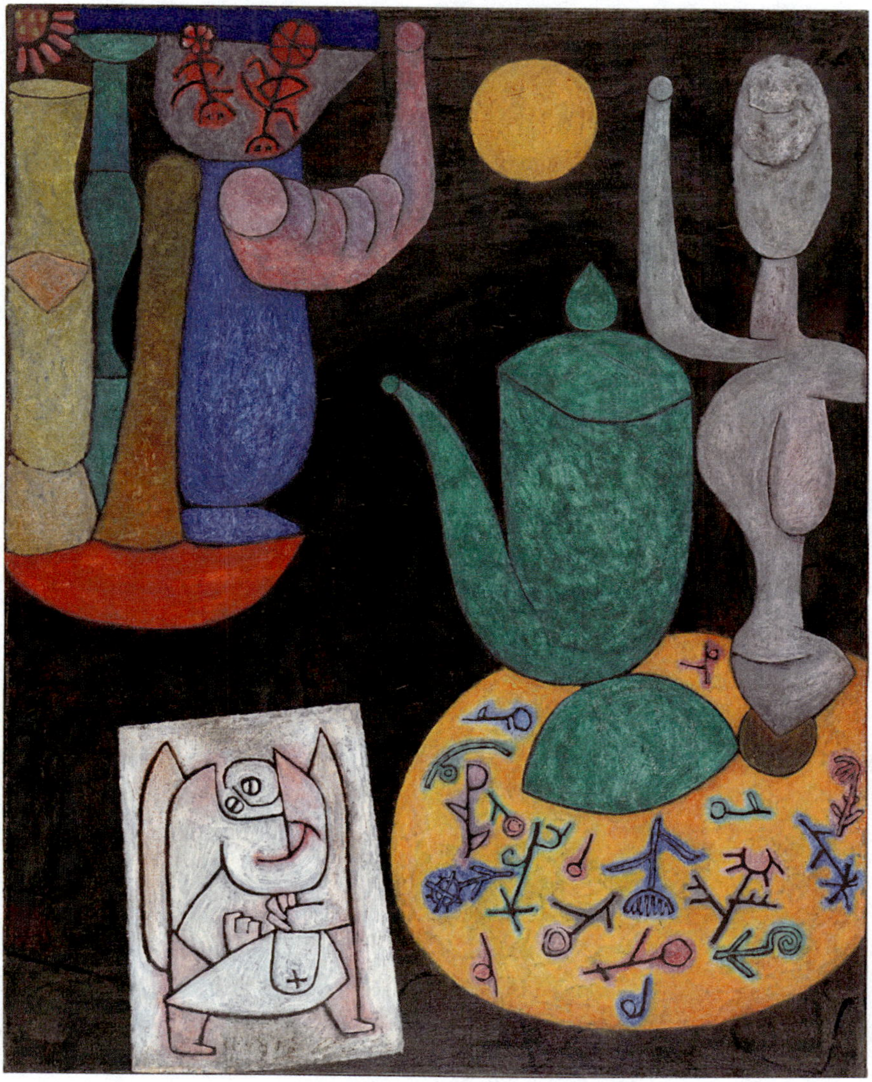

PLATE 3 (see also Figure 2.11) Paul Klee. *Ohne Titel (Letztes Stilleben)* [*Untitled (Last Still Life)*]. 1940. Oil on canvas. 100 × 80.5 cm. Zentrum Paul Klee, Bern, Livia Klee Donation.

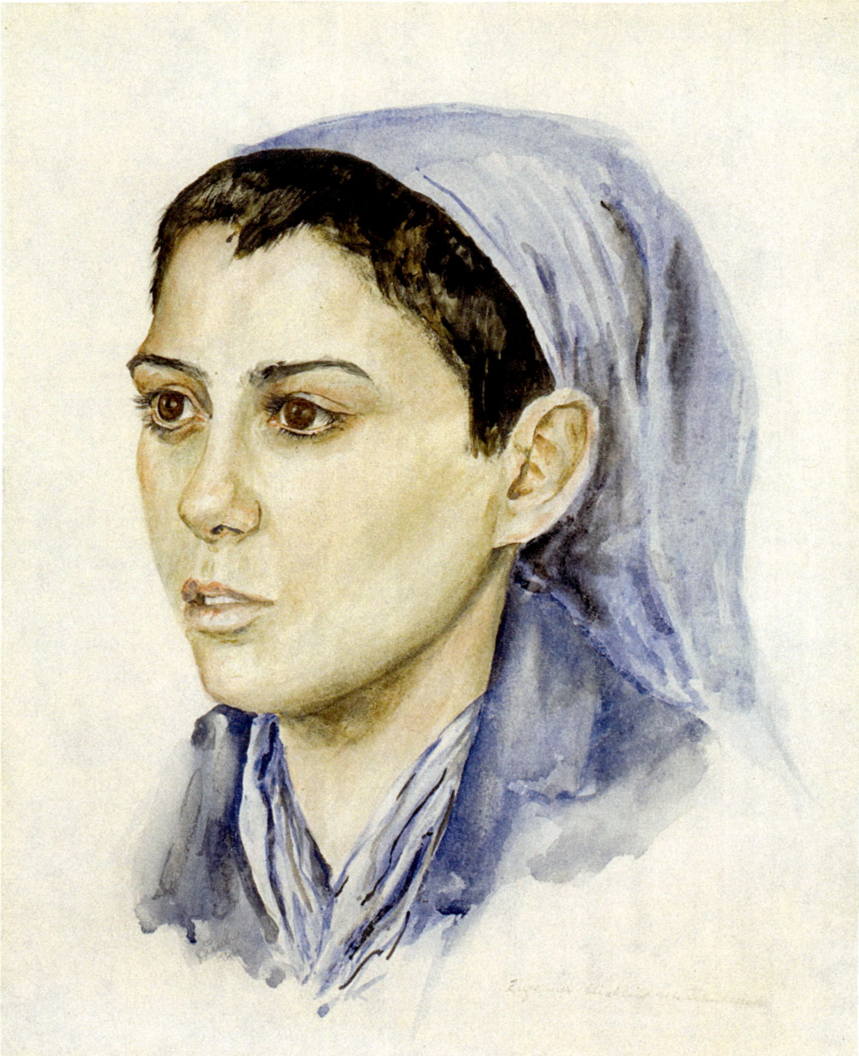

PLATE 4 (see also Figure 3.1) Dina Gottliebova Babbitt. *Zigeuner-Mischling aus Frankreich*. 1944. Watercolor. 38.5 × 31.1 cm. © KL Auschwitz.

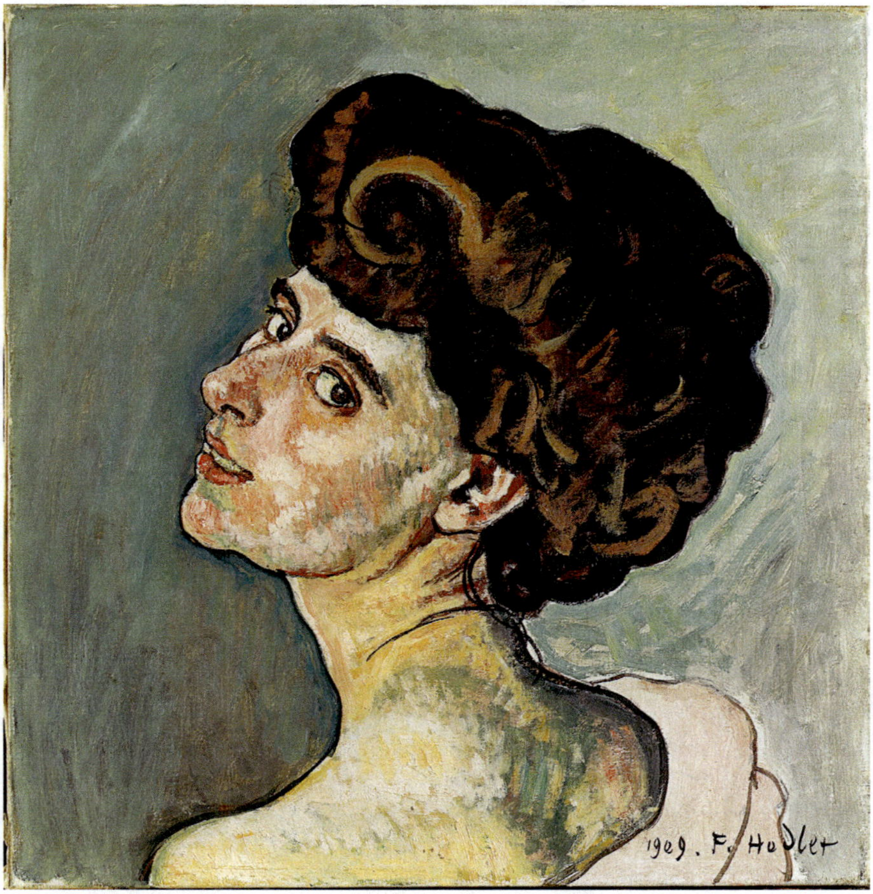

PLATE 5 (see also Figure 4.2) Ferdinand Hodler. *Bildnis Valentine Godé-Darel (La Parisienne II)* [*Portrait of Valentine Godé-Darel (La Parisienne II)*]. 1909. Oil on canvas. 41 5 × 40.5 cm. © Private Collection, SIK-ISEA, Zürich.

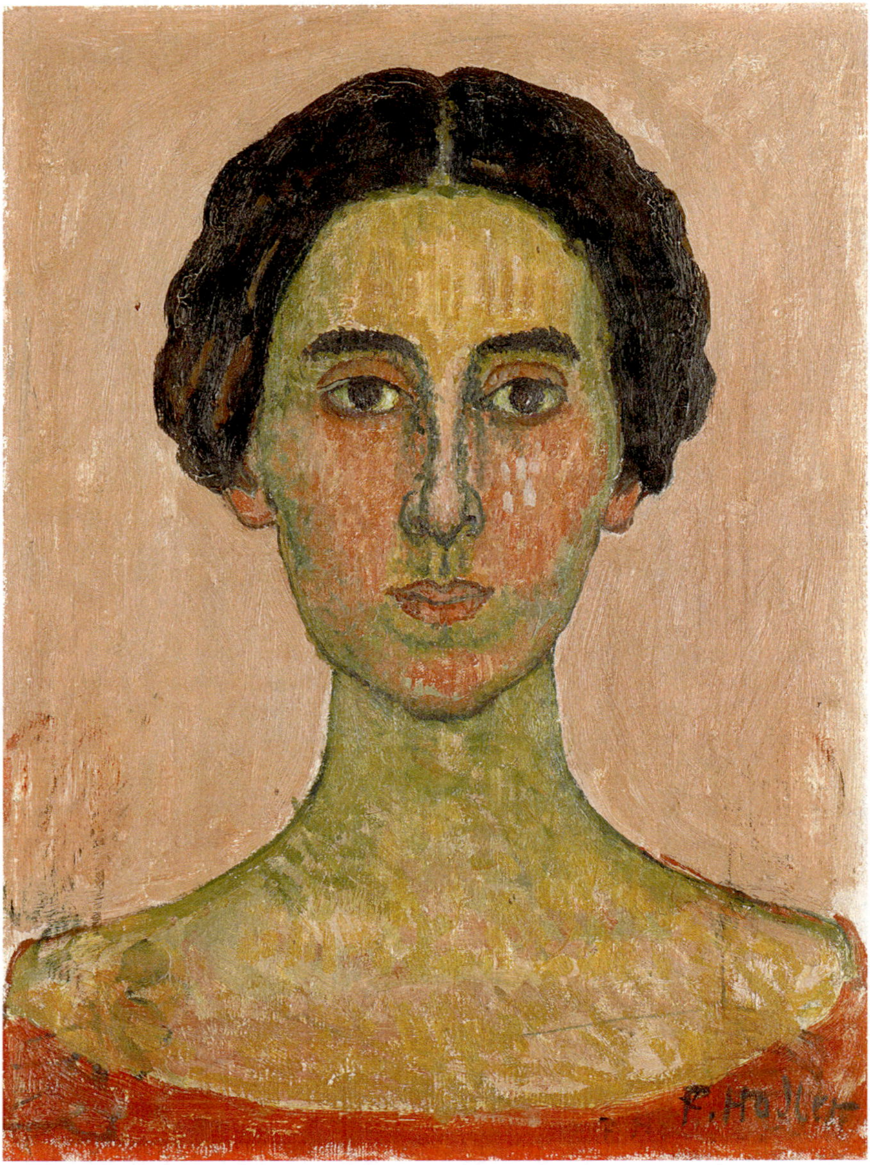

PLATE 6 (see also Figure 4.4) Ferdinand Hodler. *"Rotes" Bildnis Valentine Godé-Darel* [*"Red" Portrait of Valentine Godé-Darel*]. c. 1910. Oil on canvas. 43 × 33 cm. © Kunsthaus Zürich, Vereinigung Züricher Kunstfreunde.

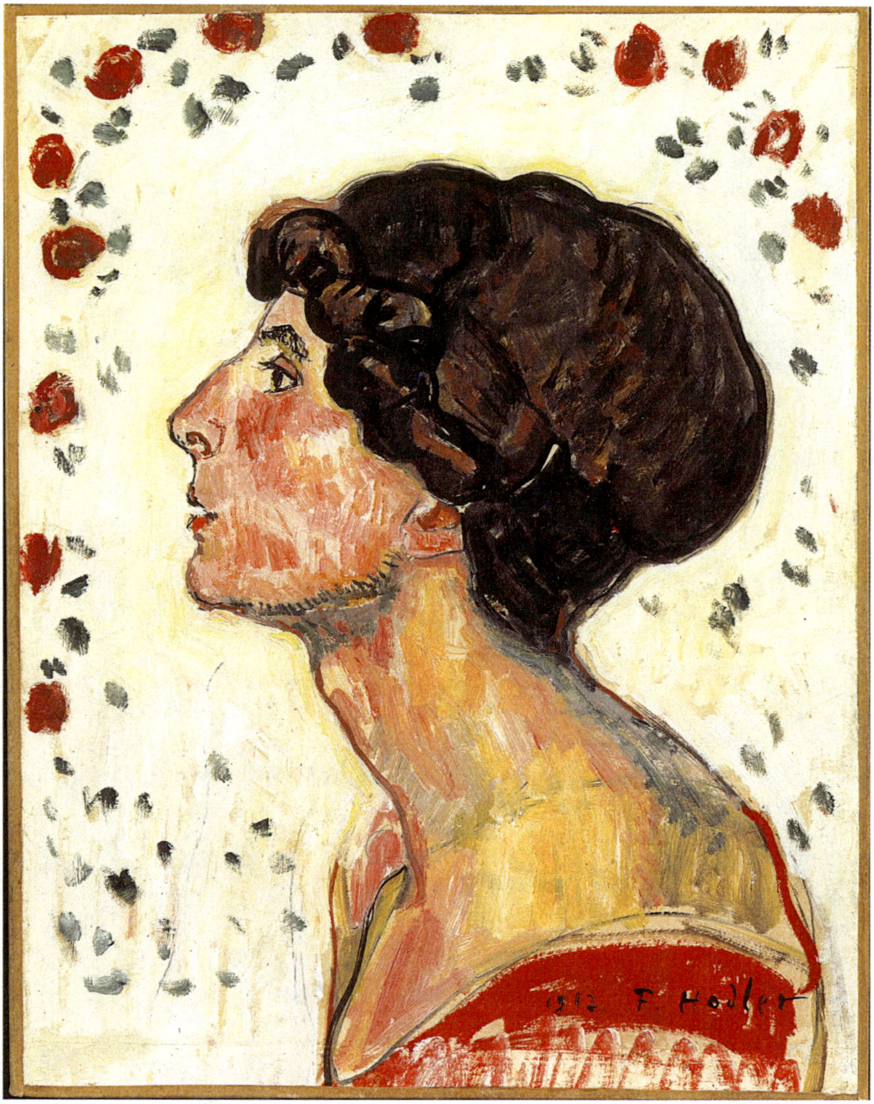

PLATE 7 (see also Figure 4.5) Ferdinand Hodler. *Bildnis Valentine Godé-Darel von Rosen umgeben, Linksprofil* [*Portrait of Valentine Godé-Darel Surrounded by Roses, Left Profile*]. 1912. Oil on paper, put on wood. 39 × 31.5 cm. © Private Collection, SIK-ISEA, Zürich.

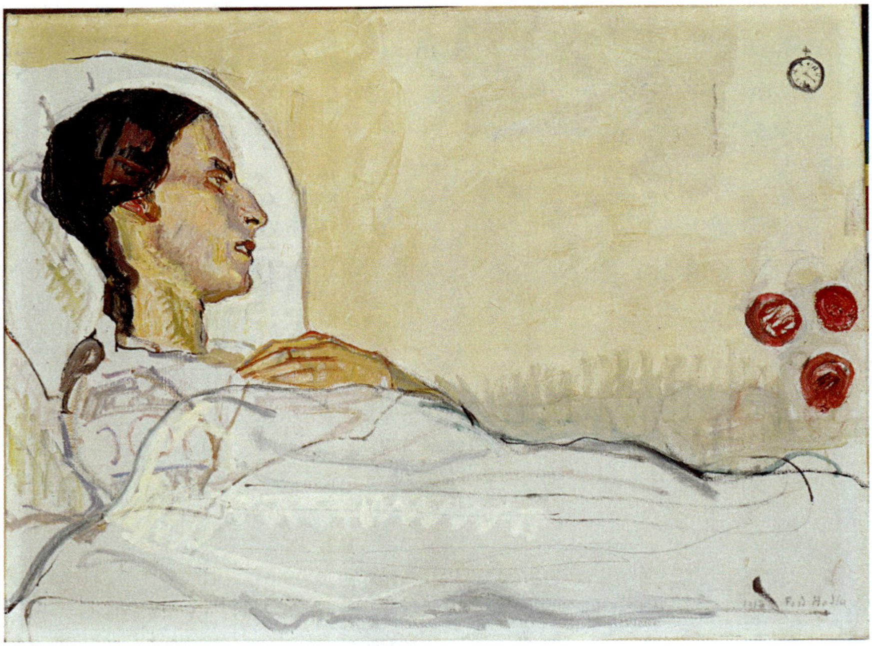

PLATE 8 (see also Figure 4.7) Ferdinand Hodler. *Valentine Godé-Darel im Krankenbett mit Uhr und Rosen* [*Valentine Godé-Darel on Her Sickbed with Pocket-watch and Roses*]. 1914. Oil on canvas. 63 × 86 cm. © SIK-ISEA, Zürich. Dübi-Müller Stiftung, Kunstmuseum Solothurn.

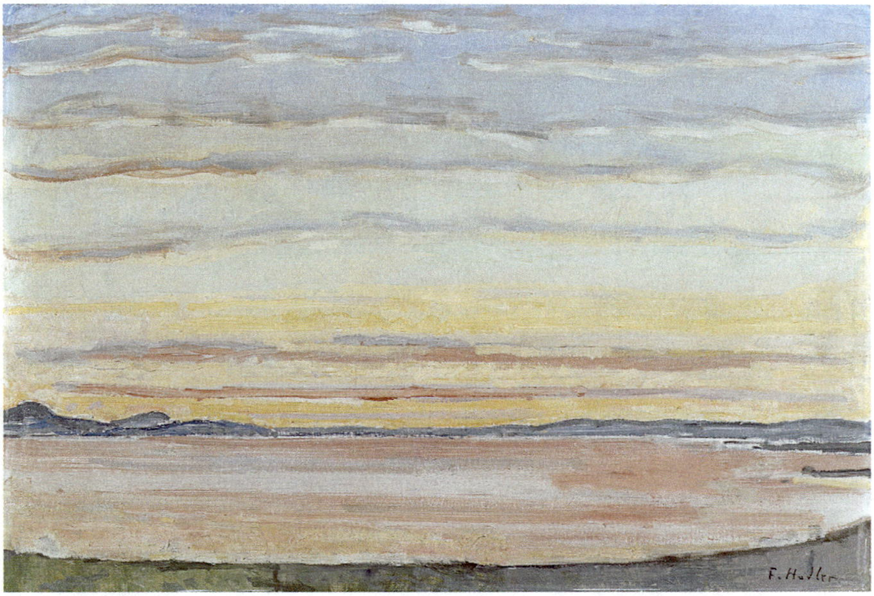

PLATE 9 (see also Figure 4.10) Ferdinand Hodler. *Sonnenuntergang am Genfersee* [*Lake Geneva with Sunset*]. 1915. Oil on canvas. 61 × 90 cm. © Kunsthaus Zürich, Gift of the heirs of Alfred Rütschi.

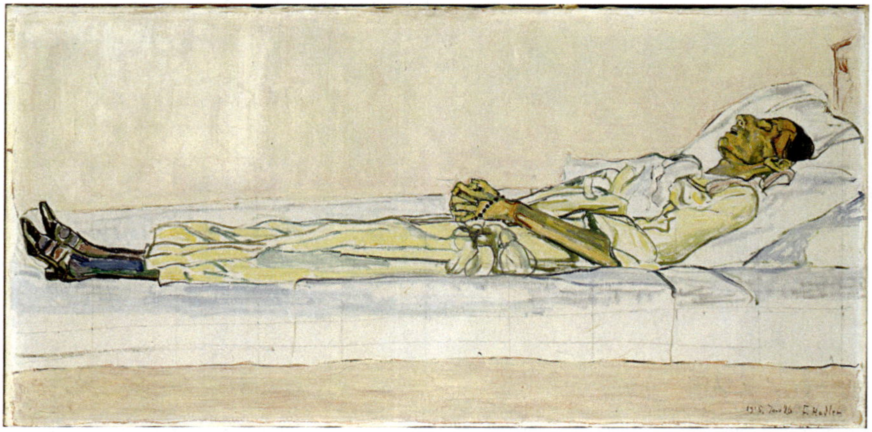

PLATE 10 (see also Figure 4.11) Ferdinand Hodler. *Die tote Valentine Godé-Darel* [*The Dead Valentine Godé-Darel*]. 26 January, 1915. Oil on canvas. 60 × 124 cm. © SIK-ISEA, Zürich. Kunstmuseum Solothurn. Schenkung Frau Erica Peters im Andenken an Herrn Dr. Rudolf Schmidt, 1971.

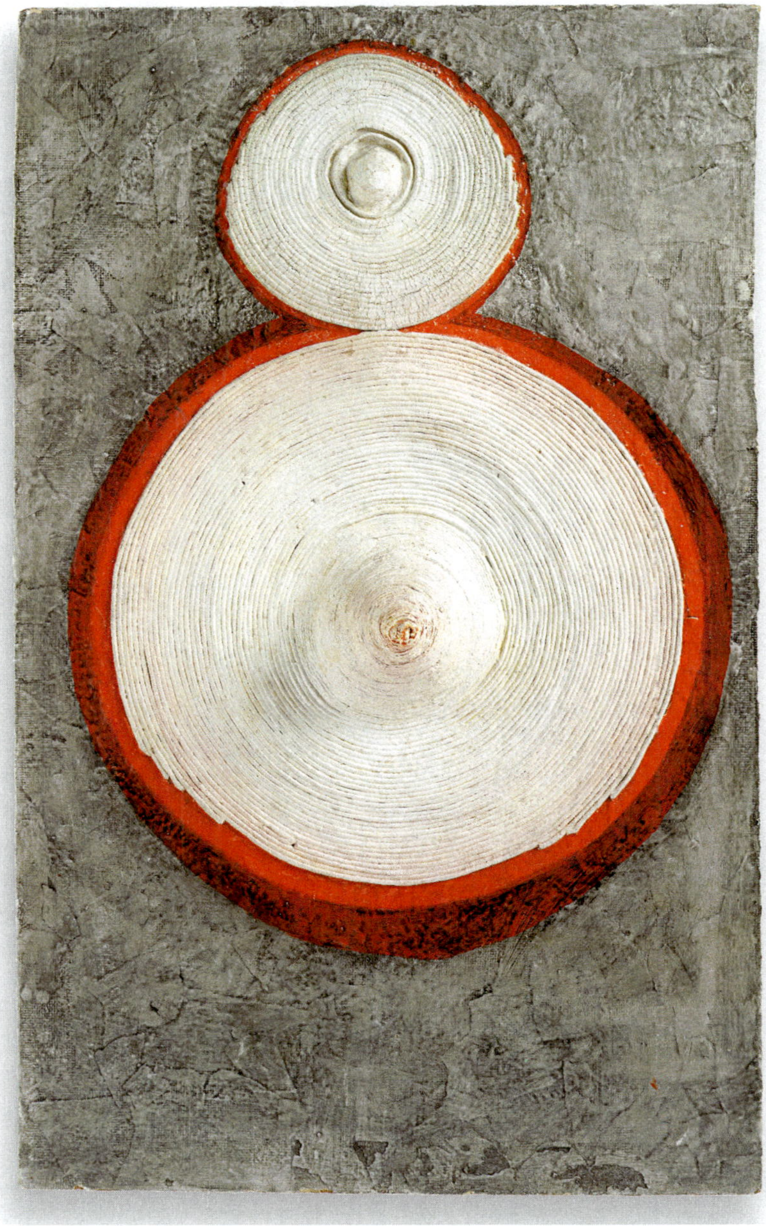

PLATE 11 (see also Figure 5.2) Eva Hesse. *Ringaround Arosie*. 1965. Varnish, graphite, ink, enamel, cloth-covered wire, papier-mâché, unknown modeling compound, Masonite, wood. 67.5 × 42.5 × 11.4 cm / 26½ × 16¾ × 4½ in. Museum of Modern Art, New York, fractional and promised gift of Kathy and Richard S. Fuld, Jr., 2005.

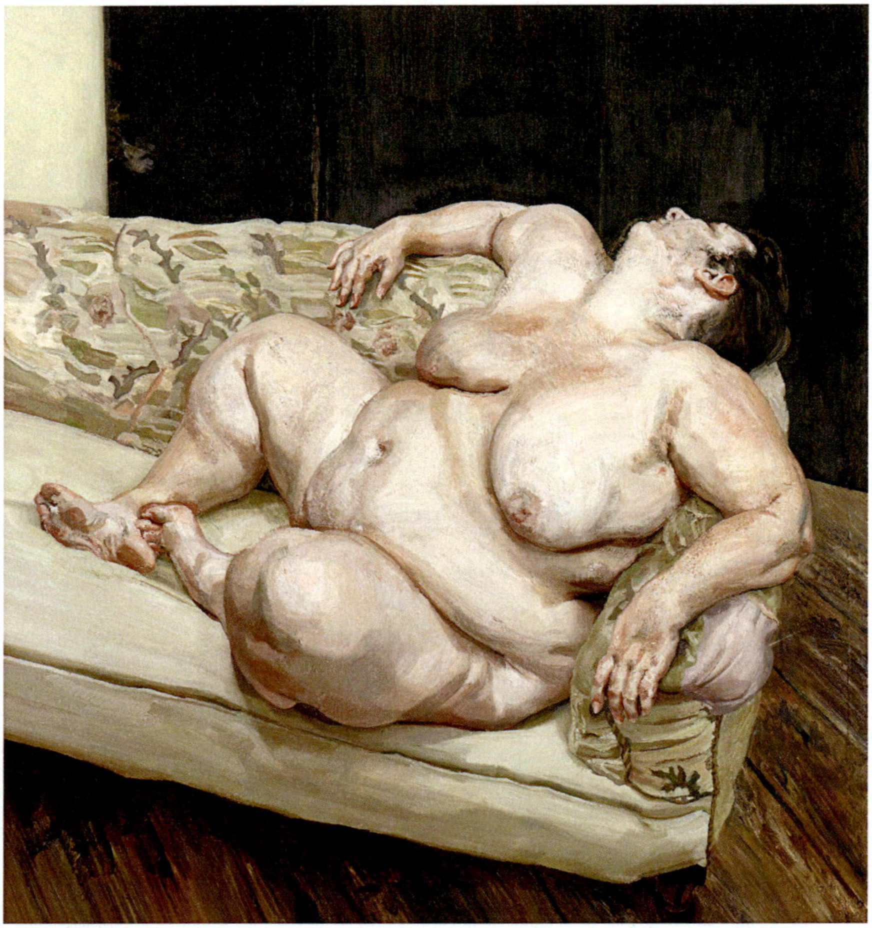

PLATE 12 (see also Figure 6.1) Lucian Freud. *Benefits Supervisor Resting*. 1994. 63 × 59¼ in. Oil on canvas. Private Collection. © The Lucian Freud Archive/Bridgeman Images.

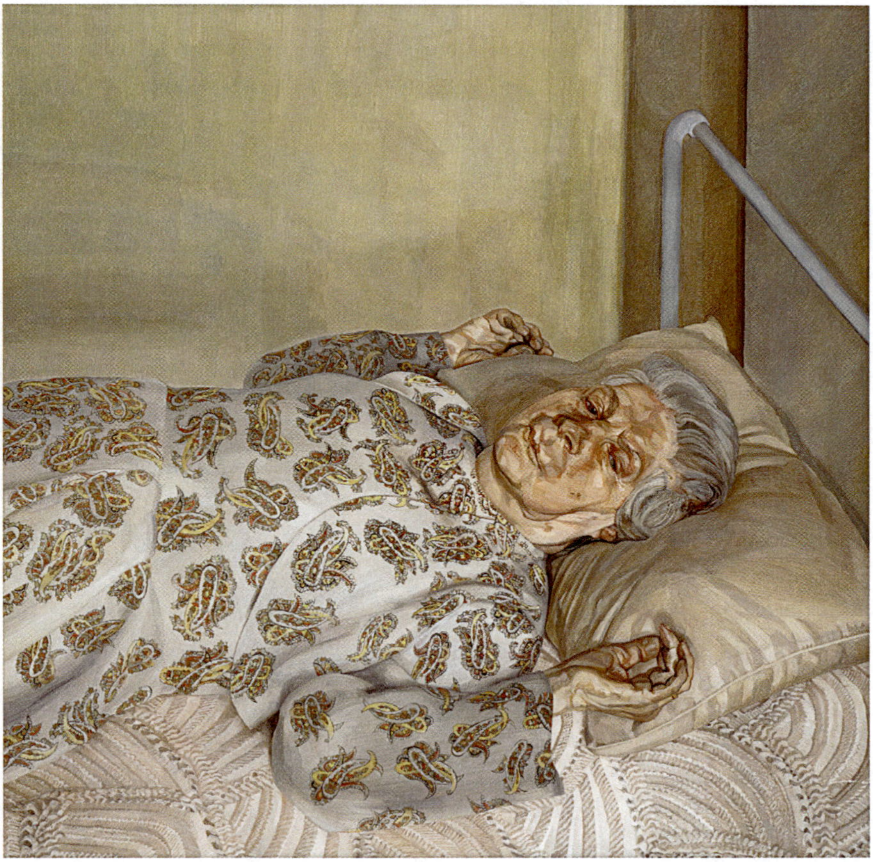

PLATE 13 (see also Figure 6.4) Lucian Freud. *The Painter's Mother Resting I.* 1975–1976. Oil on canvas. 35½ × 35½ in. Private CoLection.

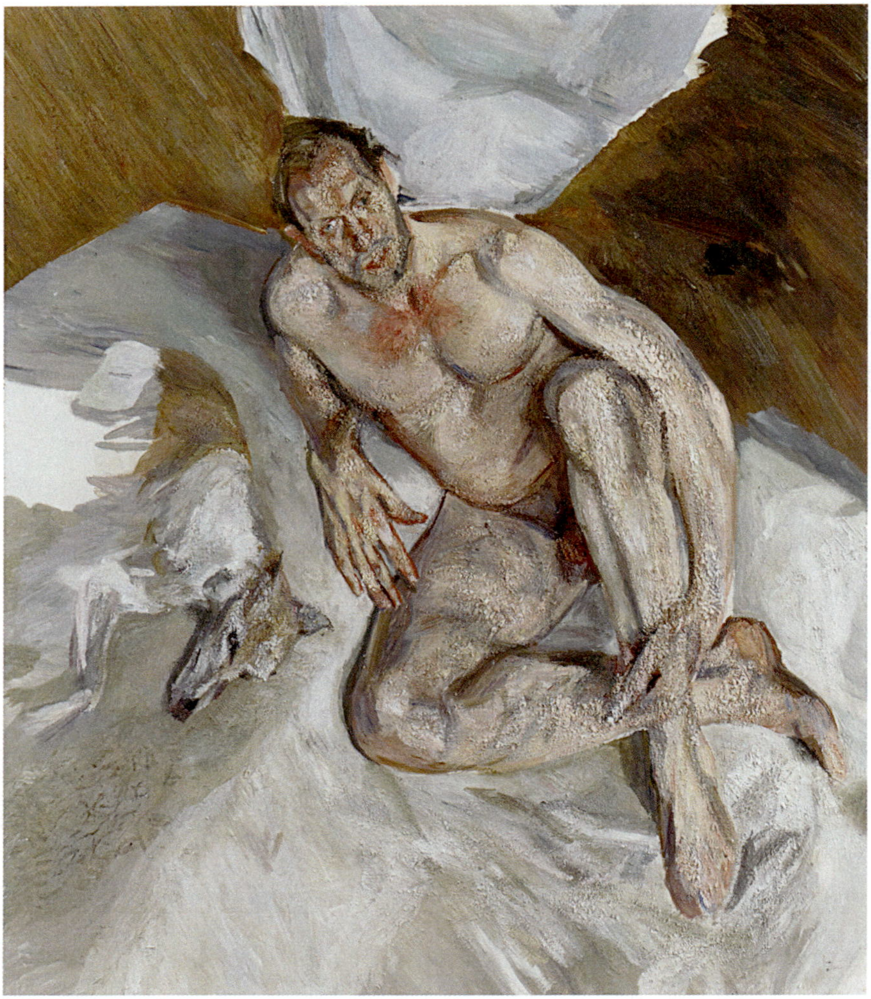

PLATE 14 (see also Figure 6.7) Lucian Freud. *Portrait of the Hound*. 2011. Oil on canvas. 1.58 × 1.38 m. Private Collection. © The Lucian Freud Archive/Bridgeman Images.

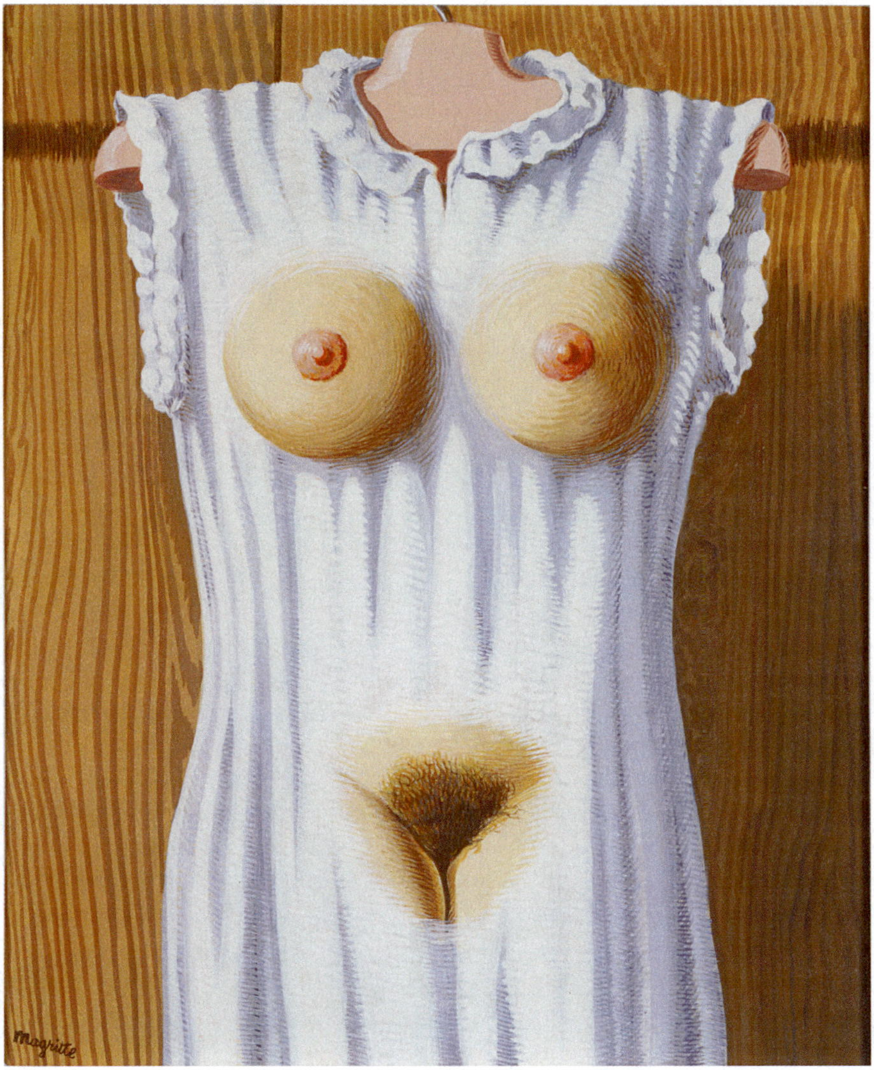

PLATE 15 (see also Figure 7.2) René Magritte. *La philosophie dans le boudoir* [*Philosophy in the Bedroom*]. 1948. Gouache on paper. 46 × 37 cm. © 2014 Herscovici/Artist Rights Society (ARS), New York.

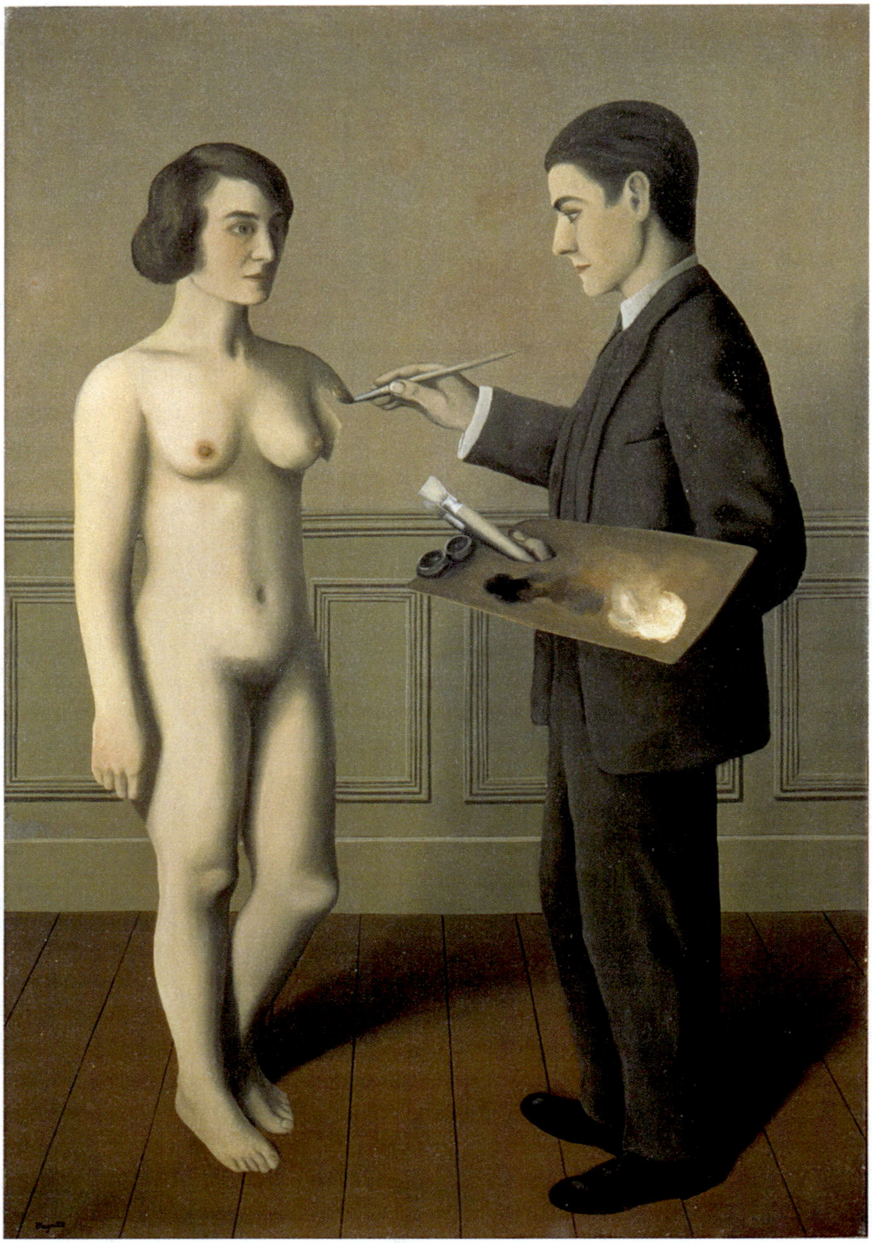

PLATE 16 (see also Figure 7.6) René Magritte. *La tentative de l'impossible* [*Attempting the Impossible*]. Oil on canvas. 116 × 81 cm. Galerie Isy Brachot, Brussels.

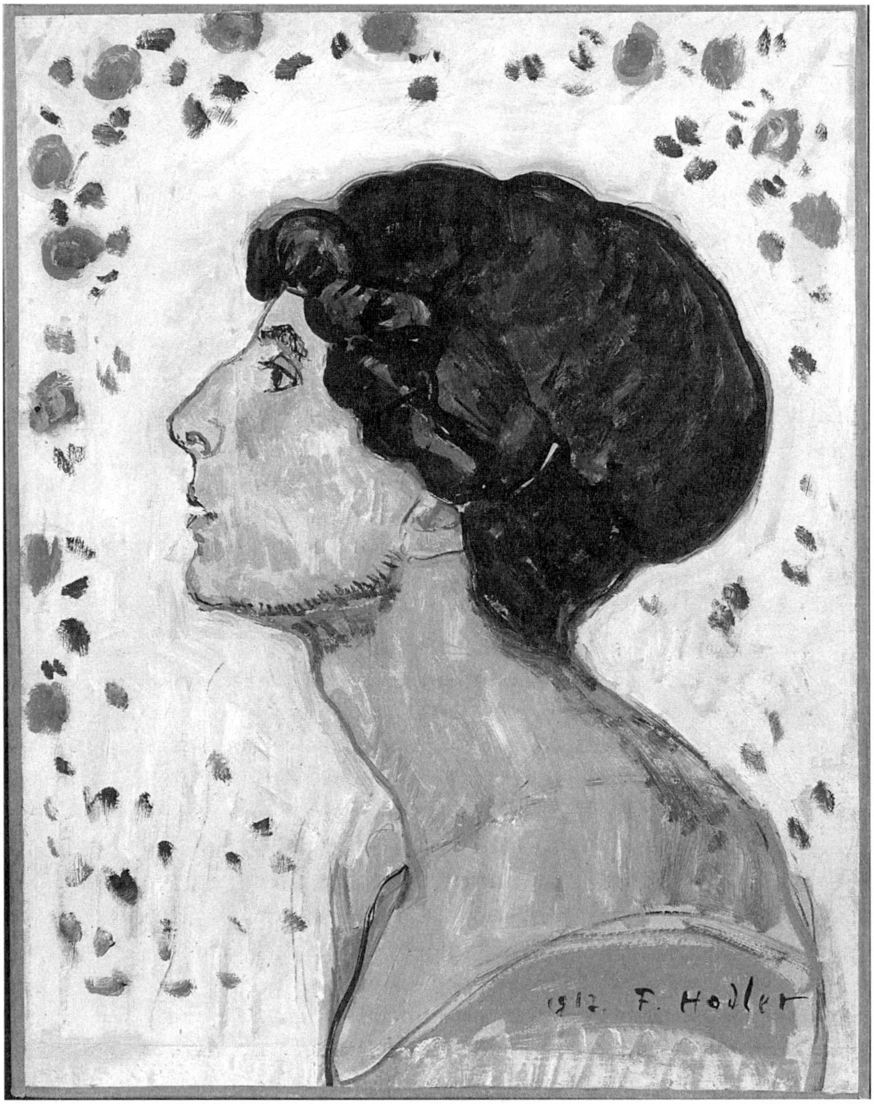

FIGURE 4.5 (see also Plate 7) Ferdinand Hodler. *Bildnis Valentine Godé-Darel von Rosen umgeben, Linksprofil* [*Portrait of Valentine Godé-Darel Surrounded by Roses, Left Profile*]. 1912. Oil on paper, put on wood. 39 × 31.5 cm. © Private Collection, SIK-ISEA, Zürich.

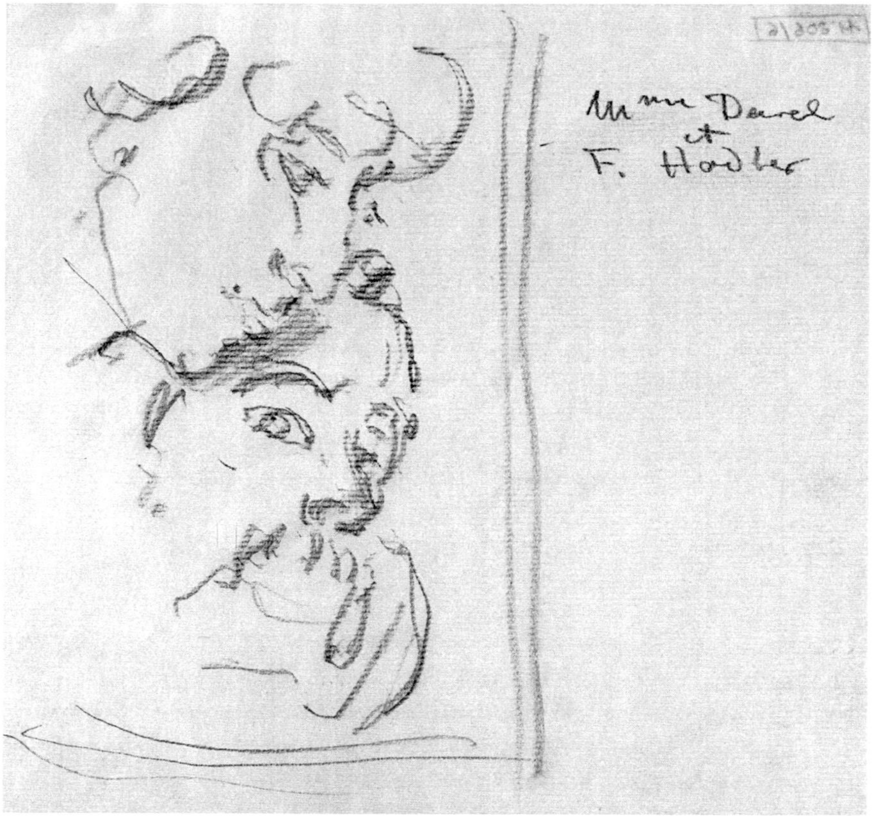

FIGURE 4.6 Ferdinand Hodler. *Selbstbildnis mit Valentine Godé-Darel* [*Self-portrait with Valentine Godé-Darel*]. 1912. Pencil on Suhl-Miss paper. 27.5 × 21 cm. © Kunsthaus Zürich, Grafische Sammlung.

reaches beyond her shoulders in two large strands. Her head is slightly tilted to the right, and her gaze expresses tired longing. Her beautiful face, with slightly open lips and half closed eyes, is full of loving intimacy. A veil of exhaustion and the inkling of an impending serious illness are illustrated in the features and colors of her face. Hodler masterfully expresses this mix of strong emotions and physical vulnerability. "Your *rayonnement* [physical expansion, glow] is a real testament to love," wrote Hodler in a letter after the birth of their daughter (Brueschweiler, 1976, p. 21).

Another painting in this series is *Portrait of Valentine Godé-Darel*, 1914 (not shown). It is often considered the most beautiful picture of this series, and expresses both true love and Godé-Darel 's deep suffering. It was painted in the very beginning of the year and Hodler's ailing lover is shown in her full beauty, as the artist's sensitive rendering of Godé-Darel's face that grants the viewer a glimpse into her soul. Shadows are painted under her eyes and cheeks, as the former red coloring gives way to browns and greens. Her once straight, proud posture is now slightly turned to the right, which makes her more vulnerable and her distant gaze hints at her fears of the future. Her eyes now focused more towards the inside, expressing humility and melancholy. Does the viewer recognize an expression of quiet longing for a supportive mother she had just lost, and for the consistent presence of a lover? In this spiritual portrait the painter effortlessly balances both closeness and distance, intimacy and the threat of separation, love and death.

On February 21, 1914, Godé-Darel underwent a mastectomy to remove her breast. Before the operation, Hodler created his only sculpture of her, as though needing to create Godé-Darel with his hands before allowing her to go under the surgeon's knife. Hodler often felt that his paintings were not good enough, not concrete enough, not real. It is for this reason that Hodler felt compelled to sculpt Godé-Darel before her mastectomy. Kraft (1984) quotes the artist: "This beautiful head, this whole figure . . . this nose, mouth—the eyes—all this the worms will eat! Nothing of it will remain, nothing at all! Or this stuff here? [pointing offhandedly at his pictures] Just shreds, smeared and dirty rags! Can one grasp them with one's hands? Can one take these rags and shreds into one's arms? Can one hug them?" (p. 320). Thereupon, Hodler screamed with a pain-filled face, Kraft records. "My poor Valentine, oh her cancer moves fast," Hodler wrote to a friend. "One treats her with radium" (Brüschweiler, 1976, p. 22).

A painting *Sick Valentine Godé-Darel*, 1914 (not shown), illustrates how quickly Valentine's illness progressed, as the once proud, beautiful Parisian is barely recognizable in this sad picture. Her distraught, ghostly face looking straight at us and the painter with brown and green shadows around her eyes, cheeks, and her forehead illustrates the suffering of a frightened woman. Sad, scared, deep-set eyes and worried eyebrows, and discolored skin highlight the woman's pain and sadness. But her posture, still vertical, and her décolleté remind the viewer of her past seductiveness and beauty. Both model and artist share a deep knowledge of an insecure future and despair.

On May 30, Godé-Darel required more surgery and the artist documents the progression of her illness in the picture *Valentine Godé-Darel on Her Sickbed with Pocket-watch and Roses*, 1914 (Figure 4.7, see also Plate 8). This beautiful and moving portrait portrays the very sick Godé-Darel lying in bed, her head resting on a pillow, holding her hand over her breast. She is gazing into space, away from the artist, perhaps in the direction of the three roses and the little pocket-watch attached to the wall. The watch as well as the fading roses are not only gifts from her lover, but symbolically represent time passing and the passing of her own withering life. Her thinned face and her detached, distant look surround Godé-Darel with a sense of melancholia and sadness. The touch of red on her lips and on the roses remind the viewer of the once passionate, happy life that she and Hodler shared. Her still vertically positioned head with her dark long hair demonstrates her dignity, which the empathic but desperate artist tries to preserve.

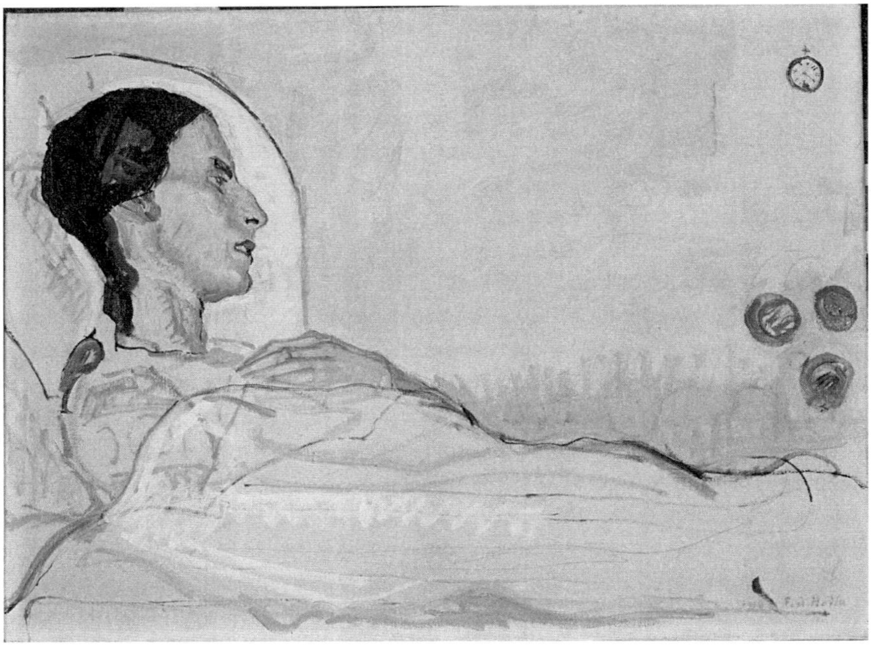

FIGURE 4.7 (see also Plate 8) Ferdinand Hodler. *Valentine Godé-Darel im Krankenbett mit Uhr und Rosen* [*Valentine Godé-Darel on Her Sickbed with Pocket-watch and Roses*]. 1914. Oil on canvas. 63 × 86 cm. © SIK-ISEA, Zürich. Dübi-Müller Stiftung, Kunstmuseum Solothurn.

Godé-Darel's housekeeper revealed that the relationship between the artist and his lover was, either in spite of or because of terminal illness, a stormy one (Brüschweiler, 1976). As a result of one of their fights, the artist did not visit the sick patient for four months. This is borne out by the fact that the artist completed a painting in June 1914 and then only created the next drawing in November 1914. At the end of the summer, with the beginning of World War I, Godé-Darel and her caretaker returned to the town of Vevey, and Hodler often rode on the first train in the morning from Geneva to visit her. He frequently brought her red roses, created portraits of her, and visited his little daughter, Pauline.

Hodler spent New Year with Godé-Darel in Vevey. The painting *To the Side, Sunken Head of the Dying Valentine Godé-Darel*, 1915 (Figure 4.8) is very touching, emphasizing the diagonal dimension as Valentine's head is turned to the right and her body is hidden below blankets or sheets. "Her eyes are closed, she is sleeping or unconscious as if buried in her sleep," wrote Hodler (Brüschweiler, 1976, p. 28). However her expression is somewhat relaxed or seems free of pain. Hodler again noted in his diary the questions that Valentine had asked him during this time period. She asked, "What will become of me, I don't want to stay on this earth much longer" (Brüschweiler, 1976, p. 28). Between January 13, 1915, and

January 19, 1915, as he was forced to witness her slow process of dying, the artist sketched his friend in many drawings in an attempt to maintain control of his own mounting despair. These drawings express agony and pain as Godé-Darel's face becomes thinner, more transparent and her features more haunting.

In another portrait from this time period (not shown), Valentine's head is supported by a pillow, and she faces both the viewer and the artist. Her mouth is half open. Again Hodler includes roses, picking up the faded color of her lips. A thinned tired hand rests on her breast. Her deep-set eyes and her very defined, thinned bony nose, illustrate the further progression of the illness. Her gaze reveals a combination of defiance and irritation. She might wonder why her lover still needs to paint her image, requiring the distance of the canvas to relate to her, in this time of great despair and pain. The flame red roses with their green stems reflect the theme of defiance and express how both model and artist try to cling to their passionate but fading love and life. It was at this time that Hodler brought his little daughter Tintine to his own home. His wife Berthe, who had no children of her own, took care of her. In a photograph taken by the photographer Gertrude Müller a few years later in 1918, a day before Hodler's own death, the viewer can see how affectionately he holds his young daughter, embracing the child as though holding on to his own life (Brüschweiler, 1998).

In December 1914, Hodler drew many sketches and drawings of his dying friend, and from this point forward her head always rested on the pillow and her eyes were always shut. On Christmas, December 25, 1914, he noted in his journal that Valentine posed to him a question: "Is it true that I will die? Tell me the truth" (Brüschweiler, 1976, p. 27). The artist's response to his lover's question remains unknown, but an analysis of his pictures below implies that he probably answered truthfully, as his painted images of his dying lover could not lie.

On January 19, Godé-Darel spoke to Hodler for the last time. Hodler documented her words in his notebook. "I wish to see you. That's what pleases me most. I am afraid of dying here" (Brüschweiler, 1976, p. 28). After stating these words and securing her lover's presence in her last struggle with life, Godé-Darel withdrew and turned to face the wall. This painting (Figure 4.9), executed in pencil, gouache, oil and charcoal, is a very touching portrait expressing pain and the end stage of life. The artist is able to demonstrate the intense agony of his dying friend for which no words remained. The picture illustrates how the dying Godé-Darel is unable to relate to the artist any longer, but is focused and turned towards her inside world in an attempt to contain all her strength. Her open mouth illustrates her struggle with pain and exhaustion. Brown colors are chosen, and the painter's strokes are forceful, illustrating his inner agitation, as he also loses the battle to keep his lover alive. The brown colors remind the viewer of the earth to which Godé-Darel will soon return, or the color of stale blood which will cease to flow shortly. The sleeping or unconscious patient now is lying nearly horizontally, as she approaches her death.

Hodler's pictures are deeply moving as they demonstrate not only the struggle of the dying Valentine, but also allow the viewer to become witness to the painter's

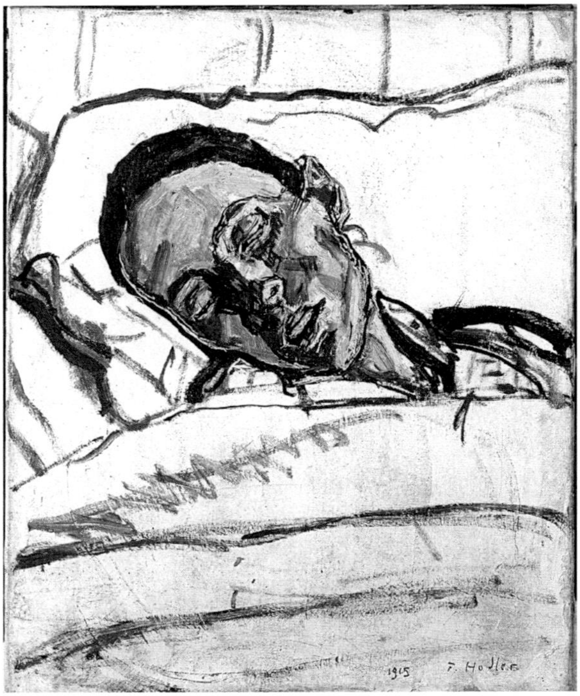

FIGURE 4.8 Ferdinand Hodler. *Zur Seite gesunkener Kopf der sterbenden Valentine Godé-Darel* [*To the Side, Sunken Head of the Dying Valentine Godé-Darel*]. 1915. Oil on wax fabric. 53 × 40.5 cm © Private Collection, SIK-ISEA, Zürich.

struggle as he records the death of his great love. These paintings move beyond their personal struggle with death and mourning, as they so movingly demonstrate the human tragedy with which we all can identify.

The last picture Hodler painted of Godé-Darel before her death is titled *The Dying Valentine Godé-Darel, Half Figure in Left Profile*, January 24, 1915 (not shown). Now the patient lies horizontally in bed, covered with the white sheet like a death shroud, her skull-like head is deeply buried in the white pillow. Her once beautiful face is now composed of only bones, her facial expression tense with pain as she fearfully waits for death to take her away. In the photograph of this painting, the artist noted: "Died January 25 at 5:00 p.m." and on the back of the photograph he added: "Monday the 25th." It seems that Hodler had to record the event twice, in order to make himself believe and understand the finality of her death.

While no more of Hodler's sketches are dated to January 25, art historians believe that three landscape images of the setting sun over Lake Geneva became the symbolic expression of Godé-Darel's departure for the artist that day. These three landscapes are beautiful and touching with their soft aching colors, their flat, equally horizontal hills, similar to Valentine's sick body stretched out on her deathbed. The clouds are hanging in the morning sky as though waiting to

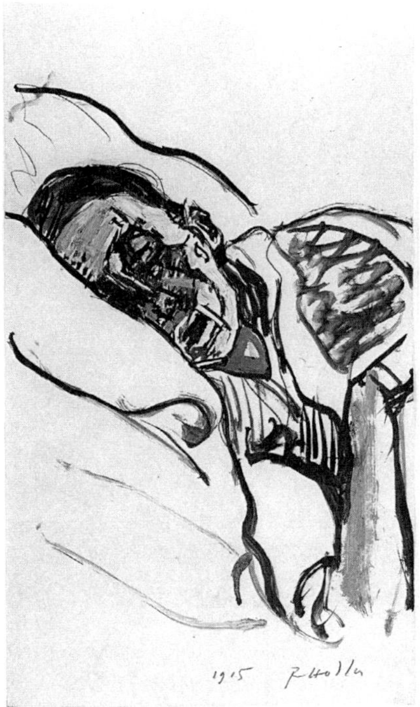

FIGURE 4.9 Ferdinand Hodler. *Die sterbende Valentine Godé-Darel* [*Portrait of the Dying Valentine Godé-Darel*]. 1915. Pencil, gouache, and oil on Belgian vellum. 39.7 × 23.3 cm. © Private Collection. SIK-ISEA, Zürich.

accompany her departing soul (Brüschweiler, 1976). Hodler illustrates the unity of the human being and nature, the fusion of the cosmos with the dead, a real reunion between matter and space according to his philosophy documented in prior years.

Art historians believe that the artist gained his inspiration for his final landscape, *Lake Geneva with Sunset*, 1915 (Figure 4.10, see also Plate 9), from the three views of the sunset out of Valentine's window after her death; thus, they seem to be colored by the strong emotions he felt after his lover's passing. The long, horizontal mountain chains appear to fuse with the water and sky, illustrating longing and mourning expressed in the most beautiful, soft colors. This sensitively painted picture might have foreshadowed the artist's wish to soon follow her departed soul.

After Valentine's death, Hodler began to create seven studies and three paintings of the deceased Valentine Godé-Darel. The following quote by Hodler demonstrates his philosophy about death: "Death is the permanence of motionlessness, the absolute immovableness of language. The permanence of non-life is so impressive because the observer realizes that he himself and all others will also have to go there. All have to go there. We must never forget that our similarity is greater than our difference," writes Hodler in his diary (Kraft, 1984, p. 313).

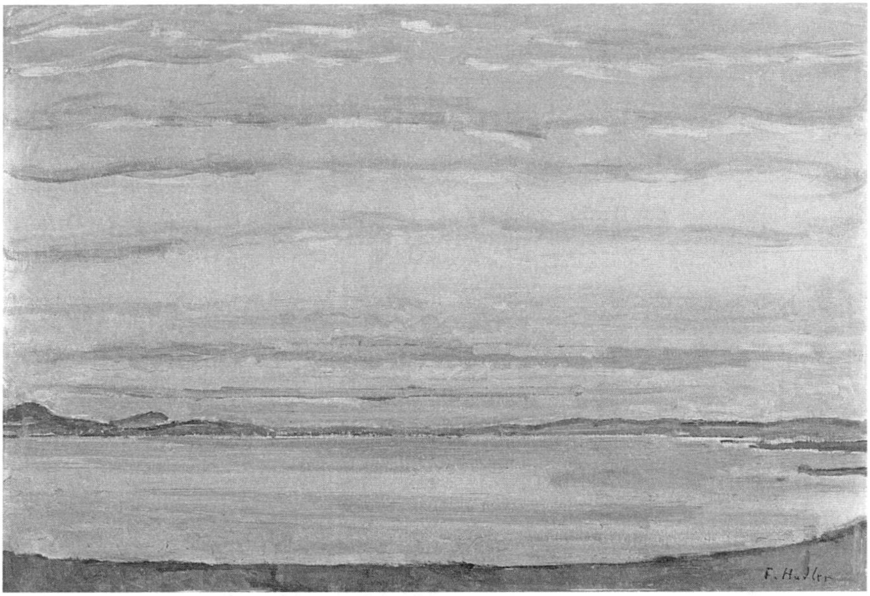

FIGURE 4.10 (see also Plate 9) Ferdinand Hodler. *Sonnenuntergang am Genfersee* [*Lake Geneva with Sunset*]. 1915. Oil on canvas. 61 × 90 cm. © Kunsthaus Zürich, Gift of the heirs of Alfred Rütschi.

In his paintings of the deceased Godé-Darel, Hodler emphasizes the horizontal line even more than he did in his previous paintings. In *The Dead Valentine Godé-Darel* (Figure 4.11, see also Plate 10), she appears ready to return to mother earth. Like the waters in his last landscape paintings, she lies completely flat, but dressed in an elegant pale yellow dress. Her breast, the location of her cancer, is covered with a white bow. The dark green stockings and black elegant leather shoes remind the viewer of the earlier times of "La Parisienne." The soft, light blue accents on the sheets and on her pale, yellow dress and mustard colored bed and wall give the illusion that her dead body is floating in space. Looking at this peaceful picture of Godé-Darel's body, the viewer forgets her struggles with death, as Hodler's overwhelming longing for his lover permeates the scene. In the picture of the dead body, Hodler symbolizes death. Here, Valentine's body lies more securely on the sickbed; the many parallel lines of the foreground, bed, mattress, sheet, and folds of her dress, which are portrayed again on the ceiling, give the viewer a feeling of fusion and eternity of matter in space.

Mourning, memory and creative transformation

In "Mourning and Melancholia" (1917), Sigmund Freud writes: "Mourning is regularly the reaction to the loss of a loved person, or to the loss of some abstraction . . . such as one's country, liberty, an ideal . . . Although mourning

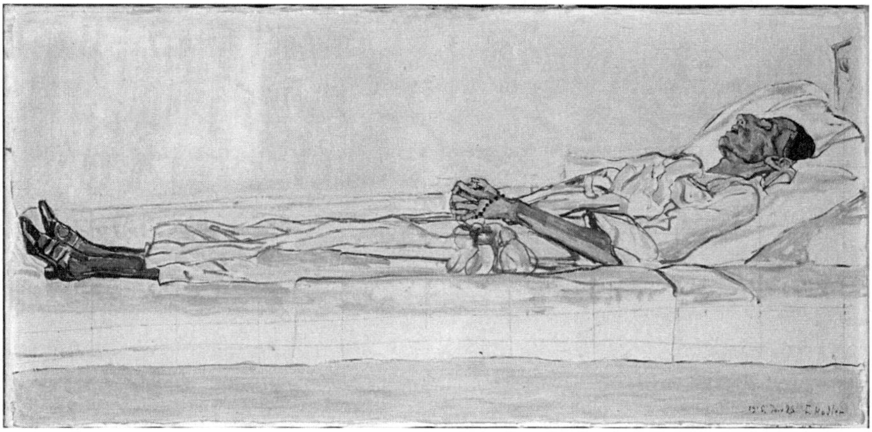

FIGURE 4.11 (see also Plate 10) Ferdinand Hodler. *Die tote Valentine Godé-Darel* [*The Dead Valentine Godé-Darel*]. 26 January, 1915. Oil on canvas. 60 × 124 cm. © SIK-ISEA, Zürich. Kunstmuseum Solothurn. Schenkung Frau Erica Peters im Andenken an Herrn Dr. Rudolf Schmidt, 1971.

involves grave departure from the normal attitude of life, it never occurs to us to regard it as a pathological condition and refer it to medical treatment; we rely on its being overcome after a certain lapse of time" (p. 244).

Freud describes the extremely painful and slow process one endures when one is forced to detach each individual memory and expectation from the object. Only later in his life, as he experienced further personal losses, did he realize that mourning is a never-ending process. Freud suffered terribly when his daughter Sophie died during the 1920 flu epidemic at the age of 27, followed shortly thereafter by her 4-year old son Heinerle, Freud's favorite grandson, in 1923. On the sixth anniversary of Sophie's death, he wrote to his friend and colleague the Swiss psychoanalyst Ludwig Binswanger, who had very recently lost his own young son, that "Although we know that after such a loss the acute stage of mourning will subside, we also know we shall remain inconsolable and will never find a substitute. No matter what may fill the gap, if it be filled completely, it nevertheless remains something else. And actually, this is how it should be; it is the only way of perpetuating that love which we do not want to relinquish" (E. Freud, 1960).

Thirteen years after Sophie's death, he showed the poet Hilda Doolittle (H.D.), a tiny locket fastened to his watch chain. "She is here," he said (Doolittle, 2005). With these words, Freud acknowledged that successful mourning work requires the reparation in one's internal world before we can sever the loving bond in the external world, thereby reestablishing a sense of inner connection (Gaines, 1997). The locket with Sophie's portrait in it allows Freud to re-remember the loss of his daughter and bring her memory into the present.

It is interesting to note that Freud, whose father died in 1897, attributes the creation of his classic, *The Interpretation of Dreams* (1900), one of the most outstanding contributions of this century, to his active mourning work for his father. Freud writes, "For this book has a further subjective significance for me personally—a significance which I only grasped after I had completed it. It was, I found, a portion of my own self-analysis, my reaction to my father's death—that is to say, to the most important event, the most poignant loss, of a man's life" (p. 25).

For Freud, as well as for the artist Ferdinand Hodler, the successful completion of mourning results in outstanding enduring creations and a meaningful life thereafter. The created product, the paintings or drawings, are located in the transitional spaces of the artist's inner world and the viewer's outer reality; the paintings become transitional objects in an intermediate space of mourning, between outside and inside, between past time and present time, allowing for a temporary defense against identification with timelessness's traumatic, fragmenting aspects.

Hodler's cycle of works documenting Godé-Darel's death, with its innovative artistic form and increasing feeling of artistic omnipotence, helped the artist face separation, mourn this specific loss and bring all painful prior losses into the present as well. The artist re-remembered the losses of his childhood and thus could establish a relationship with the new realities he was forced to encounter.

The establishment of new forms, whether through one's accustomed means of self-expression or through a novel kind of creative expression, tends to elicit pleasurable, satisfying feelings in spite of impending loss. At the same time, as in Hodler's experience, it helps to repair the narcissistic damage caused by losses, such as the process of Godé-Darel's illness and Hodler's own aging. Mourning engendered by losses of the past that are revived in the present stimulates an unconscious longing for the lost closeness with the primary object, as well as a longing for a new *gestalt* and new solution. Just as the transitional object in infancy can be utilized as a symbol for the absent mother, the picture becomes the mediating symbol of both separation and togetherness (Dreifuss-Kattan, 1994).

Artistic forms define the boundaries that govern both the connections and conflicts between wish and reality, objective circumstance, and subjective fantasy. Form mediates between that which is held inside and that which is held outside, thus granting definition to the experience. In one sense, content is but a subjective moment contained by the objectifying form.

The artist seeks to form and transform the physical experience of loss and illness into a completely new gestalt. An important aspect of this process is the use of form as a means of unifying the internal and external experience. Form becomes the carrier of another great wish, to reestablish a primary narcissistic balance undisturbed by threats of separation. In the unity of an artistic form and not only in the harmonious being-with-oneself of the creative process, the artist can search unconsciously for the original unity of mother and child. The structural coherence of a painting helps the artist overcome the painful separation of subject and object; likewise, it can temporarily suspend the passing of time, creating a new sense of a pleasurable duration where past and future are combined in the fullness of the present (Dreifuss-Kattan, 1994).

By fashioning the unity of a successfully executed work, the artist's ego secures a sense of omnipotence and self-love; from a psychodynamic perspective, the artist inwardly enjoys the love of the mother once again, thereby overcoming the past trauma of early separation. Threatening experiences are broken up into disconnected pieces; creative experience, by contrast, carries within itself its own wholeness and continuity.

Shared reparation

Ferdinand Hodler's artistic production thus entails both an internal processing and an artistic working through of cultural material. In art, these boundaries become permeable, as they negate both the psychic and the cultural, the subjective and the environmental (Schwab, 1994/1995). As a viewer, one is both pulled in and held at a distance, often at the same time, as the inner psychic and cultural spaces fuse in artistic expression. Hodler's self is bound up with memories of his multiple early objects' losses, and with the gravity of affects and a strong sense of a temporal dimension. His portraits of Godé-Darel, his lover, illustrate the exchange of inner and outer space. Because his internal memories are also expressed in the exterior, their form makes them more corporeal; thus they become anchored in his consciousness and in culture, and as a result more bearable for the artist. This "un-thought" knowledge (Bollas, 1992) becomes retrievable for Hodler from his unspoken past through his symbolic form-giving in these very moving, beautiful paintings. Through artistic expression, Hodler's self gains coherence, as his early internal narrative is retrieved and externalized onto the canvas.

In Parallelism, Hodler emphasized the harmony and similarity of forms, thus trying to foster communality and to override content. "Whenever I feel most moved by nature," he wrote, "I always feel impressed by the unity" (Honisch, 1983, p. 450). His confidence in the process of constructing unity in his art counteracted his need for the destruction of close object ties to his wives and lovers, mirroring early object losses. Art was his only reliable and stable partner throughout his lifetime.

Early in his opus, Hodler focused on the infinity of nature in his Parallelism, drawn from the world of the monumental Alps, lakes and far-off horizons, which revealed a wish for fusion with nature in its divine dimension. While his earlier work concentrated on the parallelism of forms, he later added more transparent color shading as an additional unifying entity, creating an ever deeper sense of unity and spirituality. In his late work on Valentine Godé-Darel, the artist turned his view to the finiteness of the life of his lover and of human life, documenting Godé-Darel's dying and portraying the fleeting instance of human life. With this cycle of pictures, Ferdinand Hodler was able to cope with his early object loss and his contemporary loss and mourning. He not only portrayed Godé-Darel's road to death, but also captured the human condition, creating immortal works that have survived both Godé-Darel and the artist himself. His hope of regaining his once loved and now lost inner objects is illustrated in his fantasy of death, recorded in his diary: "When we think of death, there is total unity" (Kraft, 1984, p. 313).

References

Bollas, C. (1992) *Being a character: Psychoanalysis and self-experience*. New York: Hill and Wang.

Brüschweiler, J. (1976) *Ein Maler von Liebe und Tod. Ferdinand Hodler und Valentine Godé-Darel. Ein Werkzyklus 1908–1915*. Zürich: Kunsthaus Zürich.

Brüschweiler, J. (1998) *Ferdinand Hodler Fotoalbum*. Bern, Switzerland: Benteli.

Brüschweiler, J. (2004) Über Ferdinand Hodler: Aus Gesprächen mit Jura Brüschweiler. In *Ferdinand Hodler: Das Herz ist Mein Auge*. H. Bütler (Ed.). Bern, Switzerland: Benteli, pp. 7–12.

Dreifuss-Kattan, E. (1994) *Cancer stories: Creativity and self-repair*. Hillsdale, NJ: The Analytic Press.

Doolittle, H. (2005) *Analyzing Freud: Letters of H.D., Bryher, and their circle*. New York: W.W. Norton and Company.

Freud, E. (Ed.) (1960) *Letters of Sigmund Freud* (T. and J. Stern, Trans.). New York: Basic Books.

Freud, S. (1900) The Interpretation of dreams. *The standard edition of the complete psychological works of Sigmund Freud* (Vol. 9: 141–154). London: Hogarth Press, 1959.

Freud, S. (1917) Mourning and melancholia. *The standard edition of the complete psychological works of Sigmund Freud* (Vol. 14: 237–258). London: Hogarth Press, 1957.

Gaines, R. (1997) Detachment and continuity. *Contemporary Psychoanalysis*, 33: 549–571.

Hirsh, S. (1982) *Ferdinand Hodler*. New York: George Braziller.

Honisch, D. (1983) *Das Spätwerk: Ferdinand Hodler*. Bern, Switzerland: Benteli.

Kraft, H. (1984) Object Verlust and Kreativität, Eine Darstellung anhand Ferdinand Hodlers Werkzyklus über Valentine Godé-Darel. In *Psychoanalyse und Kreativität heute*. Cologne, Germany: DuMont.

Schwab, G. (1994/1995) Cultural text and endopsychic scripts. *Substance*, 30, 1, 2: 160–170.

Selz, P. (1972) *Ferdinand Hodler*. Berkeley, CA: University Art Museum.

Vaughan, W. (1993) A view from the mountains: European art and Switzerland. In *Caspar David Friedrich to Ferdinand Hodler: A romantic tradition*. Bern, Switzerland: Insel.

5

EVA HESSE

Eva Hesse's *Hang Up* (1966)—a transition from the edge of loss to the containment of emptiness

Eva Hesse's work, especially the sculptures for which she became famous, gives visual expression to her personal history and to her dream of sexual and professional equality as an artist and a feminist.

Hesse's art—with its feminine and personal message, its visual critique of male machismo, and its allusions to dreams of sexual equality—is inseparable from the artist's personal history in the context of the 1960s. Abstract expressionism was in vogue, Minimalists were the avant-garde, and husbands were still masters of their households. It was a time when women started to read Simone de Beauvoir's *The Second Sex* and Betty Friedan's *The Feminine Mystique*. Women started to speak to each other and to their psychoanalysts about their personal histories, and together discussed their collective histories, discrimination and its political significance. These dialogues strengthened their gender identity and helped them construct a new collectivity as feminist artists within their own social space.

As a reaction to World War II and the Holocaust, a trauma too painful to face, artists fled from illustration and figuration, and as a result Abstract Expressionism emerged (Phelan, 2001). Eva Hesse was one of the greatest artists of her generation at a time when Abstract Expressionism and Neo-Surrealism competed with Minimalism, and when the artistic environment was dominated by men such as Sol LeWitt, Robert Smithson, Mel Bochner and Carl Andre, all of whom became Hesse's friends.

Hesse's artwork has great implications for the fields of gender, ethnicity and psychology. As a woman in a male dominated world, and a Jew among gentiles, Hesse certainly did not fit the typical mold of her time. She was a child of the Holocaust who could not forget her own history and who wanted desperately to survive and build a new history with her fellow female artists. All of these themes informed Hesse's artistic expressions, and her new formal and material innovations. As her leap from two- to three-dimensional forms materialized in her shift from painting to sculpture, the symbolic and affective content of her work was also transformed.

The focus of this chapter's discussions will be Hesse's sculpture *Hang Up* (1966) since it marks a formal transition from the wall to the floor, as well as an encounter between pictorial and sculptural space. From a psychological perspective, the art piece forms a bridge that shifts from a more defensive, artistically absurd attempt to deal with the artist's sense of loss to her slow acceptance and ultimate ability to contain her feelings of loss and emptiness as seen in her many sculptures of vessels. Moreover, Hesse's innovative use of new materials such as polyester resin, latex and fiberglass allowed her abstract sculptures to gain corporeality. Thus, *Hang Up* is a frame that seems to frame nothing at all and yet simultaneously frames so very much. With *Hang Up*, Hesse projected her painful personal history as well as her collective history as a feminist onto the wall and floor space.

Biographical details

In an interview, Eva Hesse said, "Life doesn't last; art doesn't last. It doesn't matter" (Nemser, 1970/2002, p. 18). A conversation she had with Cindy Nemser in a 1970 interview reveals much about her challenging, troubled childhood:

> It's not a little thing to have a brain tumor at 33. Well, my whole life has been like that. I was born in Hamburg, Germany. My father was a criminal lawyer. He had finished two doctorates and I had the most beautiful mother in the whole world. She looked like Ingrid Bergman and she was manic depressive. She studied art in Hamburg. . . . My sister was born in 1933 and I was born in 1936. Then in 1938 there was a children's pogrom. I was put on a train [*Kindertransport*] with my sister. We went to Holland where we were supposed to be picked up by my father's brother and his wife in Amsterdam, but he couldn't do it, so we were put in a Catholic children's home and I was always sick. So I was put in a hospital and I wasn't with my sister. My parents were hidden somewhere in Germany, and then they came to Amsterdam and had trouble getting us out. Somehow they got us to England.

Eva Hesse was born on January 11, 1936, in the Israelite Hospital in Hamburg, Germany. Eva and her sister were separated from their parents for a period of two months, when they took the *Kindertransport* for Holland on December 7, 1938; Eva was only two years old and her sister four. In early 1938, Hesse's mother Ruth was diagnosed with manic depression, which was exacerbated by the stress of living under Nazi rule (Wasserman, 2006). The whole family eventually reunited and arrived in New York via Holland and England in the summer of 1939. Hesse's father Wilhelm was forced to switch careers and went through training to become an insurance broker in the United States. Ruth, who initially worked as a glove maker when the family arrived in the U.S., was constantly sick and therefore unable to work most of the time. With the rise of the Nazi party, their social status had begun to decline while they still lived in Germany. Upon settling in New York and being required to train for new careers, their social status declined even more.

Ruth lost her immediate family due to the terrors of the Holocaust. Both her parents and brother were murdered in spite of enormous efforts by William to secure an exit visa for them. The Hesse's family life became increasingly unstable as Ruth's manic depressive illness caused her to frequently be admitted to various hospitals. As Eva recounted in her interview: "I used to be alone at night and used to be terrified. My mother was there and not there—there, but not there." Eva and her sister were shifted from home to home, adding to their fears. "[My father] had to tuck my blanket in tight into my German bed which had bars at the bottom which would hold me at night, and he would have to tell me that we wouldn't be poor, and we wouldn't be robbed, and he'd be there to take care of me in the morning" (Nemser, 1970/2002). This ritual between Eva and her father took place every night, as her fears never subsided. Eva's constant fears caused her to have severe abandonment issues throughout her life.

Eva began kindergarten in the winter of 1941 in a Washington Heights public school. In the fall of the same year, her mother moved out of the family's apartment, and Eva's parents eventually divorced in the spring of 1945. Around Thanksgiving time of the same year of their divorce, William Hesse married Eva Nathanson.

In January of 1946, Ruth could no longer stand her misery so she jumped out of a window, committing suicide when her daughter Eva was merely eight years old. Eva Hesse said of her childhood, ". . . My life has been so traumatic, so absurd—there hasn't been one normal happy thing" (Nemser, 1970/2002).

From the years 1949 to 1952, Eva Hesse attended the School of Industrial Art and then continued her art education at Cooper Union from 1955 to 1957, where she earned a certificate in design. In 1957, Hesse enrolled at the Yale School of Art and Architecture, where she studied under Josef Albers and there received a Bachelor of Fine Arts degree.

William Hesse kept three *Tagebücher*, diaries of little Eva, as well as five of her sister Helen. Eva's three diaries document the events beginning with Eva's birth on January 11, 1936, and ending with the holiday of Rosh Hashanah in 1946. They are very unusual diaries, a mixture of narratives, photographs, collages and documents. These *Tagebücher* were William's primary record of his children growing up, documenting milestones such as birthdays, and they provide insights into his daughters' personalities and temperament. The decade-long project served to establish some sense of order in the family's life from the chaotic era of pre-World War II Germany through their traumatic escape to New York via Holland and England. The diaries also documented the family's Jewish practice with its rituals and celebrations as they carried on the tradition of the generations before them; this provided both comfort and continuity to Hesse's family throughout their many dislocations and hardships, and allowed for a sense of rhythm in their lives. These childhood diaries left behind both a historic and personal legacy (Wasserman, 2006).

In spite of the Gestapo's arrest of her father in May 1937 and the extremely frightening atmosphere of Germany at that time, her father wrote in his diary:

"[Eva] is always joyful and makes everybody who is dealing with her happy . . . . Evchen knows a lot and much more she can articulate. First and foremost, she knows exactly what she wants" (Wasserman, 2006, p. 107). The process of documenting his children's development was one way Eva's father was able to face the threatening outside world.

Influenced by these early records kept by her father, Eva Hesse documented her own experiences through scrapbooks and extensive diaries, at first recording her experiences and insights about her relationships, but then later recording her thoughts on psychotherapy, and ultimately her art-making. Hesse's constant journaling was noticed by her friends and acquaintances: her friend and fellow artist Robert Smithson observes that Hesse "was always preoccupied with her diaries and her parents' diaries and things like that" (Wasserman, 2006, p. 101). Artist Nancy Holt recalls, "I can never remember a time that we were at her place, where she didn't bring out a memento of her past. Generally, quite a large section of the evening, at least a half an hour to an hour, would be spent looking at some log, or a diary or pictures of her parents . . . or something" (Wasserman, 2006, p. 101).

Eva Hesse's consistent feelings of loss and abandonment haunted her throughout her life from childhood to her early death. These feelings made it a necessity for her to see, handle and share both her own diaries and her father's documents about her early childhood, and helped her maintain a psychic continuity—as well as a concrete external one—which was constantly under threat in her lifetime.

Her father, who was sick for many years, suffered from his first heart attack when Eva was 13 years old. Her stepmother often used to frighten her by warning, "You can't tell him anything, or you'll make him die" (Nemser, 1970/2002).

After completing her studies at Cooper Union, Eva Hesse attended Yale University from 1957 to 1961. Her experience at Yale, from which she graduated with a Master of Fine Arts degree, was a transformative one. There, Hesse began to ask very difficult questions about her identity as an artist and as a female professional. In a letter to her psychoanalyst on December 20, 1958, she wondered: "Am I a woman? Are my needs for developing artistically and intellectually incompatible? Am I incapable of satisfying a man's need for supremacy?" (Wagner, 2002).

After graduating from Yale, Hesse married the sculptor Tom Doyle, who converted to Judaism in order to marry her. When Doyle received an invitation by a German industrialist to travel to Kettwick, Germany, he and his new wife Eva traveled there together from June 1964 to September 1965. Separated from her father and from her psychiatrist and confronted by her own traumatic childhood in Germany during the Holocaust, Eva Hesse started journaling extensively. Hesse's journaling and art-making helped her process her confusing, conflicting feelings. In January of 1965, back in New York, she received word that her father had died. On August 16, 1966, she wrote in her diary, "Daddy is dead, he is in Switzerland. I am numb" (Cooper, 1992).

Hesse's marriage to Doyle began to disintegrate. Soon after their return to New York in 1966, she and Doyle separated. Both of these losses—first the death of her father and soon after, the separation from her husband—greatly increased her sense

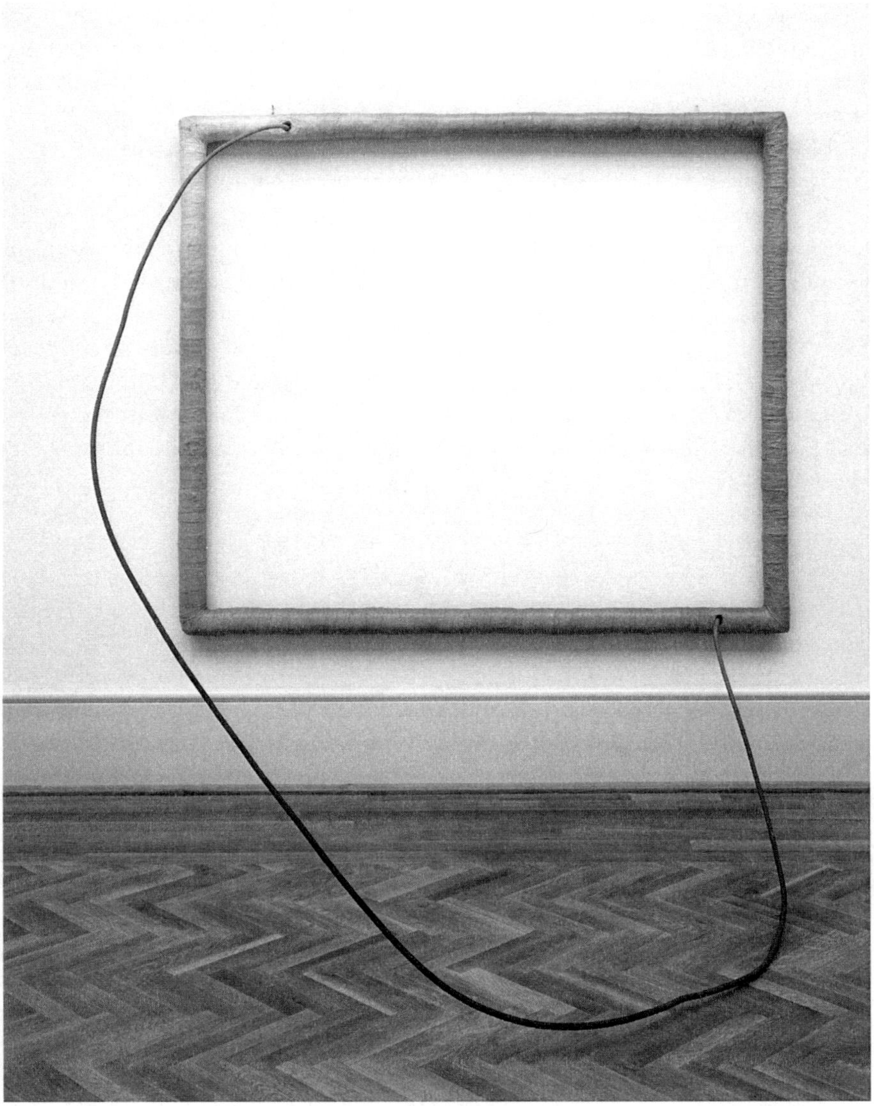

FIGURE 5.1 Eva Hesse. *Hang Up*. January 1966. Acrylic, cloth, wood, cord, steel. 182.9 × 213.4 × 198.1 cm / 72 × 84 × 78 in. The Art Institute of Chicago, gift of Arthur Keating and Mr. and Mrs. Edward Morris by exchange, April 1988. Photo: Susan Einstein, courtesy of The Art Institute of Chicago.

of abandonment and loss. Art-making, with its enduring quality, already functioned in Hesse's early life as a process of consolidation and solidification, as is clear from a diary entry written six years earlier: "I must be totally engrossed in my own work, it is the only thing that is permanent, mature and lasting" (Cooper, 1992).

From 1965 until she died of a brain tumor in 1970 at the young age of 34, Hesse felt secure in her life as an artist. Wagner writes: "It is rare in the history of art to encounter an artist (a woman) who believes so confidently in her own practice (with so much reason) and rarer still to find such an assurance echoed in the initial reception of her art" (Wagner, 2002, p. 274). Six years after her death, she had major retrospective exhibitions at the Guggenheim Museum in New York. Lucy Lippard also published her biography, *Eva Hesse*, in 1976. More recently, her art was exhibited in the San Francisco Museum of Art and the Tate Modern in London in 2002. In 2007, New York's Jewish Museum exhibited her sculptures, and both the Drawing Center in New York and the Museum for Contemporary Art in Los Angeles exhibited Hesse's drawings.

Hang Up, 1966

Hang Up (Figure 5.1) and the timing of its creation had much relevance to Hesse's life. Hesse's mother committed suicide on January 9, 1946. On December 12, 1965, as Hesse was planning and crafting *Hang Up*, she recorded in her diary: "My yearly fall into the pit of darkness is upon me . . . and I am working constantly with great intensity . . . the intensity in which I work is translated into the gloom of despair" (Pollock, 2006). *Hang Up* was thus being completed in the month leading up to the twentieth anniversary of her mother's suicide. Griselda Pollock says, "It is the nature of traumatic events to haunt us from behind consciousness, to bleed their affects into time and space, without yielding themselves to knowable form, recollections, or even conscious awareness" (Pollock, 2006, p. 41).

It took Hesse a period of seven months to complete *Hang Up* (de Zegher, 2006). What does the viewer see when looking at *Hang Up*? A simple wood frame, made of a six-by-seven-foot stretcher, wrapped or swaddled very carefully in strips of cloth, and then painted obsessively in finely gradated shades of gray. The frame or structure frames an empty space, namely the wall behind it. A flexible steel rod erupts from the structure of the frame as if lassoing the viewer into the artist's space. In her 1970 interview with Nemser, Hesse discussed *Hang Up:*

> It is close to what I feel I achieve in my best pieces . . . the first time where my idea of absurdity or extreme feeling came through. It is a frame . . . an idea piece . . . it sits on the wall a simple structure. . . . The frame, structure is all tied as hospital bandage, as if somebody had broken an arm, an absolutely rigid cord around the entire thing. It has a kind of depth I don't always achieve—a depth and soul and absurdity and life and meaning and feeling or intellect I want to get. . . . This little piece of steel comes out of this structure and it comes out a lot. It's about 10 or 11 feet out and it is ridiculous. It's the most ridiculous structure

> I ever made and that is why it is really good. . . . It is framing nothing. And the whole frame is graded—oh more absurdity—very, very finely. It was an effort and it is painted with Liquitex. It is very surreal, very strange. . . . It was done the first year of being back in America.
>
> (Nemser, 1970/2003)

As Mignon Nixon (2003) points out, Eva Hesse started to transform the art milieu of the gallery space, like other artists did in the late 1960s, as she projected the steel rod into the viewer's space "seeming to trip the viewer up" (p. 150). *Hang Up* addresses different dialectics: two-dimensional and three-dimensional, surface and depth, the pictorial and the sculptural, the artist's space and the viewer's space. The art piece also comments on feminist and personal content. Lippard suggests that Hesse's strength was in her ability to conjure opposites and make them cohabit within material form (Lippard, 1976).

The frame

In his famous essay "Parergon," Jacques Derrida discusses the significance of a frame or boundary around a work of art. Derrida's postmodern, deconstructive ideas have great relevance for the viewer's understanding of *Hang Up*. The title "Parergon," which translates as "by-work," reflects Immanuel Kant's idea that the frame is not an essential element, but rather an external complement to a work (Duro, 1996). The frame makes the work more clearly, definitely, and completely knowable and focuses the viewer's attention on the object itself, suggesting that it is the frame/*parergon* that draws an immediate boundary between the artwork [*ergon*] and its background and context. The *parergon* thus is simultaneously distinct from the *ergon* and from the milieu, and also merges the two grounds together (Derrida, 1987). Derrida suggests that the frame stands between the inside and the outside; it is a hybrid, "an inside which is called to the outside to constitute it as an inside" (Derrida, 1987, p. 63). The *parergon* tries to minimize the abyss and prevents us from falling into infinity (Derrida, 1987). The frame, which contains something that prevents its collapse, thus becomes a protection of the work, as it borders the work's absence. The *parergon* certainly becomes the marker of limits, and it points to the image it encloses. The frame pushes the work forward, onto the stage into visual immediacy.

Feminist interpretation

Eva Hesse remarked: "The way to beat discrimination in art is by art. Excellence has no sex" (Wagner, 2002, p. 183).

Unlike traditional art interpretation, which focuses on the contents inside the frame, as a window into the world, feminism emphasizes the outside, or edge of the frame. The "outside" implies being outside of patriarchal logic, history and justice, a place between the visible and invisible, the known and the unknown (Phelan, 2001).

Parker and Pollock suggest that Hesse refused to view women—including herself—as though in a frame, and therefore she made the conscious decision to leave the frame empty. She demonstrated that although women are unknown and hidden, they are very present as creators. These two scholars believe that Hesse's identity as a woman and an artist is yet unresolved, and as she approaches this tension entirely abstractly there is neither a notion of a female essence in this particular work nor in her other pieces (Pollock and Parker, 1981).

Hesse's reflections a few years later suggest that the tension she felt between her sense of self and her identity as an artist began to resolve at the end of her short life and the conclusion of her very successful career. After her first brain surgery, she wrote: ". . . this year, not knowing whether I would survive or not was connected with not knowing whether I would ever do art again. One of my first visions when I woke up from my operation, was that I didn't have to be an artist to justify my existence, that I had the right to exist without being one" (Nemser, 1970/2002, p. 59). Spoken at the end of her life, this suggests that in spite of her illness Hesse felt secure in her sense of self, her femininity, and her identity as an artist. She could imagine herself living a life no longer dominated by art-making.

We can trace the development of her artistic identity to an earlier time when she was living in Germany for a year. The shift from the art she created in Germany to the sculpture she later created in New York must not be overlooked. In Germany, Hesse created reliefs with hard dexterity and an emphasis on the outside, using very strong feminine and pop art colors such as pink, orange and purple. After arriving in New York in 1965, she abandoned color and turned to what we can refer to as "non-colors," namely blacks and grays; she traversed the gray scale and with it emphasized the framing edge. One has to wonder what contributed to this loss or change of color (Fer, 2007).

The gradation of color on the frame from very light gray to dark gray connects not only a feeling of lightness with a feeling of gravity, but also gives the frame depth and tactility (Fer, 2007). It seems as though Hesse has dressed up the frame with the cloth wrapping to make it appear less stark, and to prevent it from appearing naked and vulnerable. "It was the first time where my idea of absurdity and extreme feelings came through," said Hesse (Nemser, 1970/2002).

Hesse dedicated much time and attentiveness to dressing and painting the frame, as though dressing the wound of a child, perhaps a reference to herself as a child, as well as dressing up the war wounds of her mother. This act in Hesse's work represents a very maternal, feminine occupation transposed to the abstract. She followed the suggestion of her friend, artist Sol LeWitt, who wrote to her in a letter dated April 14, 1965: "Do more. More nonsensical, more crazy, more machines, more breasts, penises, cunts, whatever" (Lippard, 1976, p. 35). LeWitt seems to grant Hesse the permission to expand her mind beyond the categories of "masculinity" and "femininity," "blackness" and "whiteness," and even beyond her "personal" and "collective" history, all the way to the absurd.

At this point in her career, with her continuing artistic success, Eva Hesse was ready to claim her selfhood and push both the artistic frame and the feminist one into the viewers' space; Hesse engaged viewers in a dialogue about the limits, voids and challenges that women subjectively experience as artists (Nixon, 2006). Hesse also challenged Modernism's notion of separation and solitude for the feminist artist, and questioned her position as a female artist at the cutting edge of the artistic world. However, she did feel secure enough at this time to cross the margins, to push the frame forward onto the stage and into the limelight, and seemed prepared to take on all absurd gender "Hang Ups."

Psychological interpretation

Hang Up, which presents a picture frame and a window frame, is both full and empty at the same time. It seems to place Eva Hesse's experience of loss at center stage, with an umbilical cord protruding from its frame onto the floor and reattaching to the frame. The frame is full of the literal world behind it, and full of the emptiness Hesse experienced in her numerous violent abandonments which began in 1938 at the young age of two when she was put on the train to Amsterdam. The framed field, the window, is also the scene of her mother's suicide, a demarcating visual field, often repeated in her paintings, ink washes, drawings and sculptures. The space beyond the frame illustrates the content beyond the window and Hesse's great ambivalence in looking both beyond and behind the frame with her fear of death and longing desires for her lost mother and a more secure attachment to the world.

The empty space illustrates a blankness, where the inside content is delegated out to the border of the frame as though the support is actually the emphasis of the work (Fer, 2002). However, the biggest wound or hole exists in the middle, and the edge of the frame is like the dressing of the wound. In the words of the artist, the work is "all tied up like a hospital bandage—as if somebody broke an arm" (Nemser, 1970/2002). Hesse became aware of this hole inside of her six years earlier, as she recorded in a July 1960 diary entry: "A vacant, absent feeling . . . a void which . . . needs to be filled. In either case it is loneliness and emptiness which I constantly feel" (Chave, 1992).

In her psychoanalytic work as well as in her art, Eva Hesse made a sustained effort to process her mother's illness and suicide, to defend against her identification with her mother. Hesse felt guilty about her mother's death, and feared her own death would come either in the form of a suicide, just as her mother's had, or in the form of annihilation, just as her extended family was destroyed in the Holocaust. In the spring of 1966, just as she completed *Hang Up*, Hesse wrote in her diary: "My father and mother got divorced, she was sick, he let her go off by herself—without us children—she killed herself" (Fer, 2002).

The carefully bandaged frame evokes an image of the dead body, bandaged from head to foot, after a fall from a window, or perhaps illustrates the artist's need to contain her own body and self with bandages in order to prevent psychic fragmentation. The artist's wish to become a strong feminist who could work as an artist and live independently was counteracted by her great fear of autonomy; she felt very vulnerable, as though an empty frame was the only thing she could lean on. In her diary, she wrote ". . . that is sickness—the part of a leaning child" (de Zegher, 2006, p. 93).

Her extensive use of cord, strings and strips of cloth, with their wrapping and tying throughout her work, may serve as a metaphor reflecting her need to be connected to her mother who was "there but not there." Through a reenactment of her early loss of love, these cords reflect her wish to retrieve that love (to rope it in) with her art and, with the help of the viewer, maybe an attempt to be more anchored both as a person and as an artist.

Hang Up seen in the context of Eva Hesse's earlier works

Before we continue to further comprehend the psychological implications of the work *Hang Up*, it is important for the reader to understand this specific work within the context of some of Hesse's relief and sculptural work created between 1965 and 1970, the five years before her untimely death from cancer. Hesse's sculptural output in these five years is remarkable in both its creative expression and its size.

From 1964 to 1965, Eva Hesse lived in the German town of Kettwig, sharing an abandoned textile factory as a studio with her husband, sculptor Tom Doyle. During this time she began to reject painting and had a breakthrough with her assemblage and relief work. She combined papier-mâché with old, discarded loom parts, cotton cord and enamel paints in a group of funny, lively works.

In the work, *Ringaround Arosie*, 1965 (Figure 5.2, see also Plate 11), and *Ear in the Pond* (1965), for example, Hesse responds to Pop Art, which was a craze in both Germany and the United States. She playfully juxtaposes these very colorful reliefs with organic forms, often breast-like with mechanical parts. In dialogue with Pop Art, Hesse chose colors such as pink, purple, orange and lime-green to paint her humorous reliefs. The viewer notices two protuberant nipple hemispheres, the small one stacked above the large one, modeled in papier-mâché and encased in concentric loops of cloth and covered wire. Lippard (1976) calls it "a sort of doubly female figure." Presenting the human body in pieces was part of American art in the 1950s and 1960s. These early works demonstrate that Eva Hesse was influenced by Jasper Johns, Louise Bourgeois and Yayoi Kusama, who were all influenced by Marcel Duchamp.

Hesse's works that hang in the gallery with *Hang Up* were influenced by her return to New York after the loss of her father. The viewer finds in this gallery testicular, phallic and uterine forms in incredibly interesting, creative sculptures—full of humorous pathos and corporeality—informed by Hesse's failed marriage and her much stronger feminist identity. Minimalism became the operative feature as Hesse wrapped two inflated balloons in papier-mâché and cord, painting them

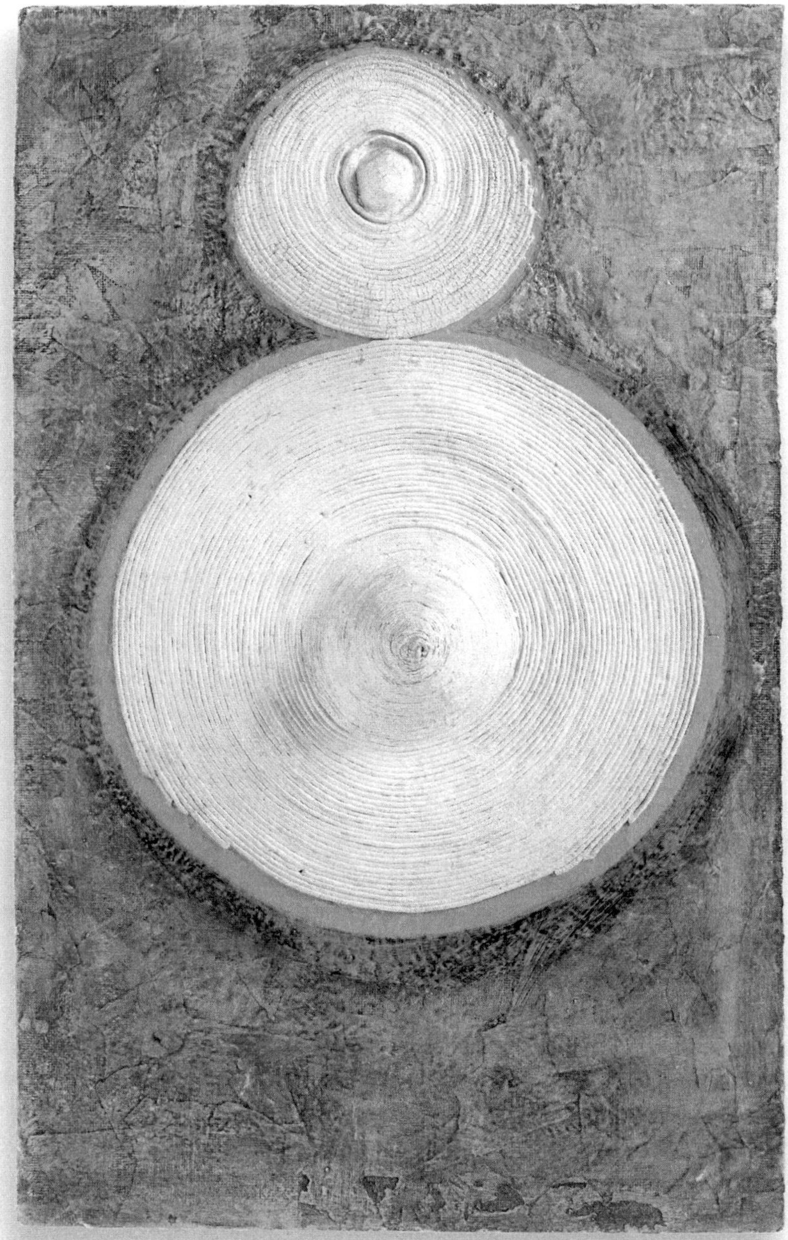

FIGURE 5.2 (see also Plate 11) Eva Hesse. *Ringaround Arosie*. 1965. Varnish, graphite, ink, enamel, cloth-covered wire, papier-mâché, unknown modeling compound, Masonite, wood. 67.5 × 42.5 × 11.4 cm / 26½ × 16¾ × 4½ in. Museum of Modern Art, New York, fractional and promised gift of Kathy and Richard S. Fuld, Jr., 2005. © The Estate of Eva Hesse. Courtesy Hauser & Wirth.

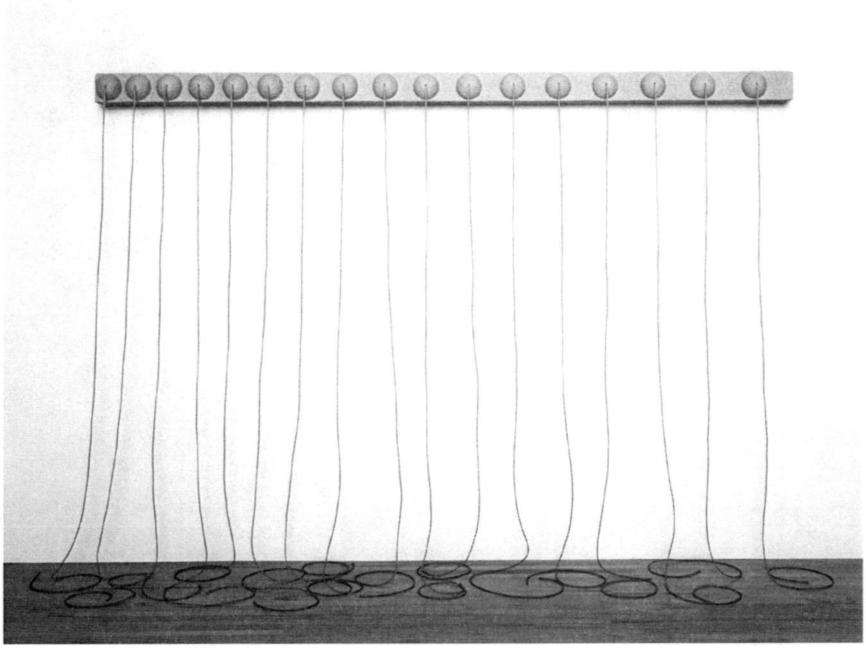

FIGURE 5.3 Eva Hesse. *Addendum*. 1967. Acrylic, papier-mâché, unkown modeling compound, wood, rope. 215 × 303 × 25 cm / 84½ × 119¼ × 10 in. (variable). Private collection, Italy, 2003. © The Estate of Eva Hesse. Courtesy Hauser & Wirth.

with black enamel paint. These twin sausage shapes are then linked together by a very long surgical hose. Suggestive forms, such as ovaries and fallopian tubes, and anatomical analogues are suggested by her title for this sculpture *Ingeminate*, 1965 (no plate shown), reiterating the themes of both mother and self conception. The word "ingeminate" could be associated with "inseminate," "disseminate," and "germinate," all of which have reproductive implications. These twin penises look like mock phalluses, bound and somehow confused with breasts or testicles, as they appear in doubles.

More circle motifs appear in Hesse's drawings and sculptures of 1966–1967. In *Addendum*, 1967 (Figure 5.3), the circles reappear as grey painted papier-mâché hemispheres on a 10-foot wall-mounted lintel. A long cord hangs from each mound, spilling onto the floor. It consists of a progression of increasing spatial intervals between hemispheres from left to right, beginning with a mound and ending with a blank space. Sue Taylor associates the process of "weaning" to this work, leading the viewer to feel a sense of separation and melancholy (Taylor, 2002).

This sense of absence is often experienced in Hesse's pieces, such as in *One More Than One*, 1967 (Figure 5.4). The viewer sees two concave hollows, appearing like

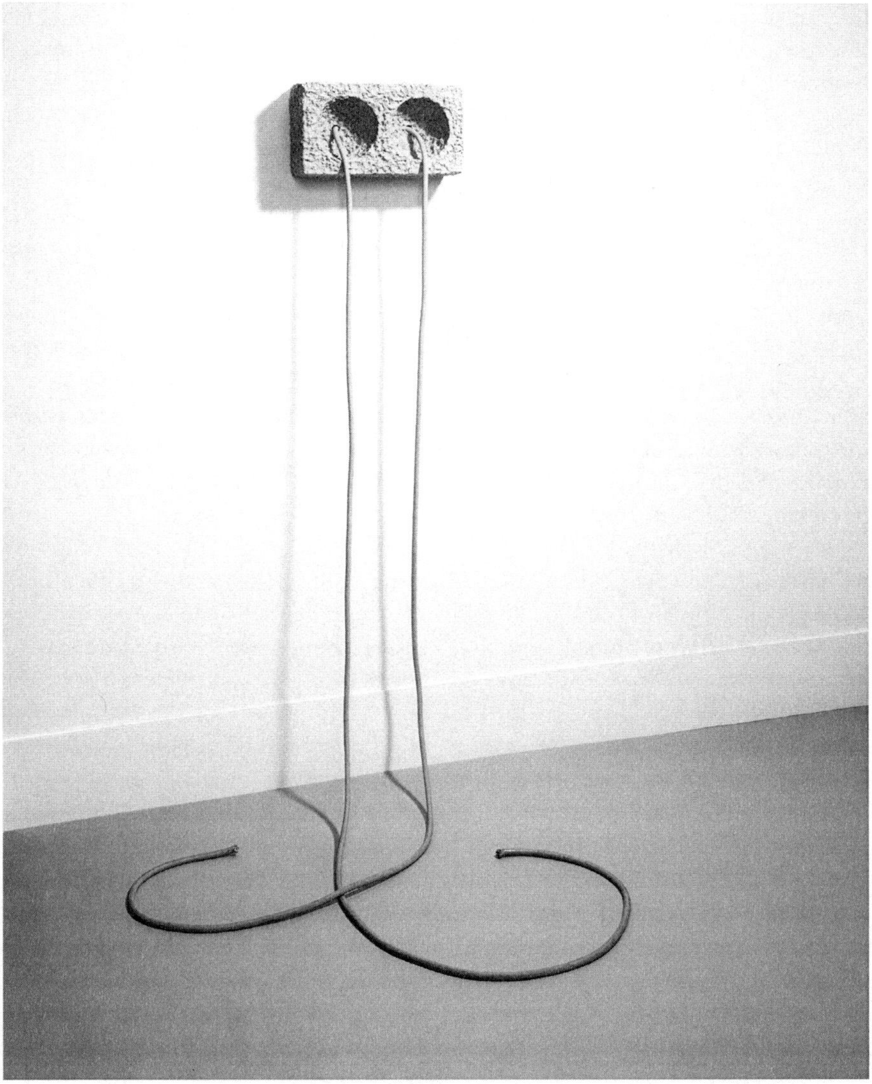

FIGURE 5.4 Eva Hesse. *One More Than One*. 1967. Acrylic, pâpier-maché, wood, plastic, rope. 21.6 × 38.1 × 14 cm / 8½ × 15 × 5½ in. (without rope), installation variable. Private collection, Italy, 2003. © The Estate of Eva Hesse. Courtesy Hauser & Wirth.

empty, absent breasts that emit cords. These two shapes also seem like two tear-streaming eyes, with the tears represented by the awkward dangling cord pouring out of the hollows. Like so many of these pieces, Hesse seems to embrace humor as well as sadness. The emphasis now seems to slowly point more towards sadness and its acceptance.

Eva Hesse discovered the amazing possibilities of new material such a fiberglass and polyester resin, which she used in the stunning *Repetition Nineteen III,* 1968 (Figure 5.6). Tender groups of knee-high, irregular and dented receptacles are placed randomly in the room, with a new element of light. In her biography, Lippard (1976) calls it the "inner glow," which Hesse achieved with the translucency of her innovative material, and associates the vessels with little children, prisoners or young trees. Taylor (2002) views the receptacles as departed souls. These associations lead the viewer to Hesse's traumatic, painful losses within her immediate family, as well as the murder of her four grandparents, aunts, uncles, and the annihilation of all of the victims of the Holocaust in her native Germany. Through abstract form, color-innovative material, and a great sense of poetry and light, Hesse was able to express in her art and in these vessels that which is inexpressible consciously. The artist seems able to contain her feeling of emptiness and mourning through forms reminiscent of huge *Yahrzeit* candles, a Jewish tradition of annually lighting a candle to memorialize the dead, as seen in her preparatory studies for *Repetition Nineteen III*, 1968 (Figure 5.5) (Taylor, 2002).

Hesse's use of container forms in her artwork continued in her sculpture *Sans II* (1968), which is composed of five aging translucent amber-colored sections. These containers are shallow fiberglass trays or boxes, sixty in all, stretching horizontally for nearly 36 feet along the wall. The artwork's French title, *Sans*, translates as "without" and refers to absence itself, the one who experiences the loss and is left "without," maybe without inner and outer stability or a secure sense of self and a way of being in the world. The images remind the viewer of a long row of foggy or smoked-glass windows, windows that offer no view. These windows are more like small containers, better able to contain Hesse's personal pain and sorrow, as well as perhaps the collective mourning for the six million Jews who perished in the Holocaust. The windows are similar to the fiberglass containers in *Tori* (1969), but so very different from the witty, absurd *Hang Up* created merely a few years earlier.

Aught, 1968 (Figure 5.7) is a four-part painting/sculpture made from latex and canvas sheets that can be viewed as yet another representation of Hesse's haunted windows. Her gouache and ink drawings of windows from 1967 and 1968 also reinforce this theme of the window. Her preoccupation with the window motif all through her work animates minimal forms and elicits fears, a more mature sense of metaphoric mourning (Nixon, 2002).

Hesse's extensive use of latex is susceptible to disintegration, as latex is known to be impermanent. Hesse was somehow aware of this fact, for her ephemeral

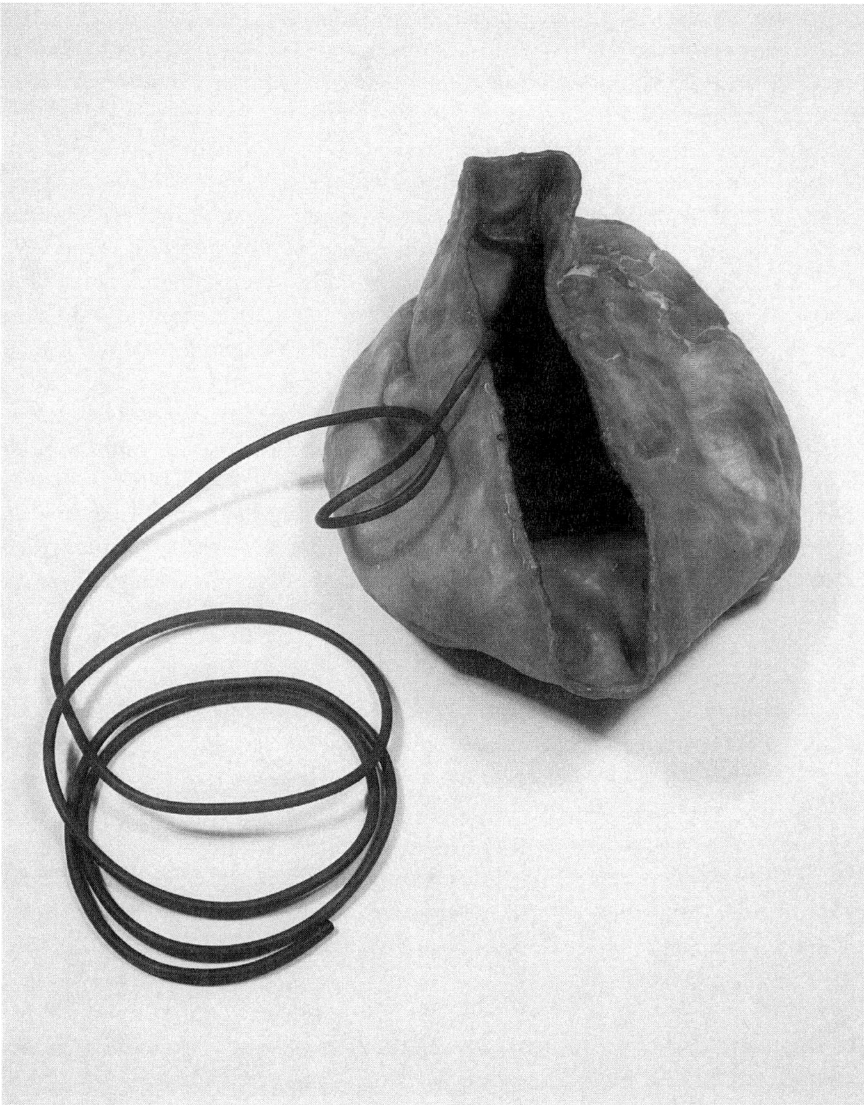

FIGURE 5.5 Eva Hesse. *Untitled* (Test piece for *Repetition Nineteen III*). 1967. Latex, cotton, rubber. 15 × 29 × 22 cm / 5⅞ × 11⅜ × 8⅝ in. © The Estate of Eva Hesse. Courtesy Hauser & Wirth.

materials are imbued with a melancholic sense of loss. As the viewer looks at these sculptures, whose material properties change over time, he or she becomes conscious of the fact that loss is already in process. It conjures up an awareness of the artist's own premature death (Nixon, 2002).

Hesse said, "Art is a total thing . . . an essence, a soul . . . In my inner soul art and life are inseparable" (Wagner, 2002, p. 96). This presentation of some of Hesse's works created before and after *Hang Up* demonstrates her exciting leap from the two- to the three-dimensional, and from the decorative, humorous, emotionally defended reliefs to richly symbolic and mature forms, containing corporeality in abstract form. From a psychoanalytical perspective, Hesse shifts from a pre-Oedipal part object state—splitting her breast and such into ideal and persecutory ones of love and hate—to the acceptance of an integrated but ambivalent awareness that lays the groundwork for deep mourning. The viewer witnesses how Hesse's feelings mature, as illustrated in these abstract sculptures. Eva Hesse seems to progress from a defensive irony in her colorful reliefs created before *Hang Up* to a gentler acceptance of loss in her later work. Because she appeared to feel emotionally stronger, she allowed herself to sculpt emptiness in her new works, creating vessels with depth. Acknowledging and containing her overwhelming feeling of loss and

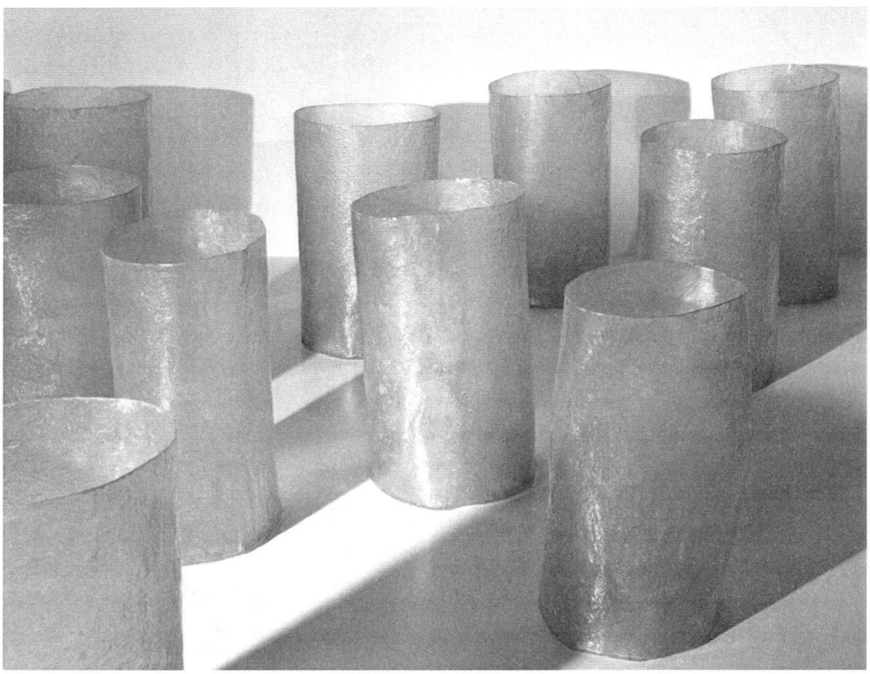

FIGURE 5.6 Eva Hesse. *Repetition Nineteen III*. 1968. Fiberglass, polyester resin. Installation variable, 19 units. Museum of Modern Art, New York: Gift of Charles and Anita Blatt. © The Estate of Eva Hesse. Courtesy Hauser & Wirth.

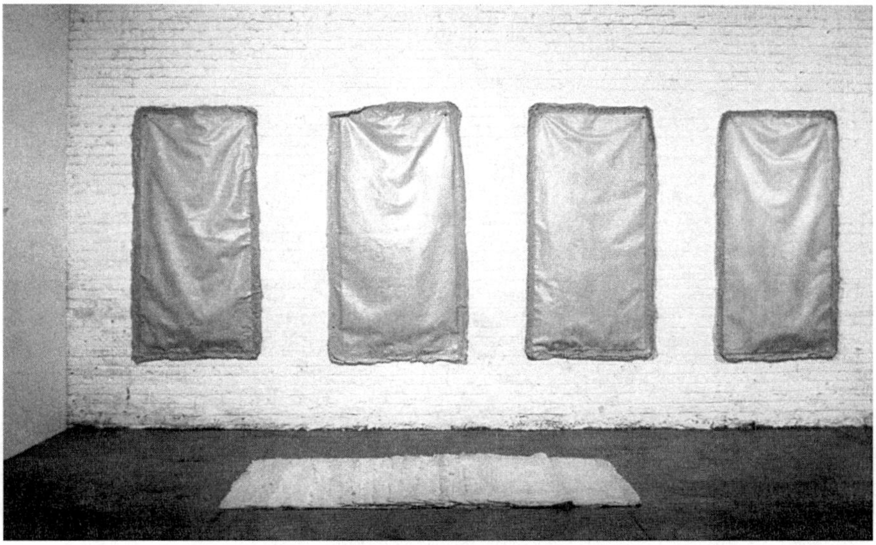

FIGURE 5.7 Eva Hesse. *Aught.* 1968. Latex, canvas, polyethylene sheeting, rope and unidentified materials, metal grommets. Installation variable, 4 units, each 198.1 × 101.6 cm / 78 × 40 in. University of California, Berkeley Art Museum & Pacific Film Archive, gift of Helen Hesse Charash, December 1979. © The Estate of Eva Hesse. Courtesy Hauser & Wirth.

absence, Hesse allowed both herself and us, the viewers, to connect to the mourning that she was unable to express in her earlier art. Hesse was able to communicate in her later work the powerful and painful dualities of chaos and order, frailty and strength, absence and presence, latex and flesh, moving as it were through the "depressive-mature" position of mourning.

Hang Up (1966) represents a transition linking the two phases of Hesse's work and her process of mourning. The viewer remembers the lovingly bandaged, carefully painted frame structure in the color scheme of gray, which frames nothing, and the wall space behind. The suspended rod, also painted in different grays, projects too far into the viewer's space, casting a shadow, and then leading back to the frame, wrapping both the artist and the viewer in a codified aesthetic discourse, a non-verbal dialogue.

We, as viewers are confronted with an empty frame, a blank space on which Hesse projects her catastrophic anxiety related to her early loss of mother, first through debilitating depression, and later through suicide. André Green (1980/2001) refers to this kind of empty space as the negative "psychic hole" that embodies traces of the unconscious breast with destructive and loving aspects. Hesse seems to search for symbolic expression of these psychic traces. Physical life has become transformed for the infant when mother retreats into her depression and/or when the small child is suddenly separated from mother and father, as love has been lost in a single blow. The infant, left with no choice, withdraws all of her affects from the disappointing object, her mother, and identifies unconsciously with the "dead" mother, and with mother's bereavement when she detached from the infant. This results in the "death" of the maternal "image" in the child's life. With time, the maternal image that used to be a source of pride and vitality, fades into a distant, lifeless figure, resulting in a catastrophe for the self (Green, 1980/2001). What is left is a hole in the relationship with mother or its substitute. It is not only an absence in the physical relationship with the mother and her non-presence, but is an absence that prevents the infant from making meaning of its confusing inner and outer worlds. When Hesse's depressed and sometimes manic mother retreated, she also took with her major portions of love and the traces of her entire being in memory, very important memories for the infant or toddler, such as her smell and her touch. In an attempt to master her traumatic loss, it was this hole that Hesse was eventually able to fill with fantasies and form in her artistic creations. She succeeded in containing her loss and thus managed to stabilize, to a certain extent, her psychic economy. The wound or hole also resurrected the physical and psychological pain and guilt connected to the dead mother. What was left then was a hole or a gap, experienced by the artist as a dreadful solitude, mourning for mother and her breast, symbolized in a blank or absent breast for which the artist still grieves.

It is the framing structure of *Hang Up*, so carefully wrapped and lovingly painted, that actually becomes the primary object, sheltering the fantasy of mother with all her ambivalences, projected into the negative space of the container, the frame. Thus the frame, even when it is empty, offers the guarantee of maternal presence, with all its positive and negative affects (Green, 1980/2001). The cord extending from the frame into the space of the viewer and back to the frame manifests itself as a kind of psychic "border linking," connecting the little girl/artist with (and differentiating her from) the mother (Ettinger, 2006). The cord also becomes the umbilical cord that reunites traumatic traces with phantasmatic ones, the unconscious connection to mother, accessing a richly layered pictorial and symbolic psychic archive (Ettinger, 2006). The extended cord in *Hang Up* connects the artist securely to her art-making abilities and is perhaps also a metaphor, as mentioned earlier, for Hesse's need to be reconnected to an internal imago of mother, a reenactment in her art of early loss of love and its concrete and absurd retrieval.

These ties and connections to her symbolic archive in art-making resulted in the artist's healing transformation. The child who has lost her mother, first through physical separation, then depression and later through suicide, always craves for her lost gaze and lost touch. Hesse learned to connect to the lost gaze and touch of mother by physically touching and manipulating soft and skin-like material in the art-making process. Hesse physically created almost all of her sculptures herself, even when they were in serials and assistance was available, as she enjoyed the touch of the skin-like materials of polyester resin, latex, polyethylene sheeting, paints, papier-mâché, and others.

Thus *Hang Up* is the first sculpture (and a witty one no less) that allowed Hesse to create a virtual home for housing all of mother, an empty space for form-giving and symbolization. The work also paved the way for Hesse's astoundingly beautiful and moving sculptures, endless repetitions of working through mourning. Through her extreme dedication to her artistic work, and her highly creative ways of implementing innovative materials in her expansive oeuvre, the artist was able to create new depths while always embracing ambiguity. In her mature sculptures, Eva Hesse was not only able to contain her sense of emptiness, but also connected her psyche with the world by roping us into her sculptural and psychic space, allowing the viewer to project personal and collective losses onto her later more mature, empty spaces, to partake of her containers. The viewer is invited in her earlier work to giggle with her erotically charged, feminist part-object imagery, and in her later work to mourn personal losses and the all-too-early-loss of the outstanding artist Eva Hesse.

References

Chave, A. (1992) Eva Hesse: A girl being a sculpture. In *Eva Hesse: A retrospective*. New Haven, CT: Yale University Press, pp. 99–117.

Cooper, H. (1992) Eva Hesse: Diaries and notebooks. In *Eva Hesse: A retrospective*. New Haven, CT: Yale University Press, pp. 17–50.

Derrida, J. (1987) *The truth in painting* (G. Bennington and I. McLeod, Trans.). Chicago, IL: University of Chicago Press, pp. 37–82.

de Zegher, C. (2006) Drawing as binding/bandage/bondage or Eva Hesse caught in the triangle of process/content/materiality. In *Eva Hesse drawing*. C. de Zegher (Ed.). New Haven, CT: Yale University Press, p. 93.

Duro, P. (1996) *The rhetoric of the frame: Essays on the boundaries of artwork*. Cambridge, UK: Cambridge University Press, pp. 183–213.

Ettinger, B. (2006) Gaze-and-touching the not enough mother. In *Eva Hesse drawing*. C. de Zegher (Ed.). New Haven, CT: Yale University Press, pp. 183–213.

Fer, B. (2002) Bordering on black: Eva Hesse on minimalism, 1994. In *Eva Hesse*. M. Nixon (Ed.). *October Files* 3: 57–85. Cambridge, MA: The MIT Press.

Fer, B. (2007) Eva Hesse and color. *October Files*, 119: 21–36. Cambridge, MA: The MIT Press.

Green, A. (1980) The dead mother. In *Life narcissism, death narcissism*. London: Free Association Books, 2001.

Lippard, L. (1976) *Eva Hesse*. New York: New York University Press.

Nemser, C. (1970) A conversation with Eva Hesse. In *Eva Hesse*. M. Nixon (Ed.). *October Files* 3: 1–24. Cambridge, MA: The MIT Press, 2002.

Nixon, M. (2002) Ringaround Arosie: 2 in 1. In *Eva Hesse*. M. Nixon (Ed.). *October Files* 3: 195–219. Cambridge, MA: The MIT Press.

Nixon, M. (2003) Eva Hesse retrospective: A note on the milieu. *October Files*, 104: 149–156. Cambridge, MA: The MIT Press.

Nixon, M. (2006) Child's drawing. In *Eva Hesse drawing*. New Haven, CT: Yale University Press, pp. 27–57.

Phelan, P. (2001) Survey. In *Art and feminism*. H. Reckitt and P. Phelan (Eds.). London: Phaidon Press, pp. 15–49.

Pollock, G. (2006) A very long engagement: Singularity and difference in the creative writing on Eva Hesse. In *Encountering Eva Hesse*. Munich: Prestel, pp. 23–55.

Pollock, G., and Parker, R. (1981) Encountering encounter: An introduction. In *Encountering Eva Hesse*. G. Pollock and V. Corby (Eds.). Munich: Prestel, 2006, pp. 13–21.

Taylor, S. (2002) Vessels and vacancies. *Art in America*, November 1, 2002.

Wagner, A. (2002) Another Hesse. In *Eva Hesse*. M. Nixon (Ed.). *October Files*, 3: 96. Cambridge, MA: The MIT Press.

Wasserman, F. (2006) Building a childhood memory: The diaries of Eva Hesse's early years. In *Eva Hesse: Sculpture*. E. Sussman, F. Wasserman, Y-A. Bois and M. Godfrey (Eds.). New York and New Haven, CT: The Jewish Museum and Yale University Press, pp. 97–132.

6

LUCIAN FREUD

The permeable membrane—mourning the transience of beauty and life itself

This chapter explores Lucian Freud's pictorial expression of an affective, inner space as he projected it onto the exterior surface of the painted flesh and skin of his subjects on the canvas. The artist's use of texture, pigment and color creates a skin-container, and the artist himself had a second skin in the form of his consistent presence with his models in his studio; both of these skins function as transitional objects, permeable membranes. The skin-container stores not only the accumulated infant experience of being touched by mother or father, fed, rubbed, and bathed, but also marks a protective boundary with the outside, providing a barrier against aggression from the outside, and forming a narcissistic envelope and thus securing physical well-being (Anzieu, 1989). The second skin provided by the artist's consistent presence forms an additional exterior protection, containing the model's affects and anxieties. The permeable skin allows the artist and viewer to visually penetrate an intimate, internal space, permitting both the artist and the viewer to mourn the transience of beauty and ultimately the loss of life itself.

Biographical details

Lucian Michael Freud was born in 1922 in Berlin, the middle of Lucie and Ernst Freud's three sons. The brothers were known as the Archangels, the oldest Stephen Gabriel, then Lucian Michael and the youngest, Clement Raphael. His father, Ernst, was the youngest son of Sigmund Freud. Ernst worked as an architect and he loved to paint in his youth. His mother, Lucie Brasch, was the daughter of a wealthy grain merchant. Lucian grew up in Berlin, next to the Tiergarten, and his family spent their summers on the Baltic or at his maternal grandparents' country estate, where Lucian loved to ride horses.

Lucian's grandfather Sigmund often traveled to Berlin for cancer treatment and visited with his grandsons. On one such occasion, Lucian remembers that he brought him a copy of *The Arabian Nights* with beautiful illustrations, and together they enjoyed reading Wilhelm Busch's *Max and Moritz*, a comic book about two naughty boys that was popular in Sigmund's youth.

Due to the early rise of Nazism and Berlin street gangs, Lucian was escorted to and from the Französische Gymnasium and was watched closely at all times by both his mother and his governess. After Hitler's rise to power in 1933, his father went to England in search of suitable schools for his sons. At the young age of 10, Lucian arrived in England and enrolled in a progressive socialist boarding school with a farm, forestry, stables and a textile studio. His love for horses often tempted him to skip class and ride instead. Eventually he completed his high school studies in a more sober public school. In 1938, while Lucian was attending art school, he applied to another school and was accepted largely thanks to his construction of a beautiful horse statue. Just after his acceptance to this art school, he was expelled from his previous program after dropping his trousers on a public street as a dare. Upon his arrival in London in this same year, Lucian also recalled visiting his grandfather Sigmund—"He made me laugh a lot" (Smee, 2007, p. 11)—which is documented in a home film recorded by Marie Bonaparte, Sigmund's good friend.

On September 23, 1939, Sigmund died: "There was a sort of hole in his cheek like a brown apple; that was why there was no death mask, I imagine. I was upset," Lucian remembered (Feaver, 2002a, p. 18). It was very important for Lucian that he had a biological and personal link to his famous grandfather. Greig (2013) felt that it was part of his core identity and formed the reason why he survived Nazism when leaving Berlin before World War II. During Lucian's late adolescence in the 1940s, he also survived the Blitz in London, a time when shell craters and corpses were a common sight. This period culminated for him in 1944 when his city block was hit by a rocket, shattering his window while a painting sat unfinished on the easel (Feaver, 2002a).

Lucian's parents and brothers called him by the nickname Lux, the Latin word for "light." He had an unusual relationship with his father Ernst. Ernst was a modernist architect and early in his life Lucian developed an aversion to the more Germanic minimalist sense of design that came with Modernism (Greig, 2013). He also felt misunderstood by his father and complained later in life that he felt an early lack of closeness to him. His mother thought it had something to do with the fact that originally Ernst wanted to be an artist himself and thus might have felt competitive with their talented artist son. When Ernst first began seeing Lucie, who came from a wealthy Jewish family in Berlin, he did not think he could make a living for a family solely with his art and he thus became an architect. In fact, Lucian kept and treasured the watercolor paintings his father had made when he was young, of German landscapes, mountains and lakes. Father and son had very different views and tastes, furthering the distance between them and leading to frequent fights. Lucian remembered one time his father was able to compliment him: in one of the early houses they lived in when the Freud family moved to London,

Lucian painted the walls of the bedrooms with a matte green color and suspended a stuffed fish in a glass case above the bathtub; Ernst was very complimentary to his young son about the choice of the sleepy green color and his sense of style (Greig, 2013). When Lucian later became a full-time artist, however, Ernst criticized his art often and Lucian felt offended by his father's rude comments. It is interesting to note that Lucian Freud's relationship with his mother only improved after his father died in 1970.

In 1942, Lucian enlisted in the Merchant Navy, but was released after only a few months due to illness. More art schools followed, and yet another attempt at a sea voyage adventure, until he eventually started to paint full time in 1944.

The year 1945 proved critical for Lucian Freud, as he met the English painter Francis Bacon and the two developed a close friendship. Their relationship deepened especially in the 1960s, when Bacon became his mentor for the next 25 years. Although Lucian Freud was envious of Bacon's early success, as it took him longer to get the acknowledgment he hoped for, the two sat and painted 18 portraits of each other, went out to bars, drank, and discussed painting. Lucian Freud was influenced by Bacon's more spontaneous approach to painting and started to imitate his broader brush strokes. Bacon was also one of the first painters to reject purely abstract art, a direction in tune with Freud's approach to realistic painting.

Lucian Freud married several times. In 1948, he married Kitty Garman (Kathleen Epstein) with whom he had two daughters, Annie and Annabel. After their divorce he married Caroline Blackwood in 1953. With Suzy Boyt he had four children: Alexander, Rose, Isobel and Susie; with Katherine McAdam another four, Jane, Paul, Lucy, and David McAdam Freud. He had two daughters, Esther and Bella, with his partner Bernadine Coverley; with the Countess of St Germans, Jacquetta Eliot, he fathered his son Francis Michael; and with Celia Paul he had his youngest son, Frank, in 1984. He acknowledged all 14 of these children and was loved and admired by his children even though he visited them irregularly and on his own terms and only very few had his phone number. In early years the different children never met each other, and some did not even know that they had half-siblings until Lucian aged and became more frail. Still, he was always the major focus of his children's world, and as he got older, it was even more important for them to be in his presence. As these many wives and lovers suggest, he was driven not only by his creative ambition but also by his libido, and he was unable to commit to any one woman—much less to a domestic family life. His focus was on painting and it took precedence over anything else. He stayed in touch with most of his partners, and he was also capable of long platonic relationships with both women and men. His models often became his lovers and friends for a time, and some stayed in touch over longer periods.

The year 1954 proved to be important for his art career. He represented Britain at the 21st Venice Biennale, followed by exhibitions every second or third year. He settled into an art studio in Paddington, London for the next 30 years before moving to one in Holland Park. His first retrospective exhibition, organized by the Arts Council of Great Britain, was held in 1974 at the Hayward Gallery in London.

Lucian Freud's figurative art developed from the Neo-Romanticism of the 1940s to Modernist Realism with an "abrasive, anti sentimentalizing objectivity, a Post-Modern scrutiny to the body in its enormous corporality" as David Alan Mellor put it (Mellor, 2002, p. 2). Mellor also links Lucian Freud's style to Alberto Giacometti's existential Realism, connecting him to Abstract Expressionists like the American Willem de Kooning and to Lucian Freud's friend Francis Bacon. Lucian actually met Giacometti in Paris, and they saw each other frequently when Giacometti visited London; indeed, it was Giacometti who introduced him to Francis Bacon.

In 1970, his father Ernst died, and this greatly affected his mother. She tried to commit suicide shortly afterwards, leaving a note that said "I left to join him" (Smee, 2009, p. 31). His mother became severely depressed and lost interest in everything "including me," Lucian Freud said (Smee, 2009, p. 31). "I always avoided her because she was so intuitive that I felt my privacy was rather threatened by her," he told Smee (Smee, 2009, p. 31). He said to his friend, journalist Geordie Greig (2013) with whom he met for breakfasts over a long period of time, that when she became this depressed he felt that he had to make up time with her. Lucian began to use his mother as a model for his paintings: for almost nine years he had her picked up in the morning, to "cheer her up" with the thought that she would have a place to go (Smee, 2009, p. 31). The transitional object of the canvas between mother and son, and the transitional protective space of his studio allowed him both the needed distance from as well as the intimate closeness with his mother that he needed. Lucian Freud told Greig (2013) that he needed his mother to forgive him for his earlier distance to her. Throughout his years of painting, Lucian chose to use close family members as his models, including his mother, wives, partners, children and long-term intimate friends, with a few exceptions for celebrities. With the exception of his four children with Katherine McAdam, he painted portraits of all his acknowledged children, alone or with others, in groups or with their own children, and six of his daughters and one son nude.

Like a caring mother or like his famous grandfather, Lucian Freud said that, "The subject must be kept under closest observation. If this is done, day and night, the subject—he or she or it—will eventually reveal the all without which selection itself is not possible" (Lucian Freud, 1954, p. 23). In Geordie Greig's book *Breakfast with Lucian* the artist elaborated on his writings from his essay in the *Encounter* magazine in 1954 saying that he puts feelings and senses into his paintings that then became form intensifying the reality (Greig, 2013). Lucian Freud's very close emotional connection to his sitters, his total focus and sensitivity, allowed him to breathe life into his paintings, often expressed by his particular strokes and color choices when painting the skin of the models. The skin on his canvases seems to breathe like the real life skin of humans and animals. He also seems to have had an almost magical, shamanistic connection or psychic power with animals, and especially loved horses and dogs. His two Whippets were part of his inner intimate circle and he drew, painted and engraved them over many years.

The skin as transitional object

In his writing "The Ego and The Id" (1923), Sigmund Freud established a link between self and body. He defined the ego as being first and foremost a bodily ego. "A person's own body, and above all its surface, is a place from which both external and internal perception may spring. It is seen like any other object, but to the touch it yields two kinds of sensations, one of which may be equivalent to an internal perception" (p. 25). One may state that consciousness appears at the surface of the body, or that it actually is the surface. The ego is initially formed based on the experience of touch. Esther Bick (1968) viewed the skin of the body as a boundary that has internal meaning, holding together the different parts of the personality. This internal function of containing all parts of the self is initially dependent on the introjections of an external object, which can be used to fulfill this function. If one cannot identify with a containing object, one suffers from a defective self-integration (Kogan, 1988).

The skin not only functions as a container for a person's skeleton and muscles, but also maintains the psyche, initially through holding and feeding, the unique ways in which a mother supports and touches the baby's body. In the beginning of an infant's life, it is the mother's or father's skin, warm hands, and soft breasts which press against the infant as she or he rubs, washes, caresses, and carries the baby. Such maternal and/or parental care is experienced by the infant as strong sensory stimulation, skin contact that ideally stimulates and pleases. The skin also becomes the baby's surface of communication to his mother or father and other important objects. On the skin, the mother draws marks and signs that will be retained inside the psyche, protected by the skin. The skin thus ideally contains and retains an accumulation of goodness and fullness, as it forms the boundary between exterior and interior (Anzieu, 1989). Willie Hoffer (1950) explained that the distinction between self and other is defined by dividing the contents inside one's body from those outside which become part of the environment, effectively creating an envelope for the content of the self, and a protective barrier through which exchanges can be filtered. The skin is also a surface containing pockets and cavities that store an individuals' early good and bad sensory memories.

Donald Winnicott (1965) suggested that every individual who has reached the stage of being a unit with a limiting membrane has an outside and an inside, called the "psychic indwelling in the soma, a limited membrane . . . the surface of the skin, and has a position between the infant's 'me' and his 'not me'. . . it gradually becomes meaningful to postulate a personal or inner psychic reality for the infant" (Winnicott, 1965, p. 45). He continued to sketch out how the child grows into a newly established unit of a localized inside and outside self, defined by a new unification, namely the skin that forms a boundary. The third phase of a human being's life is an intermediate area in which the individual's inner reality and external life interconnect. Stemming from his concept of the transitional object, Winnicot called this the birth space of creative activity, signaling the onset of a transitional stage in which the child shifts from being a primary unity with the maternal environment to developing a real self, separate from the mother. The object created within that space represents the child's first acceptable meaningful experience of the "not-me," that can be made "mine" (Winnicott, 1971).

Lucian Freud's portrayal of the skin and flesh in his paintings can be viewed as the pictorial creation of a transitional object, belonging neither fully to external reality nor entirely to the internal world, but rather imbued with both, as a living skin always is. This permeable membrane can be experienced as a veil that both reveals and conceals; the painted surface becomes like an imaginary passage through which the artist invites us as viewers to focus on the tactility and markings of his skin, eliciting from us an associative response as well as the reverie he experienced while creating (Bond, 2001). While the transitional object for the small child is initially created out of a fear of loss and provides a mode of coping with temporary loss, for Lucian Freud the transitional object became a necessary, creative defense to ward off and monitor fears and anxiety, emotional closeness and distance, and at the same time allowed for a creative space of intimacy and reverie. The experienced tactility of the paint and the brushwork in Lucian Freud's Realistic style "metaphorically and literally opens the figure for our engagement" at the same time that it feels like a screen that simultaneously reveals and conceals the represented (Bond, 2001, p. 1).

When living in dangerous prewar Germany as a small child, Lucian Freud was always protectively accompanied and supervised by his mother and others. In one published interview, he revealed that the first word he learned to speak was *alleine*, meaning "alone," which he used to indicate that he wanted to be left alone and do things alone. In contrast, however, he also revealed that he could only paint a subject or person onto a canvas if the subject was actually in front of him. He could not paint when he was alone, but rather needed to be in the company of a sitter, preferably one he knew well—or on more rare occasions in the company of his dogs or an inanimate object. Lucian Freud was simultaneously both alone and not alone while painting a subject. He painted in the same old studio—with its dirty walls, its chair that functioned as a palette, its heaps of dirty rags—and was intensely engaged with his models. He required models to sit with him for hundreds of hours, from 7 a.m. to 1 p.m. and from 7 p.m. to 1 a.m., 12 full hours, half during the day and half during the night. The night sittings were often more sexually charged, and during these long sittings with his model, presence was all-consuming and all that mattered for Lucian Freud. He transferred each inch of their body, flesh and skin onto the canvas, a father's consideration as well as a painter's. "Their fatigue is apt to enliven me," he told his biographer Feaver (2011, p. 326). He seemed intensely connected to his sitters, not only to their exterior body but also emphatically in touch with their internal world, as is reflected through their naked body, postures and facial expressions. "Freud's work will leave to posterity the vulnerability and potency of the people portrayed . . . the pressure is towards a perilous interpretation of exteriority and interiority, physical form and feeling . . ." writes Lampert (1993, p. 11).

Lucian Freud thought that painting portraits was a matter of intellect and emotion and that the human body was the most profound subject (Greig 2013). The uniqueness and value of his experience tells the viewer "I am more interested what's inside their heads. That's why I prefer working from people I know . . . To make myself as sensitive and pliable as I can to the temperament and nature of the people I work from" (Bowery, 1993, p. 2). This may sound strangely familiar, like something his grandfather could have said. In an interview with his biographer William Feaver, Lucian mentioned that "There is something about a person being naked in front of me that invokes consideration . . ." (Feaver, 2002a, p. 35). He has also said "that he is drawn to certain things . . . the insides and undersides of things" (Lampert, 1993, p. 11). This stresses his willingness to look beyond the outside layers and his ability to use his own intuition and his comfort with emotional intimacy. Lucian Freud kept a rigorous schedule for his work and his sitters; like his grandfather, he looked for the inner life of his subjects and his attunement was so intense that he even fantasized that this togetherness would create new life. By rubbing pigment onto the canvas, his brush seemed to be stroking painted skin. He hoped his subject would come alive, just as a baby defines himself or herself by mother's or father's magic touch. "A moment of complete happiness never occurs in the creation of a work of art," Lucian Freud said. "The promise of it is felt in the act of creation but disappears towards the completion of the work. For it is then that the painter realizes that it is only a picture he is painting. Until then he had almost dared to hope that the picture might spring to life" (Hughes, 1987/89, p. 17).

The basic pigment Lucian Freud used for flesh and skin is a Cremnitz white, a heavy pigment containing lead oxide flakes with much less oil medium than other whites. The particular graininess of Cremnitz white enables a painter to create a particularly real quality, akin to a deposit of raw tissue such as real skin (Hughes, 2001). "It granulates," said Lucian Freud, "and I think of granules as atoms." The artist was again pointing to the illusion of creating real life with his magic horse-hair brush. "I wouldn't use Cremnitz on anything that wasn't alive . . ." Lucian Freud said (Hughes, 2001).

In his "Three Essays on Sexuality," Sigmund Freud (1905) linked the pleasure of looking at a (naked) body with a sense of a tactile experience, integrating sight and corporeality in a field of desire (Mellor, 2002). Lucian Freud's studio became Sigmund Freud's consulting room complete with his red chair and couch. The person who entered the space later emerged as a different person, stripped not only of her clothes but also of her defenses, aware of her unconscious life. Similar to his grandfather, Lucian believed that this realistic painting style can go beyond the appearance of the Other, cutting to their essence. In a safe place over a long period of time, emotional intimacy develops between an artist and model which can eventually allow both of them—the artist and the sitter together—an intense experience of presence, fostering a state of enveloping reverie in which they can mourn their pasts and become aware of the finitude of life. This absorption, and the intense penetrating gaze of the artist creates an unusual intimacy, akin to the one between infant and mother, expanding time through a suspension of temporality (Mellor, 2002).

Looking at Lucian Freud's paintings *Benefits Supervisor Resting*, 1994 (Figure 6.1, see also Plate 12), the viewer is exposed to the special intensity of a carnivalesque woman's nudity—Sue Tilley, also known as Big Sue—stripped not only of her clothes, but also of all convention. Lying languidly on the sofa of Lucian Freud's bohemian studio, mounds and weights of flesh confront the viewer, causing the viewer to lose himself in the folds and colors of her skin. Lucian celebrates physical majesty in the flesh—a particular but powerful femininity—as well as the intense tactility of her skin and the frankness of touch. The viewer simultaneously experiences the animalistic and spiritual sides of this human being. Looking at this painting we see through her naked body, beyond the surface of the skin to her inner psyche; we also see the penetrating gaze of the artist, both anatomist dissecting his object and empathic mother with her loving gaze (Schwab, 2004). As viewers, we are forced to take part in an intense, relentless sensory encounter and an emotional engagement. These uncanny portraits with their strange ambivalence and enormous corporeality focus on the existential bareness of the Other. "I want paint to work like flesh . . . I would like my portraits to be of the people, not like them . . . as far as I am concerned the paint is the person," Lucian Freud said (Gowing, 1984, pp. 190–191). In their strange positions, their colossal sizes and enormous presence, the bodies of his subjects augment a particular awareness of physicality: stained with pigment, the canvas scraped and stressed in the process. We feel weighed down by his focused vision, yet at the same time we find ourselves uplifted by the visual truth of their dreamlike state, an uncanny weightlessness in spite of their enormous physical presence. We witness a strange ambivalence between the real and the grotesque, between the intimate and the abject (Mellor, 2002). The viewer is allowed to witness an intensely personal, truthful scrutiny of life's arresting temporality, almost a celebration of its passing, decay and death. In a passage very fitting to Lucian Freud's artistic process, Emmanuel Levinas has said that "Proximity is a disturbance of remembered time. One could call that apocalyptically the break up of time . . . the present is but a trace of an immemorial present" (1998, p. 89).

In his essay "The Uncanny" (1919), Sigmund Freud describes the recognition of uncanniness as when the distinction between imagination and reality is erased, resulting in an infantile wish that the creation will come to life. The uncanny is thus closely related to a belief in the omnipotence of thought: the secret, hidden wish of the artist to create real life in his life portraits. Lucian Freud created very real, fantastically tactile representations of people familiar to him, but he differentiated them from reality by implementing unusual postures, perspectives or slightly changed proportions. The uncanniness of his images also stems from his ability

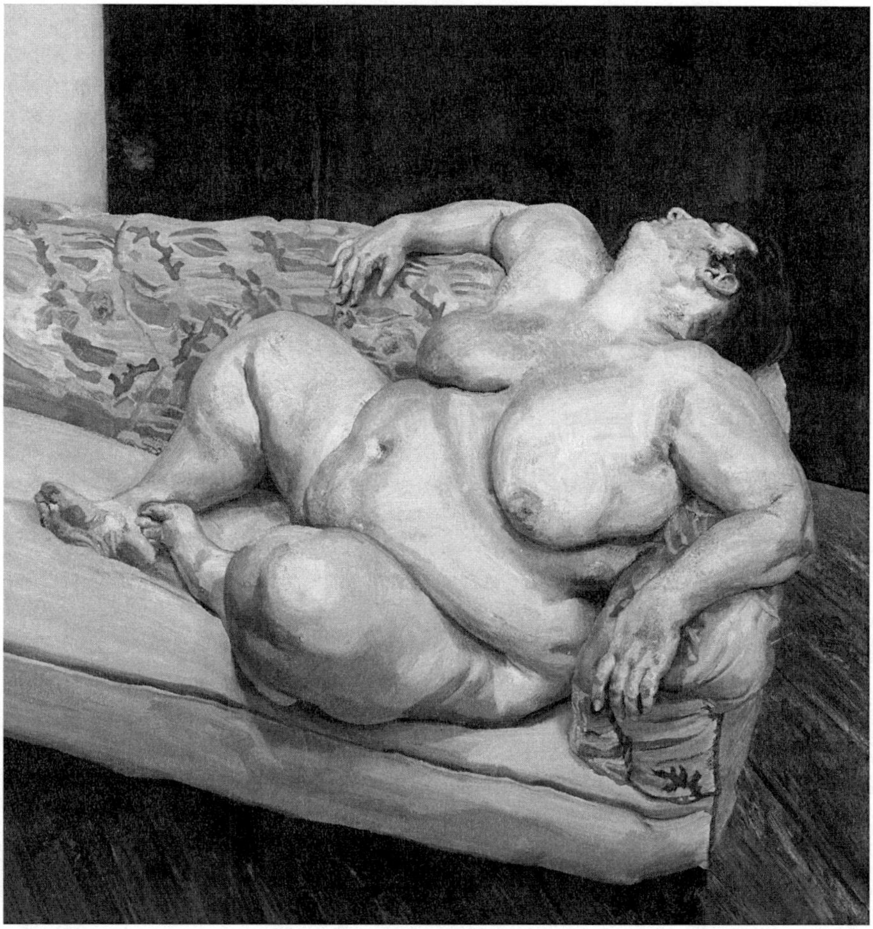

FIGURE 6.1 (see also Plate 12) Lucian Freud. *Benefits Supervisor Resting*. 1994. 63 × 59¼ in. Oil on canvas. Private Collection. © The Lucian Freud Archive/Bridgeman Images.

to expose on the skin what ought to have remained secret and hidden inside the body: his membranes become permeable. By using broken and dragged half-dried paint as similes for the enduring and aging skins of the human body, Lucian Freud simulates real skin (Elkins, 1999). Lucian Freud's nudes do not portray nudity, but rather nakedness; by exposing sexuality with an element of banality, they emphasize their reality.

In 1990, Lucian Freud met the giant Leigh Bowery, pictured in *Leigh Bowery (Seated)*, 1990 (Figure 6.2), at a show featuring the 300-pound performance artist at London's Antony d'Offay Gallery. Lucian Freud began painting the massive Bowery soon thereafter. Bowery posed for Lucian Freud dozens of times over the course of a few years, displaying his exquisite largeness and massive male power.

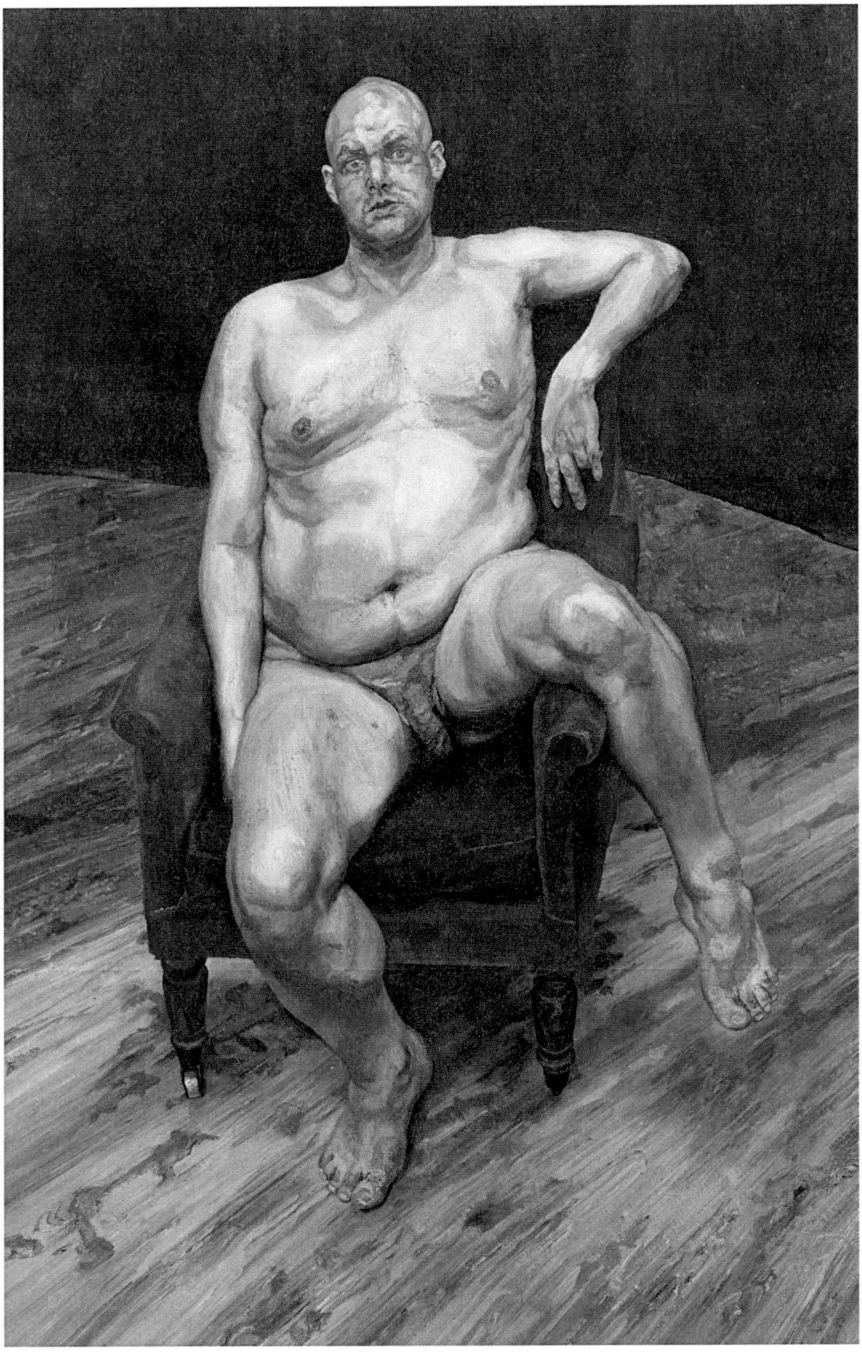

FIGURE 6.2 Lucian Freud. *Leigh Bowery (Seated)*. 1990. Oil on canvas. 96 × 72 in. / 243.75 × 183 cm. Collection of Mr. and Mrs. Richard C. Hedreen. © The Lucian Freud Archive/Bridgeman Images.

Bowery is a colossus, a corpulent man; but despite his size, which Lucian Freud reproduced sitting in his famous red chair in every detail, his body is also delicate and supple. The large canvas barely contains the overwhelming figure, and Lucian Freud paints him looking straight ahead with a challenging expression. He seems self-assured and very present. The affect Bowery and other sitters project seems at times to ooze out from the canvas into Freud's artist space and mingle with physicality, influencing the atmosphere and his composition. Toby Litt (2002) writes: "'Look at him [Bowery],' Freud seems to be saying, 'has anyone ever been more definitively there than him . . .?'" The viewer also takes in Bowery's more vulnerable and exposed fragility, however; unknown to Lucian Freud, Bowery was at the time gravely ill with AIDS.

Lucian Freud successfully brought his viewers along into the internal world of the people he portrays. The placidity of the pigment seems to fuse with the surface of the canvas, which simulates skin and flesh, allowing us to experience an evasive, psychological inwardness (Kimmelman, 1999). The permeable membrane is thus metaphorically a weakening of the skin-container's boundary, allowing the artist to connect himself to his sitters and viewers, a bond with which we can identify, "a sort of transference in the classic Freudian sense," says Feaver (2002b, p. 2).

In order to best analyze Lucian Freud's artwork, it is important to consider two artists who influenced him, namely René Magritte and Francis Bacon. Both Magritte and Bacon portray in their artwork two very different experiences and impressions of membrane containers.

In his painting *Attempting the Impossible*, 1928 (Figure 7.6, see also Plate 16), the Surrealist painter René Magritte symbolically tries to bring back or recreate his lost mother. The artist faces his model, his wife Georgette, whom he met and married at a very young age soon after his mother committed suicide by drowning. He hoped to internalize his mother in an attempt to mourn her. But due to this early violent trauma, the gradual process of introjection seems to have failed and is superseded by "instantaneous" and "hallucinogenic" incorporation, creating a surreal image (Abraham and Torok, 1994). The object inside the psyche is constructed as a "crypt," a term created by Abraham and Torok, which marks the refusal to mourn. The crypt then becomes like a "live burial of the love object" and is subsequently desired (Abraham and Torok, 1994). While Magritte uses the canvas to project the surface of his inner world, he seems unable or unwilling to penetrate beneath the surface; instead he compulsively conceals within this surface his powerful affects (Abarbanel, 1988). Thus, unlike Lucian Freud's, Magritte's membrane is not permeable at all. Magritte's work will be analyzed in greater detail in the next chapter.

Francis Bacon on the other hand believed that "Art is a method of opening up areas of feelings, rather than merely the illustration of an object, and paint should be the sensations of body not merely reproducing it." In Bacon's painting *Portrait of Isabel Rawsthorne* (1966), he portrays his friend and drinking companion Isabel. He was attracted to this beautiful woman, most likely because of her strong connection to Alberto Giacometti. In this image, the boundaries of Isabel's face dissolve altogether and the viewer witnesses a total dissolution of form. In order for Bacon to create her face, he seems to "unmake" her, and her interior spills over and dissolves into the exterior. Her skin provides an inefficient, superficial, deliquescent unity, filled with a substance that is more liquid than solid (Anzieu, 1989). In this example, the flooding of affects violently rips the skin-container.

Whereas Lucian Freud's solid but fleshy bodies have a permeable skin that keeps inside and outside separated but interrelated, Bacon's portrait of Isabel illustrates a confusion between inside and outside. Winnicott suggests that this demonstrates Bacon's wish to be seen and "mirrored" by another's gaze. To be seen and touched by one's mother signals to the infant that he exists. Looking into the mirror of a mother's face, the baby finds him or herself (Anzieu, 1989) as well, I would add, as the loving gaze of the mother. It seems thus that Bacon had to turn himself and his objects inside out in a wish to be seen and touched.

Lucian Freud was able to observe his sitters—and project himself onto them—as he gazed at them and studied their bodies for hundreds of hours. His emphasis on the flesh and skin-container provided him with necessary defensive boundaries, separating inside from outside without confusing them, opening and creating a safe space for real scrutiny and real intimacy.

Lucian Freud studied and painted the bodies of many different subjects, one of whom was his daughter with Bernadine Coverley, Esther, who was born in 1963. Lucian left her mother when Esther was three years old, after which Esther was raised by her single, "hippie" mother. Today, Esther is married with her own children, a successful author of five novels. Her first autobiographical novel, *Hideous Kinky* (1992), is based on her experience of a two-year-long trip to Morocco with her mother and sister Bella. The two words "hideous" and "kinky" became a mantra for the two sisters to protect themselves from the confusing sexual world of the adults around them, including their father's. Another book by Bella, *Sea House*, is dedicated to her father whom she views as a major inspiration for her work. She says: "[He] uses his life in his art and I always felt that was an extremely valid way to be creative."

Growing up rather poor without much stability, Esther remembers that she lived in 35 houses before she reached adolescence. She used to gaze up at the lit-up windows of other people's houses, wondering what it was like to have a stable home.

Esther was fortunate to develop a closer relationship to her father in her late teens and early adulthood, when Lucian began to paint her as a subject, including his pictures *Esther*, 1980 (Figure 6.3), and *Esther*, 1982–1983. In the first, the viewer witnesses the permeable membrane—expressed in a majestically tactile and flamboyantly physical fashion that plays with color and light—which allows the viewer to simultaneously see the outside and the inside. As we become witnesses to his never wavering gaze, Lucian tracks every inch of the surface of Esther's skin and flesh with distinct visual features. The artist's honestly stark but empathic presence for hours, days or even months in the same unchanged setting of his studio provided a container for closeness and intimacy between father and daughter that was most likely not experienced earlier in her life.

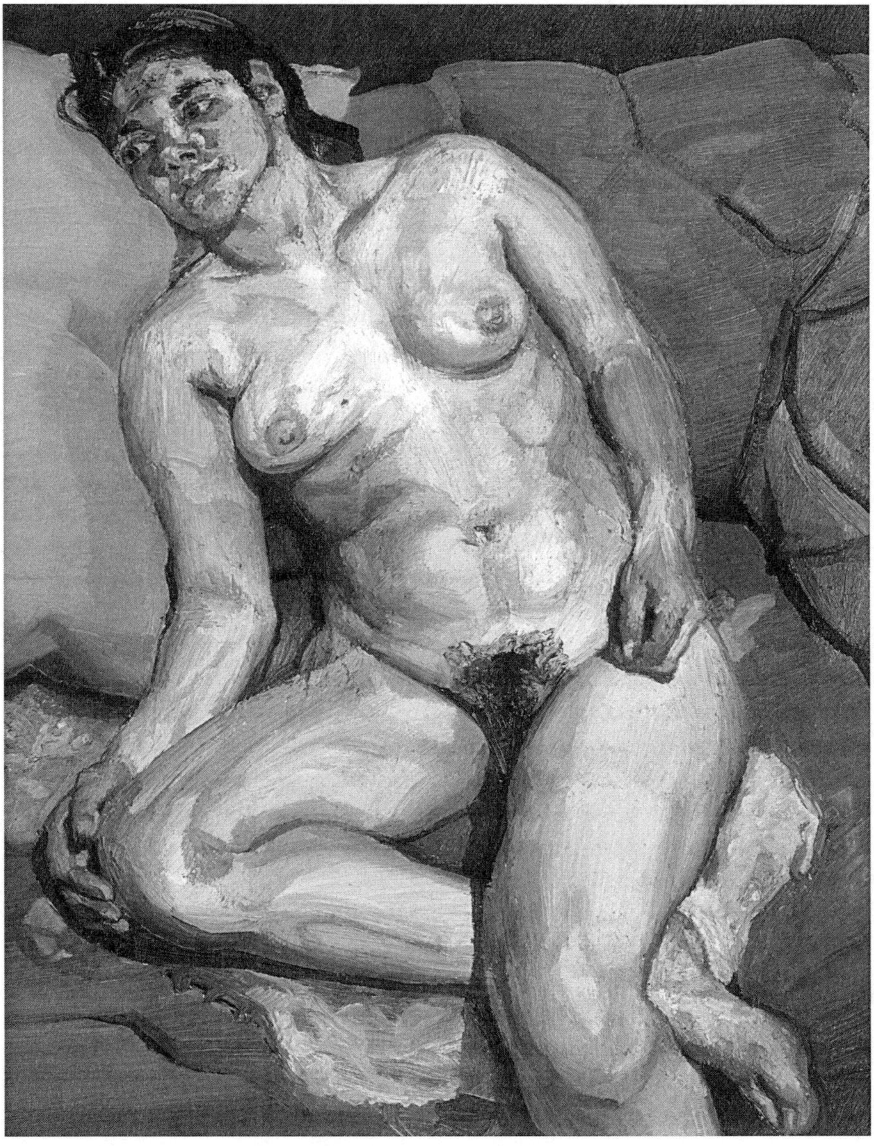

FIGURE 6.3 Lucian Freud. *Esther*. 1980. Oil on Canvas. 19¼ × 15¼ in. Private Collection. © The Lucian Freud Archive/Bridgeman Images.

It is this emotional container that Lucian Freud was able to provide to all of his sitters. As mentioned earlier, one may refer to this as a "second skin," a term created by Kogan (1988). This second skin was created through Lucian Freud's consistent, long-lasting presence and his full attention to every detail of his subjects. This emotional container held together different parts of his sitters' personalities. By providing this second skin, he was able to contain the emotions that poured out; like holding up an accepting but truthful mirror, he offered an opportunity to his sitters to internalize a real, but "good-enough" self image. His attention to the surface of their skins and to their flesh exposes their affective inner world, the "me" and the "not me," the togetherness and the potential loss of each of these relationships.

With each new, naked portrait, he allowed the viewer to perceive both life in the here and now, and to be confronted by the potential transience and mortality of the same luminous flesh and its relationship to life itself. In his images, a vitalizing and devitalizing tension is enacted again and again. Lucian Freud explained that he liked his subjects to be "tinged with death" and his colors to be "the colors of life" (Hughes, 2001). The viewer sees and experiences this push and pull. Lucian Freud left his little daughters Esther and Bella and others without consistent fatherly love and protection for many years, but then later he longed to paint them naked in the most intimate fashion for hundreds of hours. Lucian Freud might only have been able to tolerate closeness and intimacy in this transitional space of creation and in the strictly controlled setting of his studio. This creative space provided him with a defense against the overprotective, overly maternal object and was at the same time the creative space that made it possible for him to identify with his protective mother. The painted skin and flesh became the reflection of this highly ambivalent maternal encounter, an encounter on a most archaic level, absorbing the psyche as it is first reflected in the body ego.

In his short essay "On Transience" (1916), Sigmund Freud wrote that "The proneness to decay of all that is beautiful and perfect can, as we know, give rise to two different impulses in the mind. The one leads to the aching despondency felt by the young poet, while the other leads to rebellion. I could not see my way to debate the transience of all things, nor could I insist upon an exception in favor of what is beautiful and perfect. But I did dispute the pessimistic poet's view that the transience of what is beautiful involves any loss in its worth." Sigmund Freud points out to the poet Rainer Maria Rilke on their walk that even though we do know life is finite and beauty transient, being in the presence of life and nature allows us to fully partake of life and sometimes even experience time standing still.

In Lucian Freud's portrayal of skin and flesh, in its brutal banality coupled with sympathy, he disclosed an undisguised reality that brings us in touch not only with the transience of beauty but more importantly with the transience of life itself. He offers us a sight beyond the protection of the flesh and skin, deep into his models and into our own mortal souls. "I am only trying to do what I can't do," he told Michael Kimmelman (1999) as they strolled at midnight through the empty halls of

London's National Gallery for a nightcap with his two close "friends" Rembrandt and Cézanne.

It is true that he could not actually make his images come to life and have them walk out of the canvas. By extending himself as a second skin, however, as an empathic container, he demonstrated an uncanny ability to 'know' and 'share' his subjects and part of himself in his art—not unlike his grandfather Sigmund who had an uncanny ability to 'know' his patients and thus shared this 'knowledge' with his patients and with the world.

As a result of her husband's death in 1970, Lucian Freud's mother and namesake Lucie drifted into a deep, incapacitating depression. Freud painted *The Painter's Mother Resting I* (Figure 6.4, see also Plate 13) in 1975–1976. The painting *The Painter's Mother Reclining* (1982) is a culmination of several years of Freud's work with his mother that lasted through the mid-1980s. He took her to his studio five

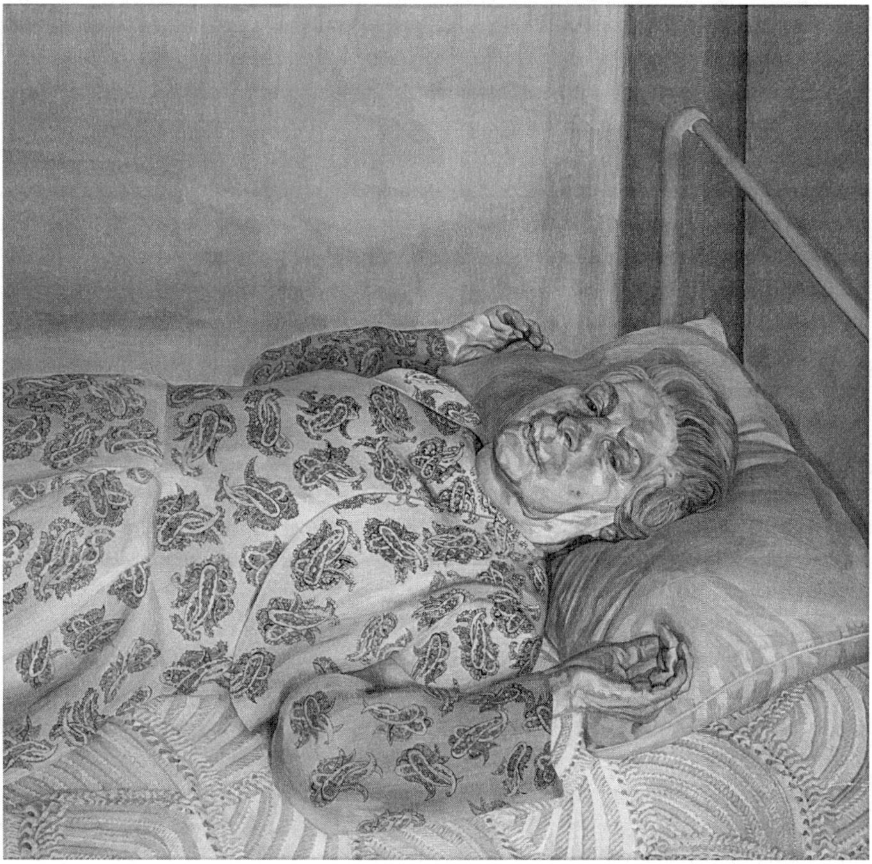

FIGURE 6.4 (see also Plate 13) Lucian Freud. *The Painter's Mother Resting I*. 1975–1976. Oil on canvas. 35½ × 35½ in. Private Collection. © The Lucian Freud Archive/Bridgeman Images

days a week to sit for him for a total of more than two thousand sessions. Lucian said that he tried to avoid his mother until he did these pictures of her. This might have something to do with his conscious fear of mourning, as he said to Sebastian Smee in an interview: "I hate mourning and all that kind of thing—I've never done it" (Smee, 2005, p. 37). Yet while painting the portrait of his mother on the canvas for so many years, he could tolerate mourning her.

In August 1989, Lucian Freud's mother died. She still sat for her son at the age of 90, walking up four flights of stairs. Earlier in life, she asked her son to give her painting lessons in an attempt to connect to him more. "She was so affectionately insistently maternal," Lucian Freud recalled, "and she preferred me" (Feaver, 2002a, p. 40). Lucian Freud's paintings of his mother are very sensitive, humane works. As viewers, we can empathize with the painter's expression of translucent skin, soft touch, the sensual light and delicate but real frankness, as well as with mother's vacant stare and regressive needs. His loose and fluid strokes of luminous skin and cloth provide an envelope, serving as a protective layer for his mother's and the viewer's psyche, providing him and us with a protective skin to tolerate loss and mourning. However, it is not the surface Lucian Freud is interested in, but a particular kind of realism or corporeality that can point to something deeper, allowing us to identify with a deeper kind of personhood, and reviving layers of his early memories of her.

Lucie eventually emerged from her despair. In the process of painting his mother, which was the final life portrait of her, Lucian Freud not only provided his mother with a new object with which to fuse, but also seemed to have repaired his own ambivalent relationship with her, allowing him to mourn her through his art making. Feelings shared with words can be very threatening, Lucian believed, but "Feeling can enter a painting in an unlimited degree" (Hughes, 2001).

In this painting we can see the delicacy of the skin on her hand and face also expresses the delicacy of their relationship. The viewer can feel the inwardness of his mother's look and know that mother does not see anything really of the outside world. Yet she seems relaxed and contained in her sadness, resting her head on a soft white pillow. She is not alone any longer and will never be alone again. Her beloved son found a way through his paintings to be loving and intimate, and at the same time distant enough to allow himself and the viewer to be moved by this very long and close encounter with her.

Most of Lucian Freud's pictures present a desire to pull the viewer in closer and at the same time keep him distant. Angus Cook (1993) asked Lucian Freud why he could only bring himself to paint pictures of his mother after his father's death when she became depressed. He answered, "She was no longer a threat to my privacy." As her favorite son, Lucian had to defend against too much closeness. This skin-container thus functions as a protective but permeable barrier for ambivalent feelings: it becomes a transitional object onto which the artist can safely project and store his ambivalent affects, neutralizing and preserving them. Skin and flesh turn into a receptacle through which the artist's internal life can be transformed and elaborated into a representational form. A similar ambivalence can be found in the paintings of Leigh Bowery and Bella Freud. While Lucien portrayed them, the canvas functioned as an acceptable defense against longing, guilt and mourning; these overwhelming emotions were projected onto and inside the skin that contains them.

As discussed earlier, the transitional object was initially introduced by Winnicott in reference to the child's first blanket, helping the little child to negotiate her mother's temporal absence. In this context, it is very interesting to understand Lucian Freud's own use and graphic depiction of dirty sheets and rags. He used hotel linen as rags for the very frequent wiping of his brushes and palette knives, and beginning in 1971 the stained rags began to appear in his paintings. Dirty cloth lay all around his workroom, first functioning as old bed sheets, then as rags stained with paints from previous paintings but not thrown away. These rags are reproduced on some of his canvases and, like his naked figures, they become subject matter and are thus memorialized. The artist states that the rags are "watery and wavy," and thus alive, similar to the clutched comfort blankets of a small child.

Although Lucian Freud painted most of the "rag pictures" between 1983 and 1990, the year when his first "rag pictures" appeared, 1971, was also when Lucian started to paint portraits of his severely depressed mother. The painting *Two Men in the Studio* (1987–1989) is a double portrait of the artist Angus Cook and Cerith Wyn Evans with rags and is another example where rags become an integral part of these portraits. In *Standing By the Rags*, 1988–1989 (Figure 6.5), we can feel the woman's weight against the pile of rags. If we include *Lying By the Rags*, 1989–1990 (Figure 6.6), as another example, all but one were completed in 1989, the year Lucian Freud's mother died. We can speculate that for Lucian, these 'rags' served as residues of security blankets, stained with memory traces of the past (Schwab, 2004). The artist attempted to discard them, but to no avail, because the impending loss of mother—first through depression and then through death—made it impossible. They become memorialized and thus kept alive forever on his most valuable canvases.

Lucian Freud was still very active in his eighties and painted every day. The last painting he made, *Portrait of the Hound*, 2011 (Figure 6.7, see also Plate 14), is also the last of 100 portraits that were exhibited in the National Portrait Gallery after his death. It depicts David Dawson on a large canvas, naked on a mattress, with Freud's whippet Eli stretched out to the side of him behind. David Dawson, himself a trained artist in his fifties, was Lucian's daily assistant, advisor, model and trusted friend for 20 years until Lucian's death in 2011. In that time David and Lucian did not miss a day of painting, seven days a week (Adams, 2012). As the painter grew older and frailer, David took care of him and it was due to his help that Lucian was able to continue to live in his house and paint on a daily basis. "I totally understood what was needed to make a painting, especially for him, so I could see how I could provide him with freedom that this could happen. It was a matter of being there for him, all the time," David Dawson remembered (Gayford, 2012). Lucian painted six or seven portraits of David during these 20 years (Adams, 2012). David also

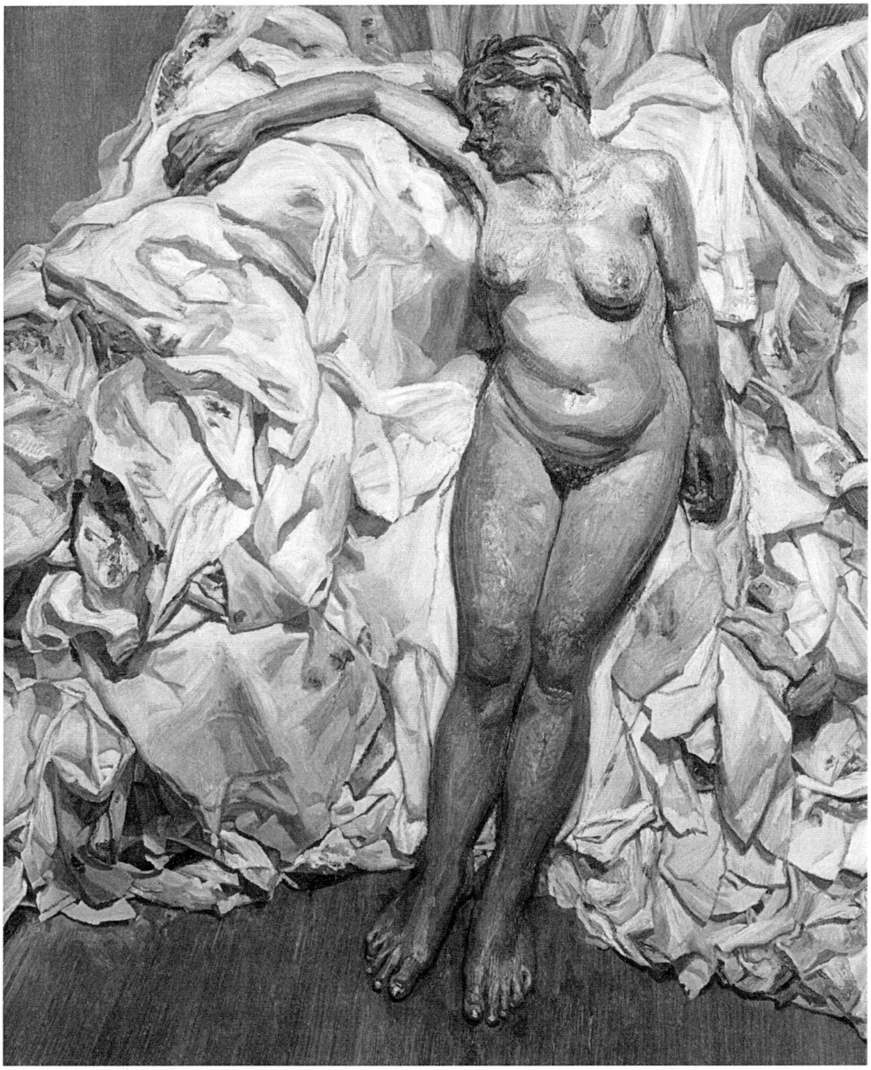

FIGURE 6.5 Lucian Freud. *Standing By the Rags*. 1988–1989. Oil on Canvas. 66¼ × 54½ in. Private Collection. © The Lucian Freud Archive/Bridgeman Images.

took photographs of Lucian working and documented the progression of works of art, as well as of the models that were sitting for the artist at a given time. He did this with great speed and care, as Lucian was known to be very bothered by flashing lights and resented any pictures taken of him. However he trusted David and thus he was able to visually record the artist at work. David Dawson was totally in tune with Lucian emotionally, not only in terms of the daily routine of the artist's work and relationships to his sitters, numerous affairs, and multi-layered family members, but also to the slow, delicate progress of each painting as it developed

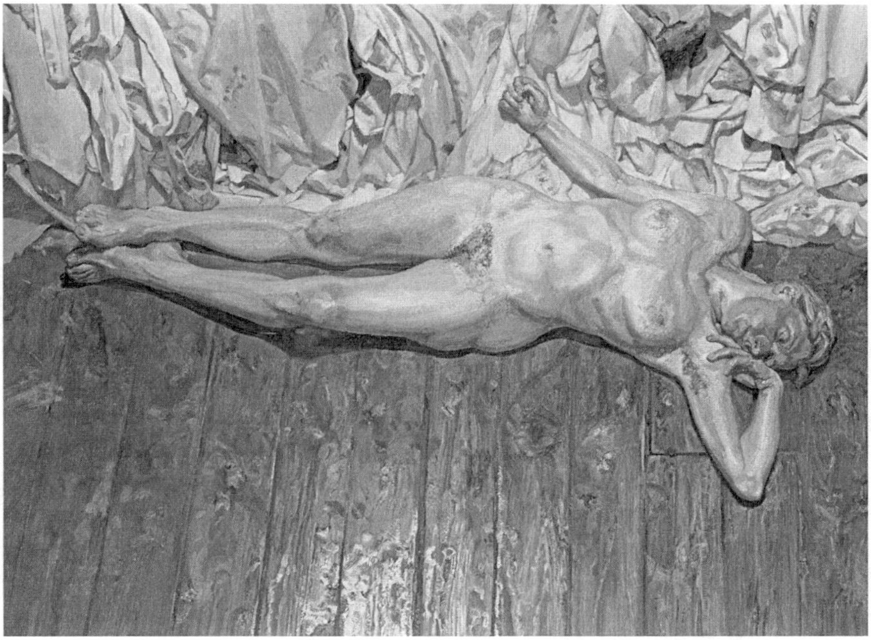

FIGURE 6.6 Lucian Freud. *Lying By the Rags*. 1989–1990. Oil on Canvas. 54½ × 72½ in. © Astrup Fearnley Museum of Modern Art, Oslo, Norway/Bridgeman Images.

over a long period of time. He was so close that Lucian would even take some of his suggestions about a particular painting; other than his life-long friend and artist Frank Auerbach, and Francis Bacon before him, David Dawson was the only person with this privilege. David was also very impressed by Lucian's great artistic talent, painting method, and intense work ethic. David and Lucian enjoyed each other's company and they shared a sense of intimacy and often laughed together. They ate breakfast and lunch together every day in one of two nearby restaurants, sitting at the same table each time.

David Dawson sat for Lucian Freud over three years for this last portrait, seven days a week, every morning from 8 a.m. to 12.30 p.m., naked on a mattress with his whippet Eli. David Dawson said "[Lucian Freud's] intimacy with those he loved was palpable and fearless . . . he gave you a wonderful feeling of 'at ease' of 'just being.' I felt enormous freedom in his company" (Barker, G. 2012). Both the dog and David were painted as equals, their bodies close and connected. David Dawson has said that both he and Lucian were the most relaxed in this last portrait of all the portraits they had done together over the years, a feeling that he knew other sitters had sometimes experienced as well. Towards the end, they both became aware that this portrait might not be finished before Lucian died. As Lucian Freud sickened, he could sometimes only paint for half an hour a day. In the end he almost completed *Portrait of the Hound*, but not quite. He very much wanted to finish it, and he worked on it until three weeks before he passed away. Time was essential in Lucian Freud's slow process: he recorded the changes over time in his sitter David, and unconsciously he tried to stretch out time as much as possible, realizing that his own deadline was approaching. When David Hockney sat for Lucian Freud for his portrait, he said that he felt that time was "layered" into Freud's pictures (Gayford, 2012). Lucian Freud was always totally focused on what he was working on, as he wanted to create the best painting possible. The constant work kept him going, and as he got older "it was what got him out of bed, to pick up a paint brush and make another mark, make another decision. So that is what he did . . ." (Gayford, 2012). In his will, Lucian Freud bequeathed his house and studio in Kensington to David Dawson, as well as plenty of money. Freud occasionally voiced to his friends concerns that he was too demanding of David Dawson, keeping him from his own artistic work. Lucian's great generosity to his former assistant and friend now gives Dawson the ability and means to pursue his own artistic career without distraction, a caring reciprocity of sorts. Dawson moved into Lucian Freud's house and studio as soon as he accomplished the repairs (Adams, 2012).

This last portrait shows an affectionate, commanding portrait of the naked David looking up to Lucian with his dog, in soft and gentle colors. Lucian Freud had two titles for it: *Davidscape* and *Portrait of the Hound*, but the latter won out. According to his friend Sarah Howgate, Lucian Freud had said that he knew David Dawson better than anyone else. He told friends that David had been "the most consecrate model, they shared a mutual understanding, a respect for one another and a love of painting" (Brown, 2011).

I suggest that the artist David Dawson's unobtrusive, competent, supportive and warm manner and close friendship over the last 20 years of Lucian Freud's life comforted him and made up for the lack of closeness he experienced from his father. Like Lucian, but unlike Lucian's father Ernst, David had an ability to tolerate and enjoy intense emotional intimacy in the protective space of the studio, with the permeable membranes of the painted skin of the sitter on the canvas in between the two. Painting allowed Lucian to feel the present time even more intensely, even as the end of his life was fast approaching. In these moments of close encounters between David and Lucian during long sitting routines, time must have been experienced as standing still for both David and the artist. A few of Lucian Freud's children described a similar sensation of enveloping closeness when they sat naked for their father in their late adolescence and early adulthood, and it allowed them to make a close emotional tie in the present that was lacking in the past when they were small children and their father was mostly absent. His relationship with David Dawson was different, however, as their love and respect for each other and their shared knowledge of painting was reciprocated between equals of sorts. It allowed them to change roles over time as the "son" became the "father" and the "father" became the "son." When younger, David cared for the vigorous artist Lucian Freud, helped him with his canvases, colors, exhibitions and meetings with his lovers, family members and sitters. As the artist grew older and later more frail, he also lovingly cared for the sick and eventually dying Lucian.

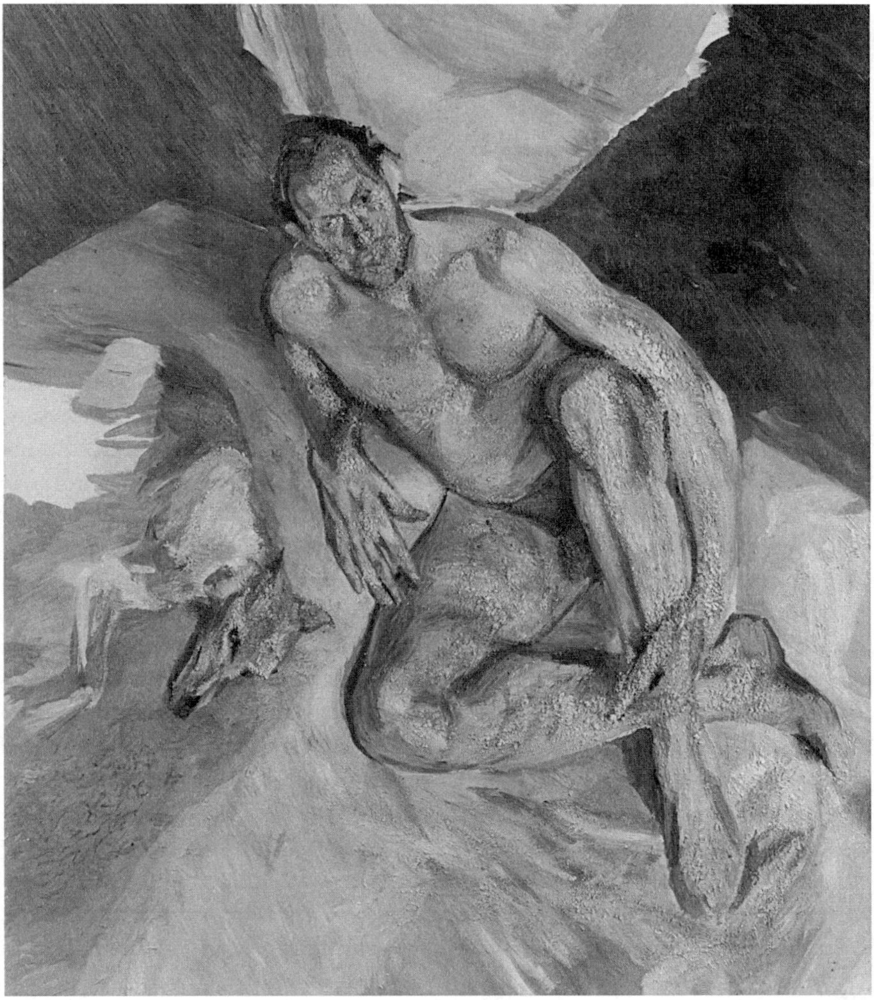

FIGURE 6.7 (see also Plate 14) Lucian Freud. *Portrait of the Hound*. 2011. Oil on canvas. 1.58 × 1.38 m. Private Collection. © The Lucian Freud Archive/Bridgeman Images.

During his last year, David moved into Lucian's house and studio and woke up every hour to go into Lucian's room to move the ailing Lucian in his bed to avoid bedsores. David had a great ability to tolerate and enjoy this close emotional intimacy and reverie with the artist and they were not afraid to mourn together his impending death and with it the end of their time together. It allowed Lucian the freedom and joy to continue painting and be happy with David in a creative play space, reminiscent of the early space and time between mother and/or father and baby in the everlasting present time and space, called *Davidscape*. The canvas in between them allowed for an intense, but non-threatening longing for a fusion with the Other while simultaneously protecting them from identification with the threatening aspects of death.

Mourning the illusionary timelessness

Lucian Freud's depiction of flesh in its skin-container became a permeable membrane, reflecting the mirroring strokes of the paintbrush displaced onto the form of the naked body. Freud's extension of empathic envelopment through his consistent presence in a never-changing setting and through his looking and being looked at for long periods of time extended a "second skin" to his sitters. This permeable membrane, the second skin and the depiction of the rags—transitional objects that are stained by the past—helped the artist and his viewers to mourn the illusionary timelessness that we consider life to be. The rags become monuments in themselves to time passed—abject, discarded, but also sacred and sublime. In both the painted objects and the rags, time seems arrested and halts the viewer's gaze (Bond, 2001). These transitional objects help us to bridge past and present time, and thus they become a temporary defense against identification with timelessness, with death. Lucian Freud allowed his viewers to mourn with him the transience of beauty, their changing bodies and their accustomed gratification, but at the very end he allowed his viewers to mourn the ultimate corporal loss—the loss of life itself. Feelings of loss are followed by longing: a longing for the transitional phase, for the supportive, protective creative play space between mother and child, and for the sense of time that was part of that space. Lucian Freud often talked about the need for emotions in a painting, not fervid expression, but rather longing, risk and compassion (Feaver, 2002a). "I've become increasingly ambitious with age. It's a fascination with the difficulties. I don't like many hours to pass without working. . . . It is not death that I fear, it is my work going off."

References

Abarbanel, A. (1988) A note on Magritte's use of the shroud. In *Psychoanalytic perspectives on art*, Vol. 3. Hillsdale, NJ: The Analytic Press, pp. 171–176.

Abraham, N. and Torok, M. (1994) *The shell and the kernel*, Vol. 1. Chicago: University of Chicago Press.

Adams, T. (2012) David Dawson: "Lucian chose people who were punctual." The Guardian/The Observer, November 2, 2012

Anzieu, J. (1989) *The skin ego*. New Haven, CT: Yale University Press.

Barker, G. (2012) Freedom in his company: David Dawson's friendship with the late Lucian Freud. *Sotheby's* magazine, July 24, 2012

Bick, E. (1968) The experience of the skin in early object-relations. *Journal of Psychoanalysis*, 49: 484–486.

Bond, T. (2001) Permeable membranes. Spatial Culture Conference, University of Newcastle. http://home.iprimus.com.au/painless/space/tonybond.html

Bowery, L. (1993) *Lucian Freud: Recent drawings and etchings*. New York: Matthew Mark Gallery.

Brown, M. (2011) Lucian Freud's final work to be shown in 2012 National Portrait Gallery show 20 August, 2011. The Guardian News Media Limited.

Cook, A. (1993) *Lucian Freud: Recent drawings and etchings*. New York: Matthew Marks Gallery.

Elkins, J. (1999) *What painting is*. London and New York: Routledge.

Feaver, W. (2002a) *Lucian Freud*, catalogue. London: Tate Publishing.

Feaver, W. (2002b) Seeing through the skin. *Guardian Weekend*, May 18.

Feaver, W. (2011) Lucian Freud and William Feaver: Conversation, November 1992. In *Lucian Freud*. New York: Rizzoli.

Freud, L. (1954) Some thoughts on painting. *Encounter*, 3, 1: 23–24.

Freud, S. (1905) Three essays on the theory of sexuality. *Standard edition of the complete psychological works of Sigmund Freud* (Vol. 7: 123–230). London: The Hogarth Press, 1953.

Freud, S. (1916) On transience. *The standard edition of the complete psychological works of Sigmund Freud* (Vol. 14: 303). London: The Hogarth Press, 1981.

Freud, S. (1919) The uncanny. *The standard edition of the complete psychological works of Sigmund Freud* (Vol. 17: 219). London: The Hogarth Press, 1955.

Freud, S. (1923) The ego and the id and other works. *The standard edition of the complete psychological works of Sigmund Freud* (Vol. 19: 1–308). London: The Hogarth Press, 1961.

Gayford, M. (2012) Portrait of the artists: Lucian Freud's final painting. Telegraph Media Group Limited, 2014.

Gowing, L. (1984) *Lucian Freud*. London: Thames & Hudson.

Greig, G. (2013) *Breakfast with Lucian*. New York: Farrar, Straus and Giroux.

Hoffer, W. (1950) Development of the body ego. *Psychoanalytic Study of the Child*, 5: 18–23.

Hughes, R. (1987/89) *Lucian Freud*. London: Thames & Hudson.

Hughes, R. (2001) *Lucian Freud paintings*. London: Thames & Hudson.

Kimmelman, M. (1999) *Portraits*. New York: The Modern Library.

Kogan, I. (1988) The second skin. *International Review of Psycho-Analysis*, 15: 251–260.

Levinas, E. (1998) *Otherwise than being: Or beyond essence* (A. Lingis, Trans.). Pittsburg, PA: Duquesne University Press.

Litt, T. (2002) Lucian Freud. In *Modern painters* (Autumn). Barcelona: Fundacio La Caixa, pp. 134–136.

Lampert, C. (1993) *Lucian Freud: Recent work*. London: Whitechapel Art Gallery.

Mellor, D. A. (2002) *Interpreting Lucian Freud*. London: Tate Publishing.

Schwab, G. (2004) Verbal communication.

Smee, S. (2005) *Lucian Freud, 1996–2005*. London: Jonathan Cape.

Smee, S. (2007) *Lucian Freud*. Los Angeles: Taschen.

Smee, S. (2009) *Lucian Freud: Beholding the animal*. London and Los Angeles: Taschen.

Winnicott, D.W. (1965) *The maturational process and the facilitating environment*. New York: International University Press.

Winnicott, D.W. (1971) *Playing and reality*. New York: Basic Books.

7

RENÉ MAGRITTE

Attempting the impossible—tracing the lost object

This chapter will focus on a leitmotif in René Magritte's art and how it relates to the trauma of his mother's suicide when he was an adolescent. In Magritte's work, trauma is not translated into a metaphor, it remains literal. While reworking adolescent trauma is but one factor in Magritte's expansive work, this chapter will demonstrate how it influences the content, tone, style and technique of many of his most famous paintings. In an attempt to defend himself against past injuries, the painter used not only defenses like isolation of affects, intellectualization, and the banning of unconscious production, but he also denied the past and the future, thus suspending time altogether. As Magritte himself said, "I detest my past and anyone else's. I detest resignation, patience, professional heroism and obligatory beautiful feelings . . ." (René Magritte, cited in Torczyner, 1979, p. 23). He hoped that the act of freezing time would protect both himself and the viewer from being re-traumatized by reality.

As I will show in my interpretations, art-making—with its repetitions in content, image and pictorial intimacy—creatively linked Magritte to the visual archives of his trauma, and provided a psychic connection to the image of his dead mother and the potential for transformation.

Biographical details

René Magritte was born on November 21, 1898, the eldest of three sons in a petit bourgeois home. His brother Raymond was born in 1900 and his youngest brother, Paul, in 1902. They lived in the Belgian province of Hainault, where most people either earned a living at the local quarry or by working in one of the glass factories. The Magritte family moved frequently in René's first 12 years, after which time they finally settled in Brussels. René's father, Léopold Magritte, owned and managed a tailor's shop, while his mother Régina worked as a milliner, or hat maker. Over time Magritte's parents were able to sustain a degree of affluence, and provided a relatively strong education for all three of their sons.

After one of the family's several moves, Magritte's mother developed emotional problems and began to suffer from depression, which culminated in several suicide attempts. Concerned about his wife's safety, Magritte's father arranged for his wife to sleep in one of her son's rooms so that the lightest sleeper in the house could keep watch over her. At other times, her husband locked her inside her own room to protect her from herself.

One night, René's young brother discovered that his mother was missing and alerted the rest of the family. It is recorded that they saw footsteps leading to the local Sambre River, and that the footprints stopped at the bridge. A search brought no answers, but two days later their mother's body washed up from the river. The family laid her body out in the house, according to religious practice, before burying her. Magritte recounted the tragedy to his friend and biographer Louis Scutenaire: "They found her nightgown wrapped around her face. It was never known whether she had covered her eyes with it, [so] as not to see the death she had chosen, or whether the head had been veiled in that way by the swirling current" (Scutenaire, 1947, pp. 71–72). René was 14 years old at the time of his mother's death.

Magritte's response to the death of his mother at this young age was repressed mourning or denial, a common response in children and adolescents who have lost a parent (Wolfenstein, 1969). Magritte later claimed that his only reaction to his mother's death was a jarring sense of pride in his new identity as "the son of a dead woman." Many years later in 1956, Magritte wrote, "I, too, have a great many bitter memories, but I shall never understand what is meant by 'repentance'; I have the feeling only of remorse" (Meuris, 1991, p. 16).

When Magritte was a young boy, he frequently played with a friend in a nearby cemetery. One day, after climbing out of an underground pipe, he came upon an artist with his easel who sought inspiration from the old graves, the beautiful trees and the peaceful atmosphere. It seems that at this time, Magritte decided that he wanted to become an artist, too. Magritte sometimes used to lie down in a coffin when he visited his friend, a carpenter. Like other Surrealist and Modernist artists, such as Salvador Dalí, Magritte was inspired by themes of death and dying. But for him, the cemetery motif, and the link between death and art were thus foundational at the very start of his artistic career, a foundation unsurprisingly reinforced by his mother's suicide into a major preoccupation in Magritte's work. Perhaps Magritte was not only affected by the acceptable new motifs of death, but unconsciously reenacting his early trauma and trying to identify with his dead mother.

In 1916, when Magritte was 18 years old, he actively began his career in art. He enrolled for two years at the Royal Académie des Beaux Arts in Brussels, after which René and his wife Georgette moved to Paris for three years. Between Brussels and Paris, they befriended likeminded artists such as Filippo Marinetti, Theo van Doesburg, Erik Satie and Tristan Tzara, as well as the Surrealists André Breton, Paul Éluard, Hans Arp, Joan Miró and Dalí. In 1919, Magritte began exhibiting his work and then in 1924, after selling his first painting, he devoted himself fully to art. In 1923, he saw a reproduction of Giorgio de Chirico's 1914 *Song of Love* and by 1925 he had begun to incorporate de Chirico's absurd conjunction of unrelated objects, leading to the painting of Magritte's first successful Surrealist picture in 1926 (Barron, 2006).

In 1928, Magritte's father died at the early age of 58. Georgette later reported that her husband did not reveal any feelings related to the loss of his father. Two years later, René and Georgette Magritte returned to Brussels from Paris, and by 1937 René's work started to be shown internationally. Before his death in 1965, at the age of 69, he saw a major retrospective exhibition of his work at the Museum of Modern Art in New York City. He influenced several generations of modern and contemporary artists who loved his provocative juxtapositions and style and who also bought his pictures, such as Robert Rauschenberg, Jasper Johns, Roy Lichtenstein, Jeff Koons, Andy Warhol, Robert Gober and others.

The non-conformist Surrealist and the power of the shadow of the object

In 1934, André Breton published a pamphlet entitled *Qu'est-ce que le Surréalisme?* (*What is Surrealism?*) with René Magritte's drawing *The Rape* (discussed below) on its cover, evidence of Breton's close relationship with Magritte. In this pamphlet, it becomes apparent that Surrealism brought together theories of psychoanalysis, language and sexuality, and proposed new ideas for social change (Greeley, 1992). Accordingly, Breton stated in his manifesto that the purpose of Surrealism was to liberate the mind from Western rationalism and go beyond restrictive boundaries of reality. The revolutionary aspects of Breton's movement focused on the release of interior reality into the external realm.

However, Magritte was a non-conformist even within the Surrealist movement. He explicitly opposed self-expression and objected to any personal or psychological consideration of his work (Hammacher, 1985). Unlike many of his contemporaries, such as Max Ernst, he believed in realism and denied the psychological conception of art; for example, he disliked using automatic writing and free association for artistic purposes and rejected the notion that dreams could be used as an inspiration for his paintings. Magritte wrote, "The word 'dream' is often misused concerning my paintings . . . If 'dreams' are concerned in this context, they are very different from those we have while sleeping. It is a question rather of self willed 'dreams,' in which nothing is [as] vague as those feelings one has when escaping into dreams . . . ! 'Dreams' are not intended to make you sleep, but wake you up" (Gablik, 1985 p. 71).

Magritte rejected the notion of dreams serving as an artistic jumpstart, and he kept up his defenses until late in his life when he wrote, "One would have to be ignorant of what I paint in order to associate [it] with a naive or learned symbolism. On the other hand, what I paint implies no superiority of the invisible over the visible, the latter is sufficiently rich to form the poetic language which evokes the mystery of the invisible and the visible" (cited after Meuris, 1991, p. 29).

After seeing an exhibition of Magritte's art, the Surrealist Max Ernst wrote, "Magritte neither sleeps nor remains awake. He illuminates. He violates methodically, without laughing" (Ernst, 1970, p. 328). This comment has particular significance when considering Georgette's memory of her husband René: "When René slept over at his friend Eduard James' home in 1937, he had nightmares. He saw ghosts in his dreams who tugged on his legs. He woke up to his own shrieks and dared not to return back to his bed for the rest of the night" (Hammacher, 1985). I would like to argue that these ghosts are the ghosts of his dead mother, split off from his conscious memory but surfacing frequently and unconsciously in his dreams and creative productions. Sleeping over at a friend's house away from his wife triggered his unconscious fear of not being vigilant enough to protect his mother from suicide, and thus his feelings of responsibility for her death. It is her ghost, the shadow of the object, that haunted him that night, in his dreams, and in most of his artwork.

In order to deny the productions of the unconscious, as many ghosts from his past might reappear in his paintings, Magritte viewed himself instead as a realistic painter who faithfully reproduced objects and people of everyday life. In truth, however, he combined objects and figures in unexpected, unusual ways reminiscent of the condensation process present in the production of dreams, which often turns traditional logic inside out and reveals secondary meanings.

It is thus not surprising that Magritte had to consciously deny the importance of his adolescent trauma; consequently, he resented people who viewed his images as symbols. He said, "If one looks at a thing with the intention of trying to discover what it means, one ends up no longer seeing the thing itself but thinking of the question that has been raised." He continued, "The interpretation of an image is denial of its mystery, the mystery of the visible" (Sylvester, 1997, p. 207). Magritte saw himself as an intellectual realistic painter who said that he painted *thought*, "objectifying the subjective" (Meuris, 1991, p. 27). He was rather solitary, very orderly and organized, as his realistic style demonstrates. His wife described him as a melancholic man, given to ennui and boredom. "The success or hatred his work aroused would interest him a short time; then he would sink into his usual mood and bizarre affliction of ennui, finding every enterprise absurd . . ." (Gablik,1985).

Magritte painted his objects very precisely, in a hyper-realistic style, without formalistic ambiguity or spontaneity. He controlled his style in such a way that the viewer cannot detect movement or action. The narrative function seems to be "frozen in time" (Rose, 1989). Even distinctions in time and gravity seem to collapse, as objects appear still and suspended in time. This suspension in time is another of Magritte's unconscious attempts to defend himself against early childhood injuries and losses, and to protect himself against new insights and thus new injuries in the present. Accordingly, his wife Georgette mentioned that her husband never spoke about the past or the future. In an attempt to protect himself he refused to make plans, even for the immediate future (Viederman, 1987).

When one studies the content of some of his paintings, one begins to recognize that the artist seems obsessed with blocked vision, blindness and invisibility. For example, he often eliminates the face of the subject in his works, perhaps in an unconscious attempt to not 'face' something. Magritte needed to veil faces in order to *not see*; he blocked vision in all kind of ways in his art in order to conceal and not face the concrete evidence of his adolescent trauma. Additionally, Magritte covers his faces; he turns the heads away, closes the eyes or makes the images transparent (Handler Spitz, 1994). He conceals faces with cloth or places objects, such as apples, flowers or birds, in front of them. By hiding the face and the eyes, Magritte might be alluding to the phenomenon that from the painted subject's perspective, the subject is invisible (for he/she cannot see and therefore feels absent), but from the viewer's perspective, the subject is merely partially covered and therefore present.

By painting both the present and the absent, Magritte illustrates that images can be simultaneously both alive and infused with death. Moreover, Magritte repeatedly surprises the viewer with his unexpected, unusual compositions. He masterfully makes important objects appear small and insignificant in his works, while making small ones loom large. The familiar becomes strange, and the strange suddenly seems very familiar. Magritte demonstrates that the act of observing is inherently different from the act of experiencing, and that art is different from life. Magritte wanted to make sure that we, the spectators, look *at* his images rather than *into* them. Sigmund Freud points out in his work "The Uncanny" (1919) that when the symbol takes over the full function of the thing it symbolizes and when the imaginary appears as the real, then the distinction between imagination and reality is erased and an uncanny feeling is produced.

Trauma and post-traumatic reactions can create a state of disorientation and agitation that can bring forth a powerful response. Magritte remained possessed and haunted by his past, whose ghosts and shrouds resist definition. His pictorial narrative of trauma often seems vacant of significant affect; instead he utilizes humor, intellectualization and disembodiment as a defense technique to divert his thoughts from the emotional content of his traumatic memory. Magritte contradicts the expectation of our perceptions as spectators. Thus we, the viewers, walk away from Magritte's paintings with feelings of ambiguity, recognizing that our perception deceives us. Sometimes we are even unable to distinguish between what is inside and outside or, more radically, our vision is blocked altogether. In this way we, as spectators, identify with the defense of the artist, who does not want to see beyond but, at the same time, cannot put the past behind. The narrative function becomes a missing element (Rose, 1989). This evokes a nameless feeling of terror and fear in the viewer (Sylvester, 1997).

Magritte's attempt to mourn his mother

According to Dominick LaCapra (1999), in the event of a trauma, the conversion from absence to loss depends on the assumption that there once existed a satisfying unity and security with the primary object (mother) that later becomes contaminated and thus lost. There is not much literature about Magritte's mother, aside from her severe depression and several attempts to commit suicide until she ultimately succeeded. Based on the information available about Magritte's mother, we cannot assume that a satisfying attachment with his mother had taken place and Magritte's father passed his responsibility to watch out for and protect his wife on to his three young sons. In Magritte's artistic output, absence is inherently ambivalent, as it produces anxiety, shock and anger, but it also engenders empowerment and infinite ways of displacement through creative means, a most potent tool of defense. While Magritte was able to represent or illustrate his trauma formally, the emotional content of the trauma is totally absent or even split off.

In this context, it is interesting to note that Magritte's mother worked as a milliner, a hat maker. When we think of Magritte's paintings, his bowler hats come to mind, as they were reproduced in multiple forms in his paintings. Magritte's bowler hat has become a symbol in popular culture. Is this a symbol for the dead and once productive mother, or does it represent the socially upward-moving father who endangered his wife's mental health and thus engendered ambivalence? Or perhaps the hat is a symbol of Magritte's need for paternal identification? René Magritte loved his own bowler hats, as one can see in multiple photographs in which he is featured wearing his three-piece suit with hat, unlike his contemporary artist-friends.

In his painting *Memory* (1948), the wound at the temple of the antique-looking statuesque head is still bleeding, illustrating that Magritte's trauma from the very distant past is still painful in the present. As Martha Wolfenstein (1973) suggests, the trauma persists in his art like an "ever bleeding wound." Magritte often juxtaposes *grelots*, the French word for old-fashioned small, round bells, with figures or objects associated with his mother. David Sylvester (1997) suggests that these bells were worn by the horses that pulled the carriages at Madame Magritte's funeral cortege.

Similarly, the bilboquets or giant balusters commonly used to decorate table legs or wooden chess pieces were also central motifs in Magritte's art, and seem to stand as a principal symbol of his mother and himself. A bilboquet is an old-fashioned wooden toy with a string attached that always lands on its feet, similar to the artist. In French, the term *bilboquet* describes a person who is psychologically unstable, and thus Magritte may have utilized this image to symbolically refer both to his depressed mother and to himself.

Magritte used compulsive repetitions in his images in an attempt, most likely, to defend against overwhelming affects and to control fragmentation and protect himself from his fear of a breakdown. The trauma is actually never really represented, but rather the structure of his traumatic feelings are translated into form or even enacted on a strictly formalistic level. These intense repetitions in content, style and form, appear to the viewer as a way of acting out, since they avoid addressing the loss directly and emotionally. The artist thoughtfully employs the surreal technique and its content to enshroud and anesthetize the theme of loss, using an impersonal, intellectual discourse of loss. The themes of the past reappear again and again but only as a haunting presence devoid of personal meaning.

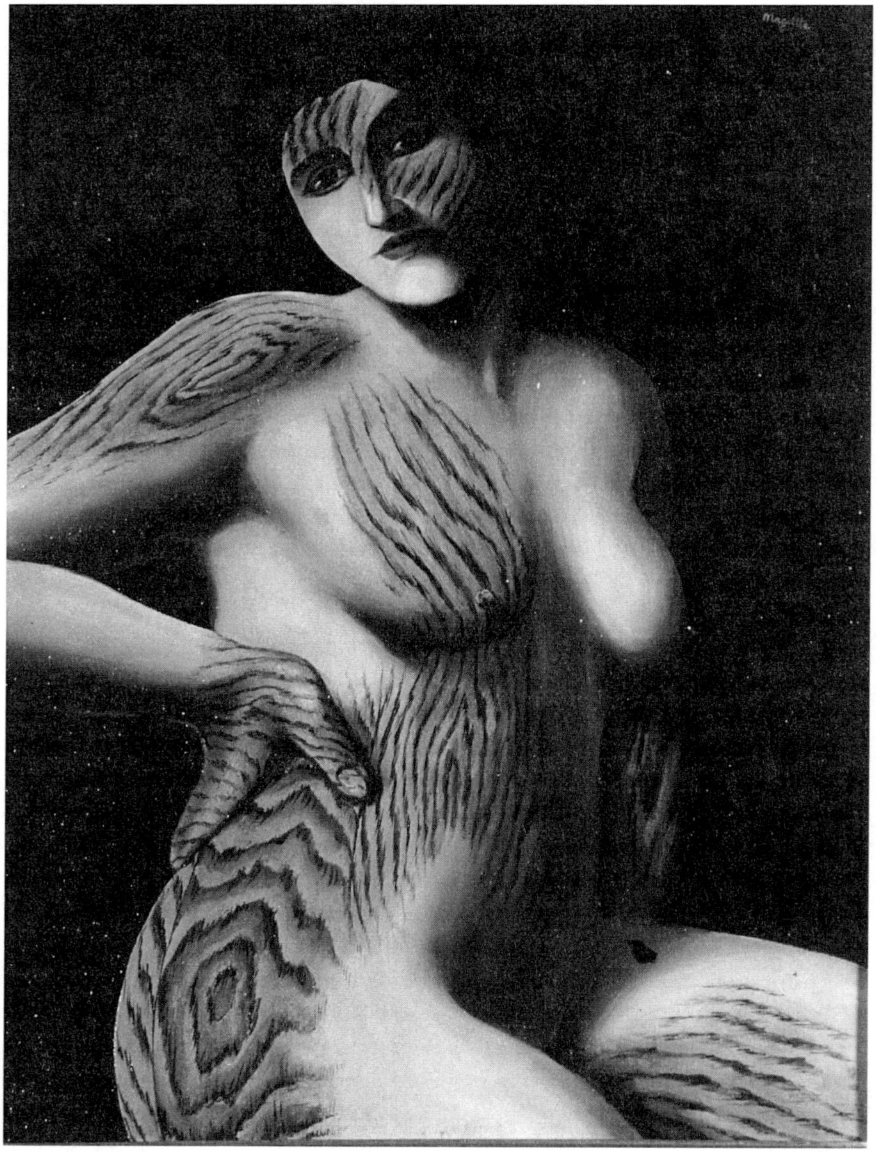

FIGURE 7.1 René Magritte. *Découverte* [*Discovery*]. 1927. Oil on canvas. 65 × 50 cm. Private Collection, Brussels, Belgium. © 2014 Herscovici/Artist Rights Society (ARS), New York. Photo Credit: Banque d'Images, ADAGP/Art Resource, NY.

In the picture *Discovery*, 1927 (Figure 7.1), the viewer sees a beautiful nude whose skin or flesh changes to wood before his eyes. A. M. Hammacher (1985) notes that Sigmund Freud saw a connection between wood and the idea of the mother. Freud recognized that the name "madera" the Spanish word for "wood," derives from the words "mater," and "mother." Perhaps through this painting, the artist shares his real childhood experience, namely watching his mother turn symbolically into wood, as she became unresponsive and uncommunicative in her depressed state, as his beloved mother withdrew from reality (Gedo, 1994). The artist projects his longings for his dead mother, but his fantasies then violently intrude and make the love object wooden. Magritte's biographer describes that the artist shared with him one of his earliest childhood memories. He recalled a large wooden chest or cupboard that stood next to his cradle. Perhaps this chest is a screen memory of his unavailable, depressed "wooden" mother who ended up in a closed chest, a coffin after her suicide.

Magritte's use of wood in this painting reminds the viewer of the implicit connection between wood and fire, suggested by the frame-like patterning of the wood grain as it consumes the flesh of the nude. Fire, an image Magritte often portrays in his art, not only elicits the idea of heat, warmth and comfort, but also excitement, danger, rage and ultimately destruction.

Magritte's painting *Homage to Mack Sennett* (1937) visualizes the sexual feeling that can be aroused when we see the clothing of someone we love, emphasized by the breasts protruding from the thin, sheer nightgown. Additionally, the clothing appears to belong to the dead, eliciting memories. In this painting, a perfectly ordinary wardrobe is opened, and a life full of promise is viewed in the woman's narrow dress, which both conceals and reveals an atmosphere of intimacy. All that remains after René's mother dies is her gown, devoid of a physical body, but still full of the fantasies of an adolescent boy and cravings for adult intimacy.

The *Philosophy of the Bedroom*, 1948 (Figure 7.2, see also Plate 15), portrays a nightgown hung on a hanger, The viewer sees a white, sleeveless nightgown suspended on a cloth hanger in front of the grained wood panels of the wardrobe. Emerging from this lifeless garment are two vibrant rosy nippled breasts and a view of the pubic hair. Like the picture *Homage to Mack Sennett* completed in 1937, this painting seems to play on the inanimate and animate, on the sexual aspects of both life and death. Like *The Rape*, this painting portrays a reoccurring image associated with the event of his mother's suicide and the recovery of her naked body from the river. According to Ellen Handler Spitz (1994), the title of this painting refers to a work by the Marquis de Sade describing a series of mutilations and assaults on an aging mother. The image alludes to the title's content and thus relates to the artist's highly ambivalent feelings towards his depressed and thus emotionally absent mother, unconsciously projecting hate and aggression, while highlighting the spooky seductiveness the painter still remembers and struggles with from his adolescent trauma.

The following quote from Magritte (1964) describes well the picture *The Lovers*, 1928 (Figure 7.3): "What I paint implies no superiority of the invisible over the

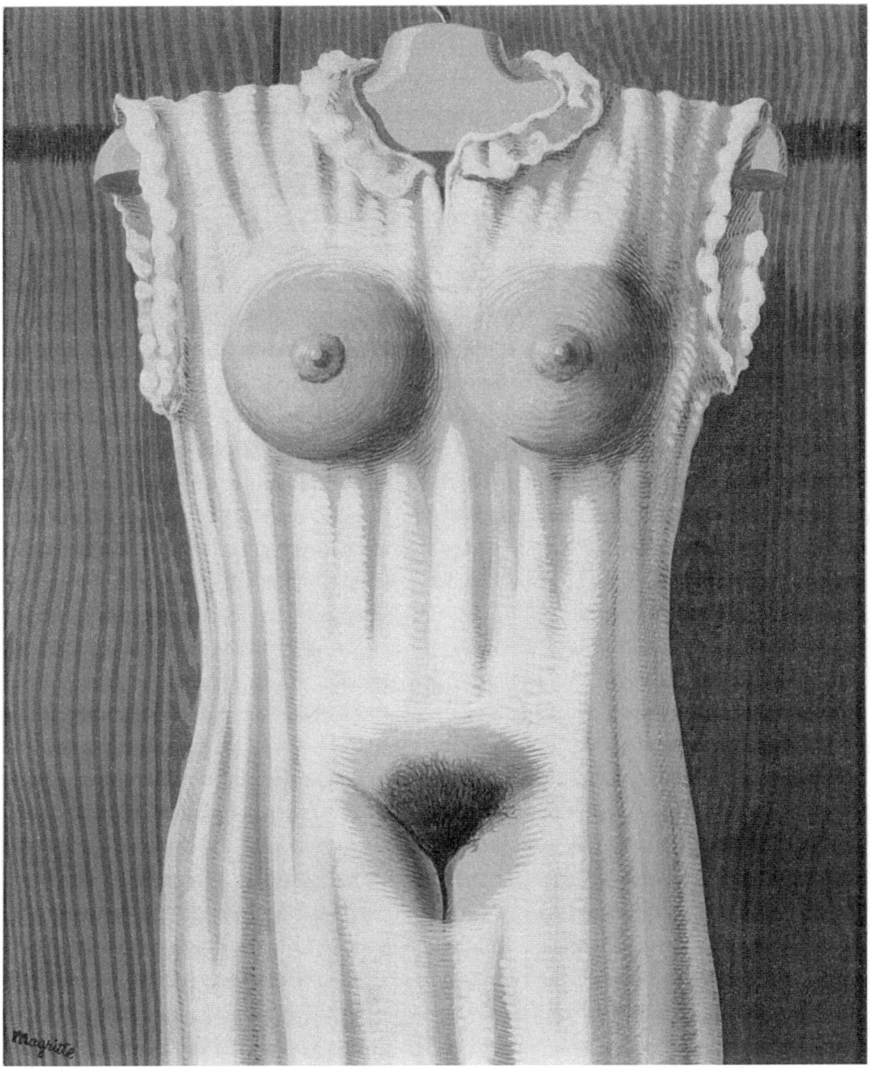

FIGURE 7.2 (see also Plate 15) René Magritte. *La philosophie dans le boudoir* [*Philosophy in the Bedroom*]. 1948. Gouache on paper. 46 × 37 cm. © 2014 Herscovici/Artist Rights Society (ARS), New York.

visible . . ." (Meuris, 1991, p. 29). Accordingly, what is concealed in this picture seems more important than what is exposed. Here the artist wraps the subjects' faces in linen or canvas, concealing the faces of the couple under a hood, achieving an effect of alienation. The enshrouded couple cannot really see each other because of the secret standing between them, namely the defended trauma of the artist's loss of his mother when he was an adolescent. The image of a face wrapped in material evokes different associations for the viewer. First, while a blanket might

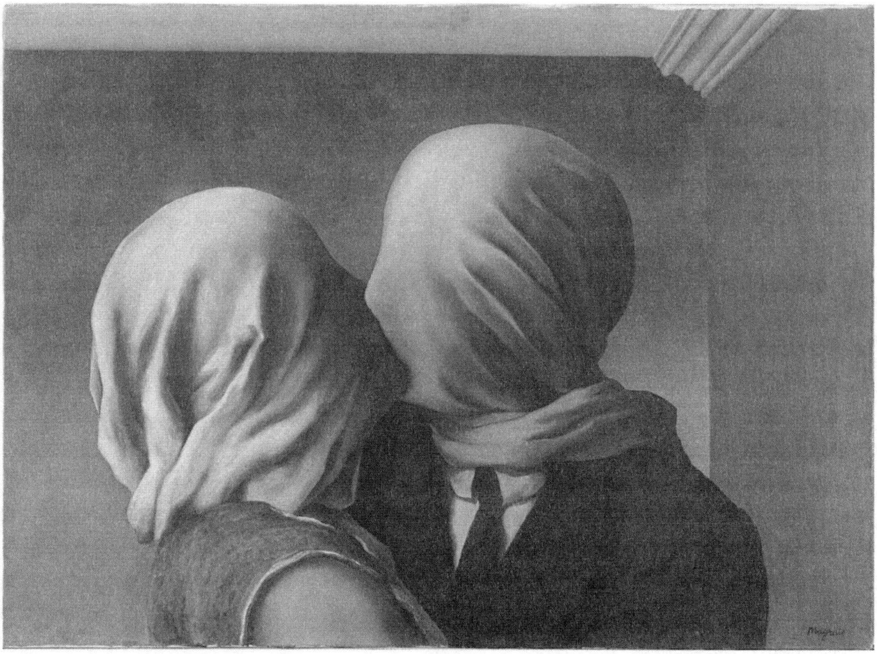

FIGURE 7.3 René Magritte. *Les amants* [*The Lovers*]. 1928. Oil on canvas. 54 × 73.4 cm. Museum of Modern Art, New York. Gift of Richard S. Zeisler. © 2014 Herscovici/Artist Rights Society (ARS), New York. Photo Credit: The Museum of Modern Art/Licensed by SCALA/Art Resource, NY.

warm or comfort a child, when it is pulled over the child's head it imposes a threat, the possibility of death. Second, people from most cultures wrap a dead body in a shroud. The idea of a covered face is eerily significant for the artist himself, as his mother's nightgown was wrapped around her head when her body washed up on the riverbank. Depressed people often describe their condition as feeling behind a veil or behind a glass wall.

In the strange, uncanny painting *The Rape*, 1934 (Figure 7.4), Magritte confuses the eye of the viewer. Does Magritte superimpose a nude body on a woman's face, or a woman's face on a nude body? He replaces the female face with her torso: her breasts replace her eyes, her naval takes the place of her nose, and her genitals displace her mouth. She can no longer speak with words, but can only communicate through her sexual anatomy. In this image, the female's access to her speech has been deleted, creating a repulsive and shocking visual experience. It seems that Magritte as well as we, the viewers, become voyeurs as we gaze onto the female, seeing her as an object instead of as a real person. The female is thus humiliated and dehumanized, but not without critique (Greeley, 1992).

This painting brings to mind many different themes. It references the union of love and death, the mind and the body, the relationship between the child and the mother, and, ultimately, the imaginary and the real. The optical fragmentation

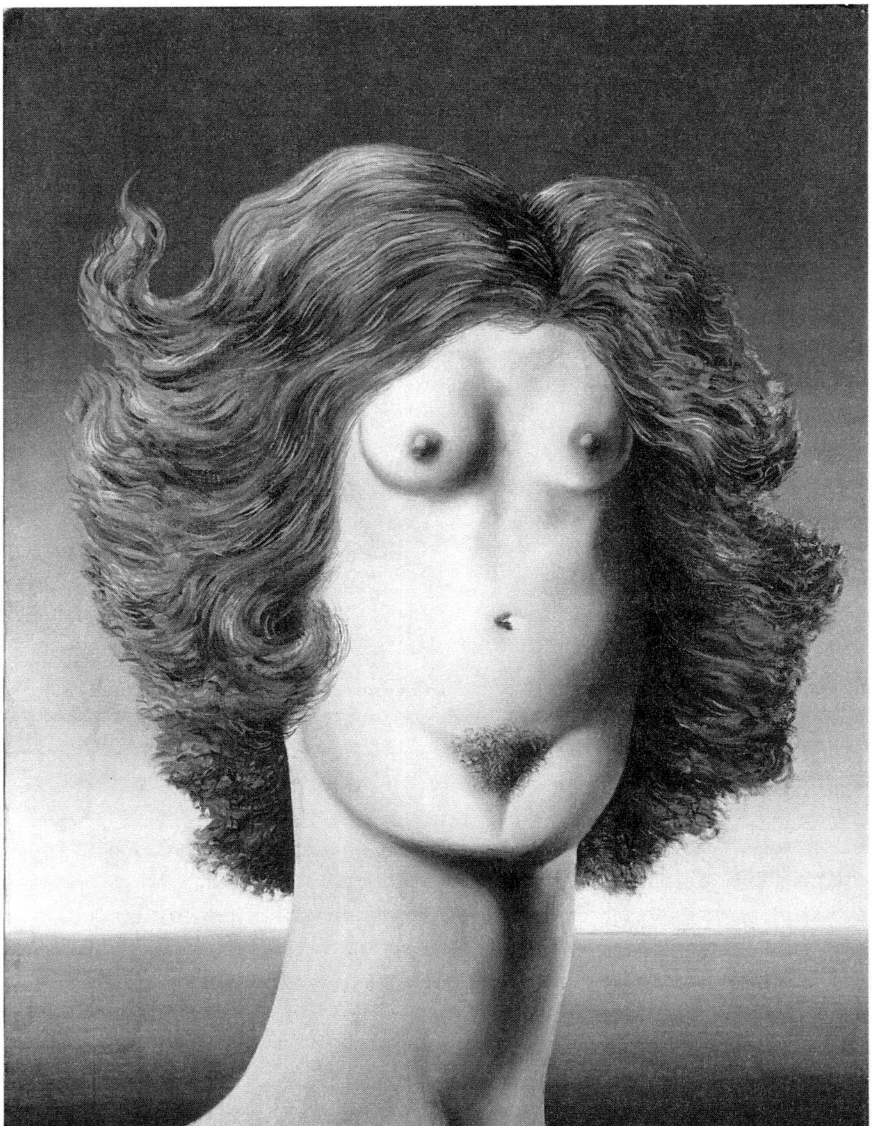

FIGURE 7.4 René Magritte. *Rape* [*The Rape*]. 1934. Oil on canvas. 73 × 54 cm. Menil Collection, Houston, TX.

mutilates not only the body, but also the spirit of the woman. The face, which used to be a window into her soul, becomes nothing but a body (Guber, 1987).

From a child's perspective, a mother's face is visible while her body is hidden and covered up. The child projects his or her desires onto the mother's face. In Magritte's memory of his mother's death as portrayed in *The Lovers* and *The Rape*, however, the exact opposite occurs. The mother's head is concealed by her nightgown, while her naked body is exposed. As a child who was confronted not only with a depressed mother but also with his mother's suicide, the artist may have needed to project his longing onto his mother's body, which stimulated confusing sexual fantasies, resulting in feelings of shame and guilt. The uncanny feeling evoked in *The Rape* condenses the temptation to merge with the object and at the same time it instills in the viewer the desire to ward off this temptation. In this painting, Magritte accomplishes the art of both revealing and concealing. The image is secretly familiar but undergoes repression and condensation, contributing to the physicality of the image. Sigmund Freud says that people experience an uncanny feeling when infantile complexes are revived after being repressed for a length of time (Freud, 1919). In Magritte's words, "a really vibrant painting has to make the onlooker sick" (Torczyner, 1979). Magritte wanted to make familiar objects "howl," a goal he accomplished in these paintings (Wolfenstein, 1997).

In Magritte's work, image and language often communicate different messages and never seem to be truly connected. There is little connection between the subject and its representation, which leaves the viewer feeling doubt, surprise and confusion at the images' illogical qualities.

The surprises and twists Magritte includes in his paintings are evident in *The Rape* and *The Collective Invention* (1934). In *The Rape*, Magritte links female genitalia to the woman's inability to speak. The artist's mother seems blinded and mute not only by her depression but also by her adolescent son gazing upon her exposed, vulnerable self.

The Collective Invention is a painting of a reversed mermaid. Instead of the mermaid image the viewer expects to see, with a human body structure from the torso up and a fish structure from the waist down, Magritte surprises the viewer by creating a figure with a fish head and human bottom. Magritte referred to this image as the "Solution to the Problem of La Mer": René's mother, *la mère*, becomes fused in her death with the sea, *la mer* (Handler Spitz, 1994). Here again, Magritte uses a realistic formal style while at the same time the content is expressed in surreal images. The deviation from realism might imply a formal reenactment of the trauma. Feelings are translated into form, because the artist is unwilling to face his trauma on an emotional level.

Magritte utilizes the element of surprise in some of his other paintings, not discussed here, in which he depicts a familiar object with a novel, surreal twist, such as a large, heavy rock that floats in space. We could interpret that this dead weight might unconsciously illustrate what it meant for him as a small boy to live with a depressed mother who was both idealized, light and beautiful, and at the same time very heavy, weighted down by her depression. Through his art-making, Magritte was able to transform his passive experience of his mother's suicide into an active one. He transformed himself from a helpless victim to a master of surprises, controlling the spectator through his art. He identified with the lost mother as well as with the aggressive mother (Abarbanel, 1988).

David Sylvester (1997) refers to René Magritte's picture *The Menaced Assassin*, 1926 (Figure 7.5) as "one narrative picture of consequence," and states that it contains a prototype or an early example of many important motifs. This picture can be understood as the recasting of Magritte's mother's suicide as a murder. Did he identify with the murderer, having not prevented her suicide?

Mary Gedo (1994) suggests that this painting represents all periods of time: the past, the present and the future. The environment—the room housing the victim and the victimizer—symbolizes the present that cannot be laid to rest. It seems that this picture also functions to make René Magritte's trauma literal, namely the secret of his dead mother that is so often enshrouded or wrapped in order to not see it. The assassin is illustrated as emotionally detached, still wearing his hat and coat, despite wielding a big weapon (a phallus). Three young men or children gaze

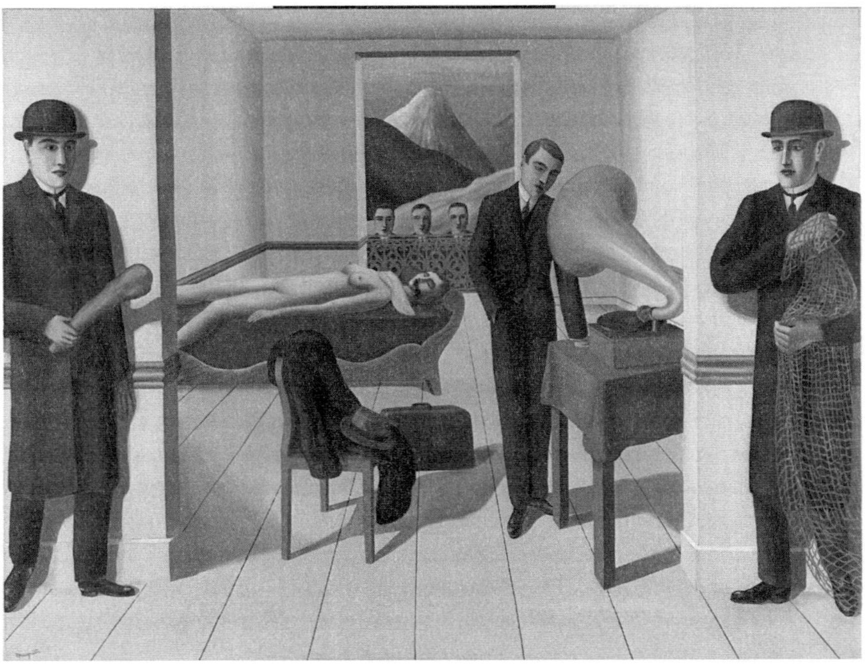

FIGURE 7.5 René Magritte. *L'assassin menacé* [*The Menaced Assassin*]. 1926. Oil on canvas. 150.4 × 195.2 cm. Museum of Modern Art, New York. Kay Sage Tanguy Fund. Photo Credit: The Museum of Modern Art/Licensed by SCALA/Art Resource, NY.

into the scene through the window, representing the past, the background. These three individuals may be the artist and his two brothers, dressed in adults' clothing, as they were asked to watch over their mother when she was depressed and suicidal. An additional viewer is evident in the painting: another gentleman, wearing a bowler hat and holding a fishnet in his hand, looks onto the scene. Magritte includes this gentleman and his pose to refer to the recovery of his mother's dead body, as if it were a big, dead fish from the river. Or perhaps the artist is implying that he wishes to catch the murderer, instead of his mother, with his net. This gentleman figure is *outside* the room, hoping to trap the murderer inside, thus representing the future.

Could this tidy yet murderous scene illustrate the initial trauma of his mother's naked, dead body, and the artist's view of his mother as both a victim and a victimizer? Who holds the weapon? Is it the angry adolescent, the irresponsible father or the grown artist stuck between feelings of rage, responsibility and a sense of great loss? Does Magritte illustrate a wish that the murderer—himself or maybe his father—be caught and judged for his crime in order for him to properly mourn his past, be relieved of his depression and be free to paint what he chooses?

As the philosopher Michel Foucault said, "All modern thought is penetrated by the law of thinking of the unthought." Foucault describes man searching for the "other one," the unknown stranger and dark companion, similar to Magritte's Surrealist friends, who attempted to uncover the unconscious through their artistic expressions and to open it up for conscious exploration. Such was not the case for Magritte, who defended his intellectual, formalistic, absurd style and set himself apart from other Surrealist artists who were inspired by Sigmund Freud, particularly by his *Dream Book*. In a letter to Foucault, May 23, 1966, Magritte wrote: "Only thought resembles. It resembles by being what it sees, hears, or knows, it becomes what the world offers it. It becomes completely invisible as pleasure or pain. But painting interposes a problem. There is the thought that sees and can be visibly described" (Foucault, 1982). The viewer recognizes that Magritte has a need to defend the cognitive, formally expressed link to his art and thus must deny, or even split off the powerful affective connection to his childhood trauma. Christopher Bollas (1987) called it "the unthought known," something the artist senses and acts upon, but cannot articulate in a fully rational discourse or artistic statement. However, the "unthought known" is something the artist does know as a fact. His mother's suicide is the unthought in the paintings, but something the artist does need to mold and create as he actively uses it within the cultural process. Still it remains outside of an intellectual discourse. As Bollas (1987) points out, the unthought known is thoughtful, even though the core of its significance has yet to be discovered by the artist. It is the shadow of the object, his mother's suicide, that hovers over so many of Magritte's paintings.

In Foucault's booklet *This Is Not a Pipe* (1982), he described the problematic relationship between Magritte's paintings and their titles. He points out that Magritte titled his paintings in order to focus on the act of naming. He often created the titles together with friends in an attempt to avoid unconscious thoughts from surfacing. His titles nevertheless offer us a glimpse into the artist's unconscious thoughts and give us insight into his traumatic past.

Magritte's images are perfectly casual. As he said, "They are what they are, explicit, matter-of-fact with an air of innocence" (Sylvester, 1997, p. 206). Magritte's art illustrates well that traumatic experience can resist true dialogue. The past and the present are experienced as the same. While the art-making process helped Magritte to bind his affects in an image or composition, they only seem to belong to his immediate present, and therefore cannot be re-contextualized in a current timeframe bearing personal, historical significance. The artist never truly succeeded in moving from absence to loss. While his artistic expression must have had some cathartic function, he was unable to reorganize his memory in order to properly mourn the past and move forward.

The beautiful, intimate portrait *Attempting the Impossible*, 1928 (Figure 7.6, see also Plate 16), portrays a man and a woman, a painter and a model, a creator and his creation. Yet the woman is incomplete as the viewer catches the artist in the act of finishing the model's arm. The title suggests that he would like to achieve the impossible, to create a living woman through his artistic endeavor. Just as in his famous painting *This Is Not a Pipe*, in this painting the subject is not a woman, but rather she is merely the visual representation of a woman and an incomplete one at that. Instead, the figure is static and smoothly painted with darker colors; she lacks the full glow of life. The woman is realistically represented, facing the artist, and both figures gaze at one another. Interestingly, as photographs show, Magritte's wife Georgette posed as the model for this picture.

Is the artist indeed attempting the impossible? The maternal body, with her psychic movement, forms an aesthetic environment for the infant. Visually, the mother's maternal gaze and her bodily presence inform the desires of the child. Thus, maternal depression and death were catastrophic for the child, as it transformed the living being (object)—the mother, who was at one point a source of vitality for the child—into a distant, inanimate object. When the mother disappeared, she took along with her the major portion of love—her gaze or look, her voice, smell and memories (Green, 2001). Consequently, the longing for a mother becomes a "mad passion" for the child, who secretly looks for her constantly (Ettinger, 2006).

Art-making, with its repetitions, allows the artist to reopen the path to the phantasmatic dead mother. Through the act of painting, the dead mother can once again become a part of an imaginary archive. The artist portrays his dead mother in the hope of regaining visual wholeness. When art is linked to the trauma with its visual imagery, the art can revive and reveal a psychic connection to the dead mother, and thus the painting or piece of art can have transformational potential and open up a space for mourning.

If the maternal image cannot be revived through artistic expression or psychoanalytic exploration, then the unconscious could become an endless source of pain, and the traumatic aching is encapsulated and remains hidden and, as Nicolas

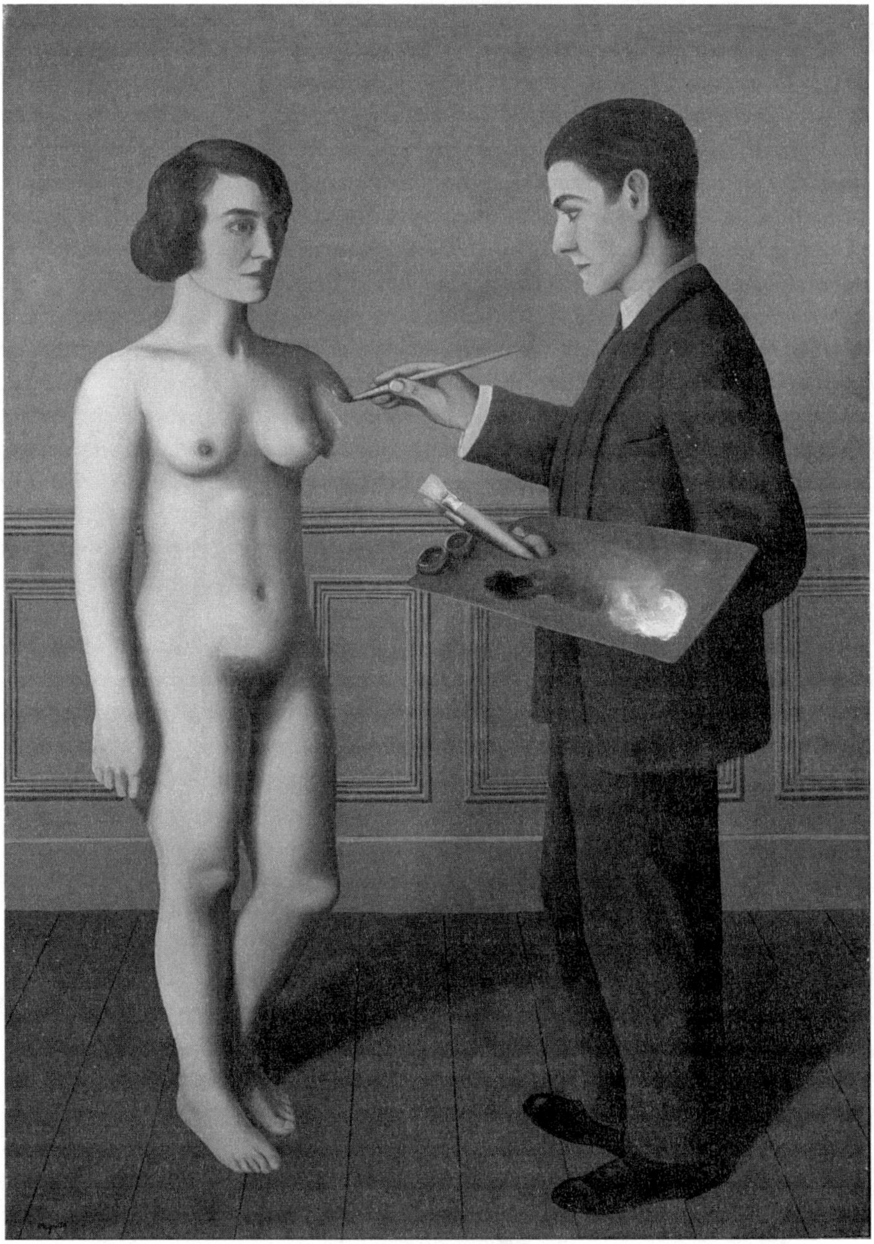

FIGURE 7.6 (see also Plate 16) René Magritte. *La tentative de l'impossible* [*Attempting the Impossible*]. Oil on canvas. 116 × 81 cm. Galerie Isy Brachot, Brussels. © 2014 Herscovici/Artist Rights Society (ARS), New York. Photo Credit: Banque d'Images, ADAGP/Art Resource, NY.

Abraham and Maria Torok (1994) describe, the trauma is kept in a crypt inside the self like the living dead. The struggle to bring unconscious material to the fore is therefore doomed.

In Magritte's art, a screen of surreal phantasm hides the object that exercised both fascination and horror for the artist. By joining together partial images and memories of his dead mother, the artist succeeded in reconnecting a visual and tactile link to her, and thus seems to transform the "dead mother" into the memory of the "enshrouded mother" seen in different paintings.

Art-making helped Magritte transform the invisible into the visible, in the hope of making the lost object more present (Ettinger, 2006). It appears however, that Magritte was not able to move from a sense of absence of mother to a feeling of loss of mother, with its consequent difficult mourning work. By denying the pain, Magritte was ultimately unable to fully assimilate and restore the lost object within himself. However, with his great artistic talent, he was able to use in his art the memory of the enshrouded mother as a very creative, adaptive solution that helped to consolidate his identity as an artist and husband, as well as to safeguard him from breakdown. It was not enough, though, to save him from his own ennui, boredom and depression.

References

Abarbanel, A. (1988) A note on Magritte's use of the shroud. *Psychoanalytic perspectives on art* 3. (171–176). Hillsdale, NJ: The Analytic Press.

Abraham, N. and Torok, M. (1994) *The shell and the kernel* (Vol. 1). Chicago: University of Chicago Press.

Barron, S. (2006) Enigma: The problem(s) of René Magritte. In *Magritte and contemporary art: The treachery of images*. S. Barron and M. Draguet (Eds.). Los Angeles: Los Angeles County Museum of Art, pp. 9–27.

Bollas, C. (1987) *The shadow of the object: Psychoanalysis of the unknown thought*. New York: Columbia University Press.

Ernst, M. (1970) *Max Ernst écritures*. Paris: Gallimard.

Ettinger, B. (2006) Gaze and touch the not enough Mother. In *Eva Hesse drawing*. New Haven, CT: Yale University Press.

Foucault, M. (1982) *This is not a pipe* (J. Harkness, Trans.). Berkeley: University of California Press.

Freud, S. (1919) The uncanny. *The standard edition of the complete psychological works of Sigmund Freud* (Vol. 16: 219–250). London: The Hogarth Press, 1959.

Gablik, S. (1985) *Magritte*. New York: Thames and Hudson.

Gedo, M. (1994) Looking at art from the inside out: The psychoiconographic approach to modern art. Cambridge, UK: Cambridge University Press.

Greeley, R (1992) Image, text and the female body: René Magritte and the Surrealist publications. *Oxford Art Journal* (15: 48–57).

Green, A. (2001) *Life narcissism, death narcissism*. New York: Free Association Books.

Guber, S. (1987) Representing pornography: Feminism, criticism, depictions of female violation. *Critical Inquiry*, 13, 4 (Summer): 712–741.

Hammacher, A.M. (1985) *René Magritte*. (J. Brockway, Trans.). New York: Abrams.

Handler Spitz, E. (1994) *Museum of the mind*. New Haven, CT: Yale University Press.

LaCapra, D. (1999) Trauma, absence, loss. *Critical Inquiry*, 25, 1 (Summer): 696–727.

Magritte, R. (1979) *Écrits complets*. A. Blavier (Ed.). Paris: Flammarion Lettres.

Meuris, J. (1991) *René Magritte*. Cologne, Germany: Benedikt Taschen Verlag.

Rose, J. (1989) "The man who mistook his wife for a hat" or "A wife is like an umbrella": Fantasies of the modern and postmodern. In *Universal abandon: The politics of postmodernism*. A. Ross (Ed.). 237–250.

Scutenaire, L. (1947) *René Magritte*. Brussels: Librairie Selection.

Sylvester, D. (1997) *About modern art*. New York: Henry Holt and Company.

Torczyner, H. (1979) *Magritte: The true art of painting*. New York: Abrams.

Viederman, M. (1987) René Magritte: Coping with loss, reality and illusion. *Journal of the American psychoanalytic association* (35: 907–998).

Wolfenstein, M. (1969) Loss, rage, and repetition. *Psychoanalytic Study of the Child*, 24: 433–456.

Wolfenstein, M. (1973) The image of the lost parent. *Psychoanalytic Study of the Child*, 28: 433–456.

8

ALBERT EINSTEIN

Creativity and intimacy

Albert Einstein (1879–1955) was the most significant scientist of the twentieth century. His life and work have been the subject of numerous scholarly and popular biographies, and his major contributions to modern physics have been examined carefully by historians of science. However, Einstein's personal and emotional life and its connection to his extraordinary creativity and productivity deserves further study, which will hopefully lead to a modification of some basic assumptions found in earlier works.

This chapter explores how Einstein's emotional life and his relationships to those closest to him shed light on his mode of thinking about his creative, scientific productivity. Einstein's dialectic will be investigated, specifically his wish to disengage from the "momentary and the merely personal," that is, from complex, unpredictable personal relationships, and his great ability (and preference) to venture into a world of complex universal laws governed by objectivity, simplicity and predictability. I will argue that both of these modes of thinking are mediated by Einstein's strong belief in intuition, namely a sense of beauty and a strong feeling of fusion with the world. For Einstein, this belief forms a bridge or a transitional space between his personal, fragmented experiences and the harmony of his overarching worldview.

This chapter will trace the linkages in Einstein's psychobiography between emotional intimacy in object relations and his interest in intuition and states of reverie in his creativity. Einstein's letters and pattern of relationships with those closest to him, such as with his children, wives and long-term colleagues and friends show a great power of intimacy and passion, but an equal difficulty in sustaining them over space and time.

Biographical details

"Man tries to make for himself in the fashion that suits him best a simplified and intelligible picture of the world; he then tries to some extent to substitute this cosmos of his for the world of experience" (Einstein, in Seelig, 1956, p. 225).

Albert Einstein was born on March 14, 1879 in Ulm, Germany to Herman and Pauline Einstein-Koch. Both of Albert's parents descended from a cultured Jewish-German background. Einstein's Jewish family members were Swabians who had lived in German lands since the year 1750, and they belonged to the educated elite who valued German music and literature and fostered the same values in their children (Folsing, 1997). Albert's father, Herman Einstein, was also mathematically talented and would have liked to have continued his schooling in the field of mathematics. Due to financial reasons, however, his schooling was cut short and he became a merchant-businessman; after his apprenticeship, he was hired as a partner in his cousin's firm in Ulm. When Albert was one year old, the family moved to Munich in order for Herman to open a factory that manufactured dynamos and other instruments for urban electrification. Two years and eight months after Albert's birth, his sister Maria (Maja) was born. Told he would receive a little playmate, a *Maedele* ("little girl" in German Swabian dialect), Albert promptly inquired about the whereabouts of his new toy's little *Raedele* (wheels). This is most likely the earliest example of Albert's delight in composing little rhymes, a hobby that he continued to have for the rest of his life. It is also the first example of little Albert's preference that his competitor be a wooden toy with which he could play, rather than a delicate baby which he would need to truly consider. In his sister's biographical sketch (Einstein, *CPAE*, vol. 1, 1987), she mentions that Albert learned to speak at the late age of two, but that once he started to speak, he immediately spoke fluently. He always repeated his own words quietly, however, until he started to attend school. She attributed this "peculiarity" to her brother's lifelong thoroughness. Einstein remembered that even at the age of nine, he exhibited difficulty in his fluency of speech and expressed himself only after thorough consideration and reflection (Frank, 1947).

Maja Einstein points out that the family taught Albert early independence. Between the ages of three and four years old, his parents sent him through the active streets of Munich: first they showed him the way, and then they merely observed him unobtrusively. He learned to peer cautiously to his left and right sides and, with great confidence, to cross the streets of the city. Little Albert loved to play quiet games as a child. He built and constructed objects in wood and metal or, as his sister recalls, patiently built houses of playing cards as many as 14 stories high.

When he was a small child, between the ages of four and five, while he was sick in bed, his father presented Einstein with the 'famous' compass. "That the needle behaved in such a determined way did not at all fit into the nature of events . . . this experience made a deep and lasting impression on me. Something deeply hidden had to be behind things," wrote Einstein in his autobiography (Einstein, 1970, p. 9). He described his observations and emotions as "indeed a wonder." Later, when he was around the age of six, his mother introduced him to what became his beloved violin, shared first with her. Einstein later shared his dear violin with his first wife Mileva who played the piano, with his two sons who were both talented in music, and with friends and colleagues.

Albert attended a Catholic elementary school. Contrary to myth, he was a very strong and bright student from the start of his schooling. He also received private lessons in Judaism at home, and was thus exposed to two religions and cultures at a very early age. Frustrated with his teacher, however, he attacked her with a chair, causing her to flee his home and never return. This was the first incident in which Einstein executed great resistance to enforced instruction of any kind. By the age of 12, he had received the *Heilige Geometrie Büchlein*, the "holy geometry booklet" by Euclid that fascinated him so much. He worked through and solved every problem by himself. As he later wrote, it was "One of the great events of my life . . . as dazzling as first love. I had not imagined that there was anything as delicious" (Folsing, 1997, p. 23). Albert's sister remembers that despite the chaos in their home caused by their cousins running around, Albert sat quietly on the living-room couch, balancing his inkbottle and solving geometrical problems as though all was quiet and calm around him. When he was 13, his old friend and mentor Max Talmud (who later called himself Talmey when he immigrated to America) presented him with popular science books by Aaron Bernstein, books about the cosmos by Alexander von Humboldt, and Immanuel Kant's *Critique of Pure Reason*. Talmud, a poor Polish–Jewish medical student who was invited once a week for a free meal at the Einsteins' table, allowed Albert to dive into a new scientific world and stimulated him in philosophical discussions (Talmey, 1932). His weekly visits to the Einstein home, which took place for five years, began in 1889 when the tutor was 21 years old and Albert was 10. Talmud was amazed at the speed with which the young Einstein read and absorbed these materials, and he became a spiritual and intellectual guide to the growing boy. Einstein's readings in science disillusioned him about the biblical stories he had learned previously. He gave up his interest in observing kosher dietary laws, and even refused to have a bar mitzvah. As Einstein wrote in his autobiography "It was quite clear to me that the religious paradise of youth which was lost was a first attempt to free myself from the chains of the 'merely personal,' from an existence which is dominated by wishes, hopes and primitive feelings. Out yonder there was this huge world, which exists independently of us human beings and which stands before us like a great, eternal riddle, at least partially accessible to our inspection and thinking" (Einstein, 1979, p. 5, Ed. Schlipp). Bertrand Russell writes that Galileo's older brother taught him the intricacies of geometry at the age of 11, and that he too, after developing a deep passion for the subject, decided to drop his medical studies in order to devote himself to the study of Euclid at the young age of 17 (Folsing, 1997).

Einstein's father's electricity business was never successful. Thus, in 1894, when Albert was 15 years old, his parents moved to Italy, where they opened a factory in Pavia. The new business also failed, however, and was liquidated only a few years later. Herman Einstein kept trying—unsuccessfully—to manage his business. Albert stayed behind in Munich in order to graduate from high school. Six months later, however, lonely and unhappy with the Prussian gymnasium's authoritarian methods of instruction and fearful of the impending obligatory one-year military service following high school, Albert spontaneously left school. Feeling sorry for his financially struggling parents, he surprised them by appearing unexpectedly in Pavia, Italy. In an 1889 letter to his sister Maja, Albert wrote:

> If I had had something to say in this matter, Papa should have looked for employment already two years ago, then he would have spared himself and us the worst. . . . What bothers me the most is the misfortune of my poor parents, who did not have a quiet minute since many years. In addition it pains me very much that as a grown man I have to stand by and watch without being able to do the least bit for them. I am nothing but a burden for my family. . . . It would be better if I would not live at all. The only redeeming thought is that I always did whatever my strength allowed, that year in and year out I did not allow myself a distraction or a pleasure other than what my studies offer, this keeps me upright and will have to protect me at times from my despair.
>
> (*CPAE*, vol. 1, doc. 38)

This letter demonstrates Einstein's strong sense of guilt for his parents' desperate situation and his wish that he would have been able to protect his family from harm.

Two years too young, and not proficient enough in French and other non-scientific and mathematical subjects, Einstein was not immediately accepted to Zürich's Federal Institute of Technology. He was asked to make up his last year of high school at the Kantonale High School in Aarau, a small Swiss town. There he lived with the Winteler family: Frau Pauline and Jost Winteler and their seven children. "Papa" Winteler, as Albert referred to him, was a professor of Greek and history in the gymnasium where Albert studied. Its liberal, open technique of instruction geared toward the individual student was more to Albert's liking, and his regular discussions with Papa Winteler helped Albert formulate his earliest thoughts and political philosophies.

Einstein's first love was Marie Winteler, the youngest daughter of the family. A letter dated to April 1896 from 17-year-old Einstein to Marie demonstrates his feelings for her: "Dear little treasure! Many, many thanks my little treasure for your cute little letter, which pleased me so very much. It is so wonderful to be able to hold a little paper to my heart, unto which two lovely little eyes have gazed lovingly, and over which two little hands have glided . . ." (*CPAE*, vol. 1, doc. 18).

From 1896 to 1900, Einstein was enrolled in the ETH (*Eidgenossiche Technishe Hochschule*, the Federal Polytechnic University) mathematics section, which included mathematics, physics and astronomy. During these university years, Einstein's love for theoretical and experimental physics flowered, as did his feelings for fellow physics student Mileva Maric; he also developed a love for hiking in the Swiss and Italian Alps. Einstein's parents, especially his mother, disliked his girlfriend Mileva, whom she considered an unfit match for her son. In a letter dated July 1900, Einstein wrote to Mileva: ". . . then my mother asks me: 'and what will become of Dockerl?' [Albert's nickname for his girlfriend] 'My wife,' I said equally as harmless, but I prepared myself for a real scene, which happened right away. She threw herself on her bed, hid her head in her pillow and cried like a child. . . . Then she went into a desperate offensive attack. . . . 'If she becomes pregnant then you are in a nice mess!'" (*CPAE*, vol. 1, doc. 68).

This letter did not endear Mileva to her future mother-in-law, and their relations were tense at best. In 1902, when his father was on the brink of death and Albert rushed to his bedside, he finally received his parents' consent to marry Mileva. Later in 1902, just as (or perhaps *because*) his mother had predicted, Albert's first daughter Lieserl was born in Mileva's native land of Navi Sad, Serbia, although the two were as yet unmarried. Mileva chose to return home to have her parents help with the pregnancy and delivery, as well as to protect her husband's ability to find a job.

After great financial and psychological strain and a long struggle to find work, Albert was finally hired as a technical expert third class at the Swiss Federal Patent office in Bern, with the help of his friend Michele Besso. One year later he married Mileva, but he never saw his daughter; she was probably either given up for adoption or died of scarlet fever as all traces of her after the age of two have been lost. In 1904, Albert's son, Hans Albert (Adu), was born in Bern. During the early years of their marriage, when Einstein developed his first revolutionary theories, Mileva functioned as a sounding board for his ideas, but no evidence indicates that she participated actively in his scientific work.

In 1905, a year now referred to as *annus mirabilis* or "the miracle year," the 26-year-old Einstein wrote five of the most significant scientific papers of the twentieth century; he accomplished this great task while simultaneously working in Bern, Switzerland as a patent examiner during the day and at night serving in his role as husband, devoted father to his one-year-old son Adu, and loyal friend to Conrad Habich and Maurice Solvine, with whom he created the Olympia Academy to read and debate the works of scientists and philosophers.

For two centuries, Isaac Newton's ideas about the basic laws of motion and gravitation had prevailed. By the end of the nineteenth century, contradictions arose between the newly discovered electromagnetic field and Newton's concept of the structure of light and his mechanical system. It was Einstein's scientific genius that brought these different parts together and created something completely new. His 1905 papers revolutionized the concept of space, time, energy and matter. In his first paper of that year, Einstein introduced a radically new concept, the discontinuous or quantum structure of light. In his second paper, he proved the existence of molecules by dealing with Brownian motion. Two even more influential papers dealt with the nature of space and time, and the electrodynamics of individual moving particles. Einstein's new theory became known as the special theory of relativity, which led to the most famous scientific equation of all time: $E=mc^2$, a statement of the equivalence of mass and energy. This equation is based on two postulates. First, in accordance with Newton, the laws of physics are exactly the same for all observers who move at constant velocity relative to one another. Einstein claimed secondly that for such observers, light always moves through empty space at a constant speed, regardless of how the source of light is moving relative to the observer. In Einstein's relativistic world of the Special Theory, the basic assumption is the constancy of the speed of light. These papers gradually brought Einstein to the attention of the scientific community.

In 1909, he resigned from the patent office and in 1910 his second son, Eduard (Tete or Tedy), was born. In 1911, Einstein predicted the bending of light and searched for new, more prestigious teaching jobs. After professorships in Zürich and Prague, he was appointed professor at the University of Berlin in 1914 without teaching obligations and became a member of the Prussian Academy of Science. His marriage continuously deteriorated until he finally separated from his wife and two young sons in 1914. Mileva and the two sons subsequently returned to Bern when Hans Albert was ten years old and Eduard was only four.

In Berlin, on July 30, 1914, Albert Einstein wrote, "Yesterday my wife left for good with the children. I was at the railway station and gave them a last kiss. I cried yesterday, bawled like a little boy yesterday afternoon and yesterday evening after they had gone. Haber [his friend] accompanied me to the station (9 o'clock) and then spent the evening with me. Without him I would have not managed to do it. . . . [Mileva] perceives my conduct as a crime against her and the children . . ." (*CPAE*, vol. 8, doc. 29). This moment marks the beginning of a lifelong correspondence with his two sons.

Between October 1915 and late 1917, within a span of 18 months while Einstein was undergoing a tormenting separation from his wife and sons, he produced revolutionary papers, lectured, was appointed the director of the Kaiser Wilhelm Institute for Physics in Berlin, and maintained correspondences; all of this was in the midst of World War I. Einstein completed the general theory of relativity in 1916. He also published his first paper on cosmology. In Einstein's new universe, gravity is no longer understood as a force nor tied to the interaction between objects; rather, it is the property of the fabric of "space-time" through which an object moves. Therefore, space and time are no longer passive arenas in which material bodies act out their roles, but become part of the action. Thus a massive body such as the sun curves the space-time around it, and the planets move around these curved pathways of space-time. The general theory of relativity predicted the extent to which a light beam would be bent as it passed by the sun. Einstein's prediction was indeed confirmed by the British astronomer Arthur Eddington during a total eclipse of the sun in May 1919.

Einstein's remarkable power of concentration in childhood, as well as between the ages of 22 and 26, and again between the ages of 31 and 37, allowed him to work uninterruptedly for many hours, days and weeks, often forgoing food and rest. Both of these periods of bursting creativity were preceded by years of "brooding" [*Grüblerei*], as he called it. In a 1918 speech honoring his mentor, Max Planck, Einstein wrote: "The state of mind which enables a man to do work of this kind is akin to that of the religious worshipper or the lover. The daily effort does not originate from deliberate intention or program, but straight from the heart" (*CPAE*, vol. 7). His ability to completely fuse with his scientific work during these productive periods operated as a substitute for forming truly emotionally intimate relationships, which were difficult for him to sustain over time.

After Mileva and the children settled in Zürich, Einstein wrote on January 25, 1915 to his son Hans Albert in Berlin: "My dear Albert . . . I heard that you are well and that you have a pretty apartment in the hills of Zürich [Zürichberg]. I also heard that you were allowed to install on your sled the steering fixture that you have been waiting for since last year" (*CPAE*, vol. 8, doc. 48).

One wonders if Einstein thought that this steering wheel would symbolically empower the 10-year-old to take over the leadership role from his father? In an attempt to rationalize the family's move, Einstein noted the better school system and educational philosophies in Switzerland, as compared to the ones his son left behind in Berlin.

> In a few years you will also be able to begin exercising your mind. It's splendid once you can do it. In the last few weeks I have been doing a wonderful and important experiment on magnets with Mr. de Haas. . . . When I spend some more time with you one day, I'll tell you a bit about it, maybe already during the next summer holiday. In the summer I hope to go on a hiking tour with you in the mountains [so] that you can also see a bit of the world. If all goes well the terrible war will be over by then. . . . Write to me if you have a special wish.
>
> (*CPAE*, vol. 8, doc. 48)

Unconsciously, Einstein might have hoped that "exercising his mind" would protect his little son from his great longing for his father and protect him from psychological injury; he unconsciously hoped to offer Adu the same satisfaction and protection he himself often experienced when completely absorbed in his scientific research.

In a letter written from Hans Albert at the age of eleven in 1915, the son responded to his father's invitation for a "special wish." He wrote:

> Dear Papa!
>
> We have received the postcard; however what you wanted to say with it, I do not know. But I hope that you thought: 'Yes, it would be nice, let's see. Can you imagine, Tete [younger brother] can already multiply and make divisions and I do "Geometery", as Tete calls it. Mama gives me exercises to do; we have a little booklet; this I could do with you too. But why did you not continue to write us? I just think to myself: 'On Easter you will be here again and we will again have a Papa.'
>
> Yours, Adu
>
> (*CPAE*, vol. 8, 69a in vol. 10)

By studying geometry, Adu hoped to forge a meaningful connection with his absent Papa. Young Adu was most likely disappointed by the response he received from his father. After a few months, his father wrote back: ". . . we can't see each other at Easter now. But in the summer I [will] take a trip just with you alone for a fortnight or three weeks . . . This will happen every year, and Tete will also come along when he is old enough for it." He continues later in the same letter: "I am very glad that you are enjoying geometry. It was my favorite pastime when I was already a bit older than you, around 12 years old. But I had nobody to show me anything; I had to learn it from books. I would enjoy immensely being able to teach it to you, but that's not possible. If you write me each time what you already know, I'll give you a nice little problem to solve" (*CPAE*, vol. 8a, doc. 70).

It is once again through geometry, the abstract "wonder," that the father proposes to keep the tenuous connection between father and son alive. The children's longings are no longer obscured in this correspondence, as Adu wrote:

> Dear Papa,
>
> Today we told each other dreams. Suddenly Tete said; 'I dreamt that Papa is here!' Then I thought: 'It would be so much nicer if you would be with us. I know now much more piano; not long ago I played a Haydn and Mozart sonatina. In short, I could also play with you. Now we are approaching the final exam [in school] but also Easter. Last year we were alone, do we have to pass Easter alone this year too? If you write to us that you are coming, it would be for us the best Easter Bunny. You know we live here quite well, but if Mama will be sick one day, I will not know what to do. We then have nobody other than the housekeeper. Also for that it would be better if you would be with us.
>
> (*CPAE*, vol. 8, doc. 69b)

Adu expresses his fear of the future, realizing gradually that his father is not returning to Zürich to be united with them. He fears that he will need to function as a substitute father to his little brother Tete and take over the role of a husband to his emotionally and physically unstable mother.

These letters must have fostered enormous feelings of guilt in Einstein who was productively working on his theories, and was comfortable in his new relationship with his cousin Elsa Löwenthal-Einstein, his stepdaughters Ilse and Margot, and his new colleagues in Berlin. Einstein and his son interacted very angrily and disappointedly with each other, as the letter to Einstein from his friend Michele Besso during this trying time implies: Besso writes: "I would like to lend you my glasses, which scale things down to size, and provide some objectivity; only because I think you could defend yourself better without rage. That the boy would naturally be completely different as soon as you had spent a couple of days with him is as clear to you as to me. His abrasive, almost impudent manner . . . is probably to a large part that self-defense of his heart against painful impressions which you yourself know only too well" (*CPAE*, vol. 8, doc. 164).

It is no coincidence that from 1917 to 1920 Einstein suffered on and off from liver ailments, stomach ulcers, jaundice and general weakness. The stress and guilt of being separated from his children and in a new love relationship must have also fostered these psychosomatic symptoms. Mileva also became very ill, as her son Adu feared would happen, and had to be hospitalized for extended periods of time.

Adu learned to take over responsibility of the home as the oldest male quickly, with the support of his father's friends Heinrich Zangger and Michele Besso. As both Einstein's fame and guilt increased, he reported the following dream to his friend Michele Besso on August 20, 1819:

> the following has happened and puts me in an awkward predicament. Zangger and Edg[ar] Meyer offered me a teaching position at the Univ. & Poly[technic] in Zürich, and I really cannot split myself in two. In Berlin, everything conceivable is laid at my feet . . . I want to sink into the ground with shame. (How happy I would have been 16 years ago with a measly assistantship. But it is as Heine put it in verse:
>
> If you have plenty, [then by and by]
>
> Much more you should receive besides
>
> Look up this exquisite little poem; Proof: I dreamt I had to cut my throat with a razor.
>
> (*CPAE*, vol. 8, doc. 604)

Einstein may have had some feelings of guilt toward the Swiss colleagues, but more importantly as he expressed in his dream he projected guilt onto the Swiss. The Swiss offer would have provided Einstein with the opportunity to escape war-torn Germany and move closer to his children, but it would have disrupted his scientific research and his new life with Elsa and her daughters. His guilt, therefore, was a sincere moral conflict; he wanted to serve two masters, but could not: it was either his first family with his sons who longed so much for him, or his own successful intellectual pursuits. This moral dilemma for Einstein might remind one of the earlier conflicts expressed by Einstein in a letter he wrote to his sister, discussed above, about his parents. Then too, Einstein felt extreme guilt for not being able to help his father's career and improve his family's financial situation, but instead chose to be a student.

During these war years, Einstein traveled once or twice a year to Switzerland to teach in Zürich, so long as his health, his financial situation, and wartime border crossing regulations allowed it; thus, he resolved his feelings of guilt about the Swiss institution by teaching there for a few weeks, as well as about his children by being able to visit them. On these trips to Switzerland, he and his ailing mother, who suffered from stomach cancer, would visit his sons and take small trips, such as hikes and sailing expeditions with Hans Albert. His younger son, Tete, saw much less of his father during these early years, as he was often sick and spent time recovering in hospitals or in the Alps.

Albert Einstein wrote to 14-year-old Hans Albert:

> Berlin, 25.1.1918
>
> My dear Albert,

> Your letter and your postcard delighted me. I see that you not only are my own son, but that we really are developing affectionate relations between us. Your concern about my illness was especially gratifying to me. So let it be said with pleasure: I am content with you and I am happy when I think of you. I believe the more mature and more independent you become, the better and better friends we will be.
>
> (*CPAE*, vol. 8b, doc. 442)

After Einstein described his illness to his oldest son and recounted how for four weeks he had been forced to lie in bed and to eat "peck" (*Vogelfutter* or bird feed), he wondered in his letter how much longer his younger son Tete would need to stay in the mountains to recover from his different ailments. He believed that eight-year-old Tete was being overly pampered and wondered if the high expense of the mountain cure was necessary for his health.

Hans Albert wrote back to his father just a few weeks later. He inquired about his father's illness and suggested that he too should come to the Alps for recovery. Then he launched into an attack, claiming that his father did not understand his younger brother's health situation at all. He continued:

> You cannot really judge what to do with Tete because you have no idea what he already went through. Mr. Zangger [Einstein's friend and physician] can make the best judgment since he checks Tete regularly. We can actually be very happy that he helps us that much. What would have happened to us if he wouldn't have been here when Mother got sick? Think about it that one has to take care of one's health. We actually do not know anything about each other, you have no idea what our needs are and what we could use; I know nothing about you, I know Mr. Zangger much better than anybody here, then you, and that is very unfortunate. I play now the Fifth sonata by Beethoven . . . and I am very happy with it. I try now to electrify my train and Mama is helping me as much as she can. I do it because of our lack of coal and hope to finish it by the time Tete returns. If you were here you would also be entertained by it. Herr Zürcher [a neighbor] has enjoyed working on it and I think after I finish mine, they will do theirs too.
>
> Write soon how you are. Many greetings,
>
> Yours, Adu
>
> (*CPAE*, vol. 8, doc. 442a)

Adu, now an adolescent, can express his anger and frustration but he also has learned to comfort or please his father. Perhaps his attempt to comfort his father is an unconscious reaction. After each attack against his father, he mentions a creative activity that he could have shared with his father, but now shares with somebody else, a father substitute. Adu realizes that these simple activities would have been pleasing, and would have fostered some intimacy between son and father despite divorce and long distance. It might also be an attack on his father, as if to say "I did these things with other people, but I should have been doing them with you."

In 1919, after her serious illness, Mileva finally agreed to a divorce and Einstein, under pressure from Elsa and her parents (his aunt and uncle), married his cousin. For quite some time, Einstein visited his sick mother in Switzerland on a regular basis, but later when her terminal state permitted, he was able to take her to Berlin. In a letter to his friend Ehrenfest he wrote: "I am writing only now because it was as if I had been crippled by my mother's severe illness. A week ago we carried her to her grave. It was a terrible time!" (*CPAE*, vol. 9, doc. 335).

This emotionally difficult year for Einstein was also the year when the bending of light was observed during a solar eclipse, providing proof of Einstein's theory of general relativity. He instantly became a world-renowned figure and was awarded the Nobel Prize in 1922. He gave the proceeds of the prize to his ex-wife, in accordance with their divorce agreement provisions, so that she could care for their sons, Hans Albert and Eduard. Following in his father's footsteps, Hans Albert also married a woman older than him against his father's advice right after graduating from the same Swiss university from which his father graduated. Hans Albert eventually immigrated to the United States with the help of his father and became a professor at the University of California Berkeley.

Eduard, who was only four years old at the time of his parents' separation, lived in Zürich with his mother. He was a precocious, sensitive, sickly child, an excellent student in the gymnasium, a talented piano player, and a strong essay writer and poet. He was also the head of the school newspaper and directed the school orchestra. While studying at university in 1932 at the age of 22, Eduard experienced a major episode of what was diagnosed as schizophrenia. He was taken by Einstein's friend Dr. Zangger to the psychiatric hospital Burghölzi in Zürich where he was last visited by his father in 1933 before Einstein immigrated to Princeton, New Jersey. While his mother was alive, Eduard was able at times to live at home or live with an aide at home, but after her death he was permanently hospitalized.

Einstein spent the last 22 years of his life in the United States. On April 18, 1955, Albert Einstein died of an aortic aneurysm in Princeton. He named The Hebrew University in Jerusalem in his last will and testament as the ultimate repository of his personal papers.

Intimacy, reverie and creativity

In *The Born–Einstein Letters*, Max Born wrote that "For all his kindness, sociability and love of humanity, [Einstein] was nevertheless totally detached from his environment and the human beings in it" (2005, p. 130). This section will investigate the accuracy of this statement.

Einstein was capable of sustaining long-term friendships, some for over half a century, such as with Marcel Grossman, Maurice Solovine, Heinrich Zangger, Max Planck, Hendrik Antoon Lorentz, Michele Besso, his sister Maja, his children and others documented abundantly in hundreds of letters, in autobiographical writings, and even in his public pronouncements. Unlike many other individuals, he was able to manage both intense creative work and long-term relationships simultaneously. The patterns of his relationships demonstrate a great power of intimacy and passion with family members and long-term friends, but a difficulty in sustaining them.

The image of Einstein to be presented here will be a stark contrast to the simplified descriptions of a remote and disengaged man that have appeared throughout most biographical studies. None other than Erik H. Erikson wrote, "Yet, I must say that when one reads some of his letters and sees his reflection in some of his surviving members of his inner circle, one cannot doubt that this man knew how to give some intense sense of intimacy" (Erikson, 1982, p. 157).

One of the most prominent leitmotifs that recurs in his letters and later reminiscences is the role of scientific work as an escape from "the merely personal." At age 18, upon breaking up with his first sweetheart, Marie Winteler, Albert Einstein wrote to her mother, Pauline:

> . . . strenuous intellectual work and the study of God's nature are the angels that will lead me through all the troubles of this life with consolation, strength, and uncompromising rigor.
>
> (*CPAE*, vol. 1, doc. 34)

In an essay written in honor of Max Planck's sixtieth birthday, analyzing the motives that lead men to a career in science, Einstein stated: "I believe with Schopenhauer that one of the strongest motives that lead men to art and science is escape from everyday life with its painful crudity and hopeless dreariness, from the fetters of one's own ever shifting desires" (*CPAE,* vol. 7, doc. 7).

The same year, urging intellectuals to embrace international reconciliation and cooperation after the end of World War I, Einstein wrote: "The most valuable contribution to a reconciliation of the nations and the permanent fraternity of mankind is in my opinion contained in their scientific and artistic creations, because they raise the human mind above personal and national aims of a selfish character" (*CPAE*, vol. 7, doc. 47).

In his *Autobiographical Notes* at age 67, Einstein wrote: "In a man of my type the turning point of the development lies in the fact that gradually the major interest disengages itself to a far-reaching degree from the momentary and the merely personal and turns towards our striving for a mental grasp of things" (Einstein, 1970, p. 7).

Contrary to extant simplified notions, and his own pronouncements, Einstein was not only drawn away from the intensely personal and from ambivalent feelings into the comfort of space, abstract concepts, visual images, or Platonic forms, but he also was capable of immersing himself in intimate relationships, love and passion with his partners, lovers, and very close friends. In 1900, he wrote to his then lover and later wife Mileva, "I long terribly for a letter from my beloved witch . . . only now I see how much in love with you I am! Pamper yourself so you will become a radiant little sweetheart and as wild as a street urchin!" (*CPAE*, vol. 1, doc. 69).

Or, in another love letter to Mileva:

> My dearest Dolly,
>
> . . . Soon I'll be with my sweetheart again and can kiss her, hug her, make coffee with her, scold her, study with her, laugh with her, walk with her, chat with her . . . + ad infinitum! . . . When I think of you now, for a second I don't want to anger or tease you ever again, only to be an angel all the time! What a nice illusion! But you will still love me, won't you, even if I am the same old rogue I've always been, full of whims and mischief, and as moody as ever.
>
> (Renn and Schulman, 1992, p. 31)

In Western culture, the accepted notion of the origins of modern science is intricately bound to the belief that it was the ancient Greeks who, by inventing natural sciences (specifically mathematics and astronomy), elaborated upon the human capacity to separate the factual and verifiable from the emotional and traditional. The scientific mode of thinking emerged, whereby the rational—the ability to sustain by argument and realism . . . became the lingua franca of the Western intellectual tradition (Buchwald, 2003).

Evelyn Fox Keller, in her book *Reflections on Gender and Science*, writes that "feminism . . . seeks to enlarge our understanding of history, philosophy and sociology through the inclusion . . . of those domains of human experience that have [historically] been relegated to women: namely, the personal, the emotional, and the sexual" (Keller, 1995, p. 3). She continues, "I cling to the belief that, like other human activities . . . scientific change cannot be adequately understood without an understanding of the individual actors through whose hearts, minds, and hands, the imperatives of history make themselves felt" (Keller, 1995, p. 8).

Understanding Einstein's more personal side, with his intense ability for love and passion both in his friendships and love relationships and at the same time his great ambivalence in long-term close intimacy with his wives and his children, also helps us to understand Einstein the scientist. The following quote illustrates how his friendship with Michele Besso helped him to clarify his ideas in 1905. As Einstein (1949) wrote, "Without the sense of fellowship with men of like mind, of preoccupation with the objective, the eternally unattainable in the field of art and scientific research, life would have seemed to me empty" (Einstein, A., 1954, p. 9).

Following a night's sleep after an intense dialogue with his colleague and friend Michele Besso in May 1905, after sending his paper on the Brownian motion for publication, Einstein was inspired to write to his friend: "Thank you. I've completely solved the problem. An analysis of the concept of time was my solution. Time cannot be absolutely defined, and there is an inseparable relation between time and signal velocity" (Folsing, 1997, p. 155).

Five weeks later, 26-year-old Einstein wrote a 30-page paper titled, "On the Electrodynamics of Moving Bodies." "It was a treatise beyond compare and without precedent, one of the greatest scientific achievements," writes Folsing (1997, p. 156). Many years of pondering, hard work and important dialogues with his friend and colleague Besso resulted in the relativity principle in electrodynamics. Scientific research and intimate scientific discussion with one of his best friends resulted in this great discovery.

Available historical literature about emotion and motivation in the lives of scientists is scarce both in studies of the history of science as well as in psychoanalytic literature. However, it is interesting to note that in general, negative or excessive emotions have been the focus of most psychological research. Historians and sociologists of science most frequently consider negative emotions and themes—such as competitiveness, acquisitiveness, thirst for power and influence, pursuit of fame, or, in private life, sexual and amorous transgressions—as they seem to have become acceptable topics. Researchers imply that negative emotions should have been sublimated, or alternatively, that scientific life should be impervious to human frailty. There is a disjunction between the language of science and the language of history, but both have little possibility of incorporating the language of affects and the unconscious world of fantasies and dreams.

Such was not the case for Einstein, who wrote in his *Autobiographical Notes*, "What, precisely, is 'thinking'? When at the reception of sense-impression, memory pictures emerge, this is not yet 'thinking.' When, however, a certain element turns up in many such series, in that it connects series, which in themselves are unconnected. Such an element becomes an instrument, a concept. I think that the transition from free association or 'dreaming' to thinking is characterized by the more or less preeminent role which the 'concept' plays in it" (Einstein, 1970, p. 7).

Interestingly, Einstein and other scientists place great emphasis on their power of intuition, visual images, and unconscious productions: "For me it is not dubious that our thinking goes on for the most part without the use of signs (words) and beyond that to a considerable degree unconsciously" (Einstein, 1970, p. 9).

Transitional and creative space

Earlier in life, the transitional space is initially utilized to form boundaries to separate the individual from the object; later in life it is used to keep boundaries flexible and establish them according to the individual's need at a particular time. The extension of the transitional space into adulthood functions as the space for one's own aesthetic experiences, between conscious and unconscious, self and other, differentiating between the cognitive and the affective level of communication. The more the primary process mode has to be repressed due to familial, educational and cultural pressures, the more the imagination will take on the function of holding on to these experiences within the transitional space and connecting them with what has been repressed during development. It is this space which can be used to create one's own aesthetic experience between conscious and unconscious, self and other, a place for any creative production. Within this space, where the unconscious is more free to surface, language and symbols are also created, paradoxically revealing and concealing the unconscious. From a psychoanalytic viewpoint, these productions and words help to differentiate the cognitive and affective level of communication (Schwab, 1994). In this context it is interesting to recall that Einstein was a late talker. When he finally did speak, he constantly repeated his few sentences. He may have had a difficult time separating from this earlier developmental stage where he was closely linked to fantasy within a maternal protective environment. As Gabriele Schwab points out, within the transitional space the infant or baby also creates sounds and forms word, events that Donald Winnicott included among the transitional objects. From the infant's perspective, the sounds he makes seem to come simultaneously from inside and outside of him. He creates the sounds from the inside using his vocal cords, and hears them coming back to him from the outside. Schwab points out that traces of such play with sounds belong to the pleasure of creating verses and funny poems, a happy passion of Einstein's (Schwab, 2005).

Roman Jakobson quotes a conversation between the adult Einstein and Shankland: "'I hear words,' Einstein says. 'This reminds us of the early preverbal stage, where babies pick up clues from auditory, visual and gesticulatory type'" (Jakobson, 1982, p. 141). Schwab argues, "Perhaps Einstein deferred his entry into the realm of articulate words in order to prolong the experience of transitional sounds and speech. Words had to remain 'real creations,' namely creations that remained spontaneous from the unconscious. Speaking from within a pre-given symbolic order, by contrast, needed to be deferred" (Schwab, 2005, p. 3).

Einstein's capacity for creative play and intellectual pondering became significant later, as a creative adult, when his familial and cultural environment and intellectual influences came to the fore. Close to the end of Isaac Newton's life, the scientist remarked, "I do not know what I appear to the world; but to myself I seem to have been only like a boy playing on the seashore, and diverting myself in now and then finding a smoother pebble or a prettier shell then ordinary, whilst the great ocean of truth lay all undiscovered beyond me" (Erikson, 1982, p. 156). Einstein, his role model Newton before him, and his favorite composer Mozart were all very much in touch with their playful, childlike side, connecting them easily to their unconscious fantasies and making them comfortable with their sense of spontaneous play. Such imagination or creativeness facilitates a dialogue between inner and outer reality, or between primary and secondary process experiences. While initially the child creates a very private object in the transitional object, scientists' and artists' creations within the transitional space have to adjust to cultural intersubjective communications. As mentioned earlier, Anton Ehrenzweig (1967) believes unconscious scanning is indispensable for creative processes and indeed a superior instrument for knowing. Einstein wrote: ". . . of all our thinking of this nature of free play with concepts, the justification for this play lies in the measure of survey [*Übersicht*] over the experience of the senses which we are able to achieve with its aid" (Einstein, 1970, p. 7).

Erik H. Erikson also understands this "survey" as a form of scanning, a way "to have an overview over a wide horizon, a kind of 'Anschauung,' a German philosophical way of looking around, 'a way of looking at things,' both focused and encompassing" (Erikson, 1976). Unfocused and focused attention reveals both conscious and unconscious imagery, mediating between primary and secondary processes. Freud describes it as ". . . the true part of oneself—unconscious but knowable" (Binswanger, 1956, p. 58).

Einstein believed that "thinking" was a combination of "sense impressions" from which memory pictures emerge over and over again. These pictures then serve as an element for order, which he referred to as "concepts." One is reminded of Walter Benjamin's *Denkbilder*, that is, thought images. Benjamin believed that *Denkbilder* can exist both as images and as language. Einstein realized that "free play with concepts" was an important ingredient of scientific thought and emphasized the centrality of visual imagery: "All our thinking is of this nature of a free play with concepts" (Einstein, 1970, p. 7).

Sigmund Freud argues that consciousness is only a small part of our mental life. Albert Einstein explains it well: "I think that the transition from free association, or dreaming, to thinking is characterized by the more or less dominating role which the 'concept' plays in it" (Einstein, 1970, p. 7).

Einstein described the process of moving from unconscious seeing (invisible images) to the preconscious "concepts," to the conscious realm created by the use of words. As he explained, "The words or language, as they are written or spoken, do not seem to play any role in my mechanism of thought." He told his psychologist friend Max Wertheimer, one of the founders of Gestalt therapy, "I very rarely think in words at all. A thought comes and I may try to express it in words afterwards" (Wertheimer, 1959/1978).

Ehrenzweig assumes that individuals are capable of recognizing an unconscious form, even without the conscious formation of a visible image. Following Ehrenzweig's line of thought, abstract thought then does not exclude the primary process. As the following quote by Einstein reveals, he viewed unconscious fantasy as crucial to his creative process: "When I examine myself and my method of thought, I come to the conclusion that the gift of fantasy has meant more to me than my talent for absorbing positive knowledge" (Calaprice, 2000).

Integration of space and time in personal relationships

One must consider whether Albert Einstein may have had to forgo the gratification of object love in order to function at the peak of his creative potential. In other words, one must explore the relationships between creativity and intimacy and object love. Sigmund Freud's theory of sublimation would make plausible the existence of this relationship between creativity and object love. What is the role of creativity in intimate relationships? It is the capacity for reverie with another, and the capacity for free play, intuition and unconscious scanning; Einstein was familiar and comfortable with all of these concepts. As evidenced by his letters and correspondence, Einstein displayed creativity and warmth in the wooing periods of his intimate relationships with lovers, spouses and children. As Schwab (2005) points out, however, over time something seemed to change, which was very difficult for Einstein to tolerate. Ironically, it was the integration of space and time that appeared difficult for him to accept and sustain in his personal relationships. Like most individuals, Einstein was extremely vulnerable to distance and its effect on reverie in intimate encounters, as well as to time and its influence on connectedness in intimate relationships. Although Einstein repeatedly insisted that his interests shifted from the merely personal and momentary to the mental aspect of things, Einstein did in fact maintain many intense friendships over the period of half a century; he was very involved with his family, particularly with his children and stepchildren, and with the community at large. The strength of these relationships is apparent by their ability to withstand multiple ambivalences and conflicts. Einstein's fantastic correspondence with his mentors, colleagues, friends and family members parallels the work ethic of his scientific research.

Einstein was most comfortable in sustaining long lasting intimacy in relationships that granted space and distance. Einstein's way of being in these relationships was much like his way of being in science. The physicist Einstein arrived at his universal laws through objective thought (deduction), which he felt needed to be simple, intelligible and objective. These laws provided a semblance of a world that was certain and predictable.

Human life—with its ambivalent relationships and its ever-changing passions—is complex and often unpredictable. And daily life, with its routines, is often painful and boring. One's personal life, with its daily mood fluctuations, is far from the idea of a harmonious cosmos. For Einstein, one's perception of oneself is a disjointed and fragmented experience (Schwab, 2005). Scientific theory, he believed, can grant individuals certainty and clarity, for it is intimately connected with harmony, beauty and symmetry mediated by intuition (Elkana and Holton, 1982).

Einstein always felt closely connected to nature, a sort of God to Einstein. This strong bond with nature protected him to a certain extent from the "merely personal," from the reverie of sustained intimacy with its ambivalent love, or from often unsatisfied longings and conflicting emotions in himself as well as in the ones closest to him. It was therefore easier for Einstein to view himself and others merely as tiny particles of nature, which are part of all that is living in the eternal flow (Seelig, 1956, p. 36).

This particular feeling of being one with the world, which Freud refers to as "oneness with the universe," is supposed to restore the limitless narcissism humans lost after growing out of "the paradise of our childhood and dreams," as Marie Bonaparte called it (Bonaparte, 1940). The religious experience that Einstein described developed out of a similar sense of fusion with the world, out of a boundless, limitless experience that came to be known as Freud's "oceanic experience." One could even speculate, as mentioned earlier, that Einstein's initial refusal to speak may have reflected his reluctance to be thrown out from the imagined, unconscious order of a unified sense of self into a new form, a "wording self" (Bollas, 1999). Einstein's secret lay in his ability to retain the child's capacity to wonder. As much as he valued concepts, he never allowed them to rigidify, but instead used them as heuristic tools open to change and always attuned to a world in flux (Schwab, 2005).

During these intense periods of pondering, imagining, dreaming and constructing ideas in his scientific work, often done in isolation in his office, Einstein was able once again to withdraw and be contained within a safe space of motherly protection that predated social responsiveness and language; it was this isolated, safe space that enabled Albert to crystallize his theories. Throughout these times, even the basic needs for food and rest were eliminated, allowing for the illusion of an "indissoluble bond of being one with the external world as a whole," as Freud refers to it (Freud, 1930, p. 167). Such a merging with the universe constitutes not only a defensive attempt to transcend the painful limitation of the merely personal's loneliness, but it also constitutes a restitutive act. The creative, scientific search then satisfies a strong narcissistic desire to rediscover a lost sense of unity, bringing back together the ego and its ideal (Dreifuss-Kattan, 1994).

References

Binswanger, L. (1956) *Erinnerungen an Sigmund Freud.* Bern, Switzerland: Franke.

Bollas, C. (1999) *The mystery of things.* New York and London: Routledge.

Bonaparte, M. (1940) Time and the unconscious. *International Journal of Psychoanalysis,* 21: 427–468.

Born, M. (2005) *The Born–Einstein letters 1916–1955: Friendship, politics and physics in uncertain times* (I. Born, Trans.). New York: Macmillan.

Buchwald, D. (2003). Unpublished document.

Calaprice, A. (2000) *The expanded quotable Einstein.* Princeton, NJ: Princeton University Press.

Dreifuss-Kattan, E. (1994) *Cancer stories: Creativity and self-repair.* Hillsdale, NJ: The Analytic Press.

Ehrenzweig, A. (1967) *The hidden order of art.* London: Phoenix Press.

Einstein, A. (1954) *Ideas and opinions based on Mein Weltbild.* C. Seelig (Ed.). New York: Three Rivers Press.

Einstein, A. (1970) *Autobiographical notes.* P. Schlipp (Ed.). Chicago, IL: Open Court Publishing Company.

Einstein, A. (1987–2012) *The collected papers of Albert Einstein (CPAE)* (Vols. 1–12). Princeton, NJ: Princeton University Press.

Elkana, Y. and Holton, G. (1982) *Albert Einstein: Historical and cultural perspectives.* Mineola, NY: Dover Publications.

Erikson, E. (1982) Psychoanalytic reflection on Einstein's centenary. In *Albert Einstein: Historical and cultural perspectives.* G. Holton and Y. Elkana (Eds.). Mineola, NY: Dover Publications.

Folsing, A. (1997). *Albert Einstein.* New York: Penguin Books.

Fox Keller, E. (1995) *Reflection on gender and science.* New Haven, CT: Yale University Press.

Frank, P. (1947) *Einstein: A centenary volume.* Cambridge, MA: Harvard University Press.

Freud, S. (1930) Civilization and its discontents. *The standard edition of the complete psychological works of Sigmund Freud* (Vol. 21). London: The Hogarth Press.

Jakobson, R. (1982) Einstein and the science of language. In *Albert Einstein: Historical and cultural perspectives*. G. Holton and Y. Elkana (Eds.). Mineola, NY: Dover Publications.

Keller, E. (1995). Changing the subject of science and psychoanalysis: Problems of agency and authority in a post-modern world. October 15, 1995, lecture to the APA, p. 3.

Renn, J. and Schulman, R. (1992) *Albert Einstein, Mileva Maric: The love letters*. Princeton, NJ: Princeton University Press.

Schwab, G. (1994) *Subjects without selves: Transitional texts in modern fiction*. Cambridge, MA: Harvard University Press.

Schwab, G. (2005) Personal discussion.

Seelig, C. (1956) *Albert Einstein: Biography and autobiography*. London: Stables Press.

Talmey, M. (1932) *Personal recollections of Einstein's boyhood and youth*. Scripta Mathematics, Yeshiva University, NY.

Wertheimer, M. (1959/1978) *Positive thinking*. New York: Greenwood Press.

ILLUSTRATIONS

Figures

Plates

8 Ferdinand Hodler. *Valentine Godé-Darel im Krankenbett mit Uhr und Rosen* [*Valentine Godé-Darel on Her Sickbed with Pocket-watch and Roses*]. 1914. Oil on canvas. 63 × 86 cm. © SIK-ISEA, Zürich. Dübi-Müller Stiftung, Kunstmuseum Solothurn.

9 Ferdinand Hodler. *Sonnenuntergang am Genfersee* [*Lake Geneva with Sunset*]. 1915. Oil on canvas. 61 × 90 cm. © Kunsthaus Zürich, Gift of the heirs of Alfred Rütschi.

10 Ferdinand Hodler. *Die tote Valentine Godé-Darel* [*The Dead Valentine Godé-Darel*]. 26 January, 1915. Oil on canvas. 60 × 124 cm. © SIK-ISEA, Zürich. Kunstmuseum Solothurn. Schenkung Frau Erica Peters im Andenken an Herrn Dr. Rudolf Schmidt, 1971.

11 Eva Hesse. *Ringaround Arosie.* 1965. Varnish, graphite, ink, enamel, cloth-covered wire, papier-mâché, unknown modeling compound, Masonite, wood. 67.5 × 42.5 × 11.4 cm / 26½ × 16¾ × 4½ in. Museum of Modern Art, New York, fractional and promised gift of Kathy and Richard S. Fuld, Jr., 2005. © The Estate of Eva Hesse. Courtesy Hauser & Wirth.

12 Lucian Freud. *Benefits Supervisor Resting.* 1994. 63 × 59¼ in. Oil on canvas. Private Collection. © The Lucian Freud Archive/Bridgeman Images.

13 Lucian Freud. *The Painter's Mother Resting I.* 1975–1976. Oil on canvas. 35½ × 35½ in. Private Collection. © The Lucian Freud Archive/Bridgeman Images.

14 Lucian Freud. *Portrait of the Hound.* 2011. Oil on canvas. 1.58 × 1.38 m. Private Collection. © The Lucian Freud Archive/Bridgeman Images.

15 René Magritte. *La philosophie dans le boudoir* [*Philosophy in the Bedroom*]. 1948. Gouache on paper. 46 × 37 cm. © 2014 Herscovici/Artist Rights Society (ARS), New York.

16 René Magritte. *La tentative de l'impossible* [*Attempting the Impossible*]. Oil on canvas. 116 × 81 cm. Galerie Isy Brachot, Brussels. © 2014 Herscovici/Artist Rights Society (ARS), New York. Photo Credit: Banque d'Images, ADAGP/Art Resource, NY.

INDEX